THE
ANNOTATED
CAT

UNDER THE HATS
OF SEUSS
AND
HIS CATS

THE ANNOTATED CAT

UNDER THE HATS OF SEUSS AND HIS CATS

INTRODUCTION
AND ANNOTATIONS
BY PHILIP NEL

RANDOM HOUSE 🏠 NEW YORK

We have made every effort to trace the ownership of all copyrighted material and to secure permission from copyright holders. In the event of future questions arising as to the use of any material, we will be pleased to make all necessary corrections in subsequent printings.

The Cat in the Hat TM & copyright © 1957, renewed 1985 by Dr. Seuss Enterprises, L.P.
The Cat in the Hat Comes Back TM & copyright © 1958, renewed 1986 by Dr. Seuss Enterprises, L.P.
Introduction and annotations copyright © 2007 by Philip Nel
"The Strange Shirt Spot," "How Orlo Got His Book," and "My Hassle with the First Grade Language" reprinted courtesy of Dr. Seuss Enterprises, L.P.

www.randomhouse.com/kids
www.seussville.com

Educators and librarians, for a variety of teaching tools, visit us at www.randomhouse.com/teachers

Library of Congress Cataloging-in-Publication Data
Nel, Philip, 1969–
The annotated cat : under the hats of Seuss and his cats / Philip Nel. — 1st ed.
    p.   cm.
Includes bibliographical references.
ISBN-13: 978-0-375-83369-4 (trade) — ISBN-13: 978-0-375-93369-1 (lib. bdg.)
1. Seuss, Dr.—Criticism and interpretation.   2. Cat in the Hat (Fictitious character).   3. Seuss, Dr. Cat in the hat.
4. Seuss, Dr. Cat in the hat comes back.   5. Children's stories, American—History and criticism.
6. Children's stories, American—Illustrations.
7. Children—Books and reading—United States—History—20th century.   I. Title.
PS3513.E2Z786 2007   813' .52—dc22   2006003843

Printed in the United States of America   10 9 8 7 6 5 4 3 2 1   First Edition

Acknowledgments and photo credits can be found at the back of the book.

CONTENTS

INTRODUCTION

It was 1954, and many Americans were worried: *why can't Johnny read?* In a *Life* magazine article, John Hersey said that Johnny and Susie were not learning to read because the Dick and Jane primers were boring.

Hersey proposed that Dr. Seuss write a reading primer to replace Dick and Jane.

Seuss had already published nine books for children. The first, *And to Think That I Saw It on Mulberry Street,* came out in 1937. The tenth, *Horton Hears a Who!,* would appear in the fall of 1954. He had received some acclaim for his books, winning Caldecott Honors for *McElligot's Pool* (1947), *Bartholomew and the Oobleck* (1949), and *If I Ran the Zoo* (1950).

But Dr. Seuss was equally famous for "Quick, Henry, the Flit!"—his slogan for Flit insecticide. After first appearing in an ad in 1928, it quickly became a national catchphrase. And his work in the field of advertising was his primary source of income.

The Cat in the Hat would change all that. Seuss wrote the book to teach children how to read, and its success allowed him to write full-time for children. Indeed, the Cat made "Dr. Seuss" a household name. With the publication of *The Cat in the Hat* in the spring of 1957 and of *How the Grinch Stole Christmas!* later that year, Dr. Seuss became an icon of American children's literature.

Dr. Seuss and *The Cat in the Hat*, 1957.

He was born Theodor Seuss Geisel in Springfield, Massachusetts, on March 2, 1904. His family called him Ted. As Judith and Neil Morgan's *Dr. Seuss & Mr. Geisel: A Biography* (1995) tells us, Ted's paternal grandparents, Theodor Geisel and Christine Schmaelzle, emigrated from Germany. His maternal grandparents, George J. and Margaretha Seuss (pronounced *Zoice*), emigrated from Bavaria. Grandpa Geisel ran a brewery, and Ted's father, Theodor Robert Geisel, joined the family business. Grandpa Seuss was a baker, and Ted's mother, Henrietta Seuss, worked in her father's bakery before becoming Mrs. Geisel in 1901. At bedtime, Ted and his older sister, Marnie, often went to sleep to the sound of their mother chanting to them "softly, in the way she had learned as she sold pies, 'Apple, mince, lemon . . . peach, apricot, pineapple . . . blueberry, coconut, custard, and SQUASH!'"[1] He later said that his mother was most responsible "for the rhythms in which I write and the urgency with which I do it."[2]

Ted Geisel began attaching pseudonyms to his work early on: in his high school newspaper, he signed his work under his own name and the names Pete the Pessimist, Ole the Optimist, and T. S. Lesieg—"Lesieg" being "Geisel" backward. He didn't start using "Seuss" as his pen name until his senior year at Dartmouth College.

During the spring of 1925, Geisel was the editor of and a contributor to *Jack-O-Lantern,* Dartmouth's humor magazine. The night before Easter, Geisel and nine friends were caught drinking gin in his room. As he recalled, the dean put them all "on probation for violating the laws of Prohibition, and especially on Easter Evening."[3] The dean then stripped Geisel of his editorship of *Jack-O-Lantern.* To evade the punishment, Geisel published cartoons under other names—L. Pasteur, L. Burbank, D. G. Rossetti '25, T. Seuss, and Seuss. This was the first time he signed his work with the name "Seuss." As a magazine cartoonist, he would give himself the mock-scholarly title of "Dr. Theophrastus Seuss" in November 1927, and he shortened that to "Dr. Seuss" in May 1928. Since Americans tended to pronounce the name *Soose* instead of *Zoice,* Geisel's middle name acquired a new pronunciation.

Geisel came to professional magazine cartooning by way of Oxford, where he pursued graduate studies in English during 1925 and 1926. His notebooks reveal a young man more interested in doodling than in studying literature. Fortunately, his classmate Helen Palmer noticed that his talents lay beyond academia. Looking at his notebook one day after class, she told him, "You're crazy to be a professor. What you really want to do is draw." And she said, "That's a very fine flying cow!"[4] They got engaged, she finished her M.A. . . . and he did not. In early 1927, they returned to the United States, and—with Helen's encouragement—Ted Geisel began sending cartoons to magazines. In July, the *Saturday Evening Post* published a cartoon. In it, two dumpy American tourists ride on camels in a desert. One says to the other, "I am so thrilled, my dear! At last I can understand the ecstasy Lawrence experienced when he raced posthaste across the sands of Arabia in pursuit of the fleeting Arab." By the end of the year, Geisel's cartoons were appearing regularly in *Judge,* a humor magazine.

On November 29, 1927, at the age of twenty-three, Ted married Helen. In 1928, he became a successful advertising artist with cartoons for Flit (a product of Standard Oil), which in turn led him to create ads for Holly Sugar, NBC, Ford, General Electric, and many others. Geisel often said that a clause in his Standard Oil contract prevented him from undertaking many other types of creative work. But it did not prohibit him from publishing children's books. As he told Edward Connery Lathem in 1975, "I would like to say I went into children's book writing because of my great understanding of children. I went in because it wasn't excluded by my Standard Oil contract."[5]

Ted began writing children's books at roughly the same time that he and Helen found they could not have children. According to the Morgans, by about 1931, Helen was hospitalized "with worsening abdominal pain," and "after hurried conferences doctors removed her ovaries."[6] Throughout his life, interviewers would ask him how he, a childless person, could write so well for children. His standard response: "You make 'em, I'll amuse 'em." (Though Geisel didn't point this out, such a question ignores the fact that many great children's writers have had no children of their own—Lewis Carroll, Edward Lear, Beatrix Potter, Margaret Wise Brown, Maurice Sendak, Crockett Johnson, and Ruth Krauss, to name a few.)

In 1931, Geisel wrote and illustrated his first work for children—an ABC of fanciful creatures. The publishers weren't interested, and so the manuscript never became a book. In 1936, returning from Europe on the M.S. *Kungsholm,* he began composing a story to the rhythms of the ship's engines: "And that is a story that no one can beat, and to think that I saw it on Mulberry Street."[7] Upon his return home, he worked for months writing and illustrating this tale of an imaginary parade. Again, he could not interest any publishers. Depending on the version of the story he tells, either twenty, twenty-five, twenty-six, twenty-seven, twenty-eight, twenty-nine, or forty-three publishers turned down the manuscript.

As Geisel liked to say, one day he was walking down Madison Avenue, manuscript in hand, and was thinking that he would never sell the book. He happened to bump into Mike McClintock, a friend from Dartmouth:

> He said, "What's that under your arm?"
> I said, "A book that no one will publish. I'm lugging it home to burn."
> Then I asked Mike, "What are *you* doing?"
> He said, "This morning I was appointed juvenile editor of Vanguard Press, and we happen to be standing in front of my office; would you like to come inside?"
> So, we went inside, and he looked at the book and took me to the president of Vanguard Press. Twenty minutes later we were signing contracts.
> That's one of the reasons I believe in luck. If I'd been going down the other side of Madison Avenue, I would be in the dry-cleaning business today![8]

In the fall of 1937, Vanguard published *And to Think That I Saw It on Mulberry Street*. The book won strong reviews and sales, and so began the career of Dr. Seuss as we think of him today—Dr. Seuss, the author-illustrator of books for children.

He published *The 500 Hats of Bartholomew Cubbins* (1938) with Vanguard, and then publisher Bennett Cerf wooed him to Random House. Seuss published his next two children's books—*The King's Stilts* (1939) and *Horton Hatches the Egg* (1940)—with Random House, which would be his publisher for the rest of his career. But he wrote only these four children's books before the Second World War pulled him in a new direction.

Concerned that American isolationism left the country vulnerable, in 1941 Dr. Seuss began his twenty-one-month career as a political cartoonist for New York's Popular Front newspaper, *PM,* creating over four hundred cartoons—as many as five per week. In January 1943, he and Helen left New York for California, where he became a captain in the U.S. Army's Information and Education Division—Hollywood's Fort Fox.[9] Serving under Major Frank Capra, Captain Geisel was in the same unit with composer Meredith Wilson, who would later write *The Music Man.* Also in the unit was former Disney animator Phil Eastman, who, as P. D. Eastman, would later write *Go, Dog. Go!*

and *Are You My Mother?* for Seuss's Beginner Books series at Random House. During the war, they produced documentary films, cartoons, and booklets in support of the U.S. effort. Their best-known creation is Private SNAFU, whose name is an acronym of sorts for "Situation Normal All . . . All Fouled Up," as the first SNAFU animated cartoon put it. Created by Geisel, Eastman, and civilian directors Chuck Jones and Friz Freleng, SNAFU failed to maintain his weapon, let confidential information slip, and neglected to protect himself against malaria-carrying mosquitoes. In other words, Private SNAFU taught by negative example.

Title image from a *Private SNAFU* cartoon.

After the war, Dr. Seuss returned to children's books and continued his advertising work. He and Helen bought a former observation tower atop La Jolla's Mount Soledad, then had it converted into a home, and there they would live and work for the rest of their lives.[10]

In this house, he wrote *The Cat in the Hat* for Random House and Houghton Mifflin. He struggled to keep his vocabulary within Houghton Mifflin's word lists for beginning readers and nearly gave up in frustration. As he said, upon starting to write this primer, "I figured I could knock it off in a week or so." However, "it took a year and a half."[11] Or, as he observed in one semifictional account of writing *The Cat in the Hat,* the experience was like "being lost with a witch in a tunnel of love. The only job I ever tackled that I found more difficult was when I wrote the

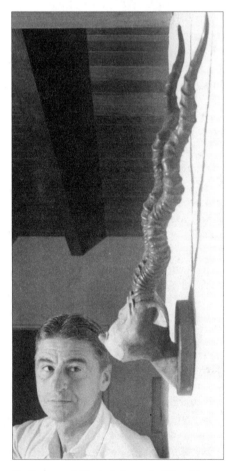

Dr. Seuss and his sculpture of a "Blue-Green Abelard," 1953.

Baedeker that Eskimos use when they travel in Siam."[12]

One part of Seuss's difficulty was that he always worried whether what he had written was good enough. This feeling motivated his perfectionism, pushing him to revise and revise again. Yet, when after much revision he finished *The Cat in the Hat,* he seemed unusually confident that the book would be a success. On June 11, 1956, he wrote to Random House:

> Don't ever show this letter to anyone, but I've got a hunch . . . (very immodest) . . . Namely, according to Houghton-Mifflin, who will be releasing my First

Dr. Seuss

THE TOWER
La Jolla, California

June 11, 1956

Hey, you:

I enclose one of the results of the publicity you started rolling. The Saturday Review piece got the San Diego Sunday Union thinking. And here's what they did. I think it's a good one to put in your files, because it's very complete and nicely put. (Tho, where they got that photo from, I don't know.)

. . . .

About the AssociatedPress. They did send a guy out to see me. What he got from me, I don't know. But I know it was skimpy compared to the enclosed. I told him, in parting, to pick up the enclosed piece from the S.D.Union. But he may not have. And if he didn't, he didn't get ~~much~~ too much information. If Bill Rogers is still on the story, it might be an idea to show him the enclosed.(Anyhow, give him my very best regards and thanks.) . . . . .

Don't ever show this letter to anyone, but I've got a hunch...(very immodest)... Namely, according to Houghton-Mifflin, who will be releasing my First Grade Reader to schools early in Jan.or Feb., we've got a possibility of making a tremendous noise in the noisy discussion of Why Johnny Can't Read. The Random House trade edition won't come out until later, and the big noise may never come off.

But Collier's is talking about an article on the reader. And, if that happens, I'll follow up with television. And if that happens, (it might or might not) I can immodestly say that it might warrant my face on the cover of the Saturday Review. (But don't tell them.)

Too early to tell yet, so you and I should just watch and wait. But if Houghton Mifflin is right, we'll be plumb in the middle of a great educational controversy.

I'll be sending the book to H-M. thru Phyllis Jackson some time in August, I believe. She will take it to Colliers and to Random House before sending it on. At that point we'll have a better idea of whether we're sending off sky rockets or not. And if it looks like sky rockets to you, we'll have a big thing on our hands.

////////

Dr. Seuss, letter to Random House, June 11, 1956.

Grade Reader to schools early in Jan. or Feb., we've got a possibility of making a tremendous noise in the noisy discussion of Why Johnny Can't Read. The Random House trade edition won't come out until later, and the big noise may never come off.[13]

Seuss then talked about potential press coverage in *Collier's* and the *Saturday Review* and the possibility of his making a television appearance to promote the book. He added, "Too early to tell yet, so you and I should just watch and wait. But if Houghton Mifflin is right, we'll be plumb in the middle of a great educational controversy."

As Seuss's letter discloses, Houghton Mifflin published the edition marketed to schools; Random House published the one sold to the general public. (Though their covers differed, the content of the books was the same.) This unusual arrangement came about because William Spaulding, a friend from his army days and then director of Houghton Mifflin's educational division, had asked Seuss to write the primer in the first place. As Judith and Neil Morgan report, Random House president Bennett Cerf agreed that Seuss "could write the reader" as long as Random House retained "the rights to market the trade edition in bookstores. Houghton Mifflin would publish only the school edition."[14]

The school edition did not sell as well as the trade edition because, according to Seuss, educators considered his book too subversive. As he told Jonathan Cott, Houghton Mifflin "had trouble selling it to the schools; there were a lot of Dick and Jane devotees, and my book was considered too fresh and irreverent. But Bennett Cerf at Random House had asked for trade rights, and it just took off in the bookstores."[15]

Published on March 1, 1957, and priced at $2.00 (later reduced to $1.95), Random House's edition of *The Cat in the Hat* was an immediate hit. Its first printing was selling so well that Random House ordered a second printing in April.[16] As the Morgans write, the book's average sales began at "about twelve thousand copies a month" and only increased thereafter. *The Cat* became a phenomenon because, "spurred by playground word-of-mouth, children nagged their parents to buy it."[17]

The overwhelmingly positive reviews must have helped to persuade parents. The first review I can find, published in *Kirkus Reviews* on March 15, 1957, says that the book "is a perfect specimen of what *can* happen and the Seuss drawings tell as much of a story as his simple verse."[18] If *Kirkus Reviews* is mostly descriptive, the *New York Times Book Review*'s March 17

review by Ellen Lewis Buell is enthusiastic, setting the tone for subsequent reviews: "Beginning readers and parents who have been helping them through the dreary activities of Dick and Jane and other primer characters are due for a happy surprise." *The Cat in the Hat,* she says, is "one of the most original and funniest of books for early readers."[19]

As Buell did, most reviewers praised *The Cat in the Hat* as a successful reading teacher. The *Saturday Review*'s Helen Adams Masten wrote, "Theodor Geisel has accomplished a *tour de force.* . . . Parents and teachers will bless Mr. Geisel for this amusing reader with its ridiculous and lively drawings, for their children are going to have the exciting experience of learning that they *can* read after all."[20] The *Chicago Sunday Tribune*'s Polly Goodwin thought that the book would make seven- and eight-year-olds "rejoice" and "look with distinct disfavor on the drab adventures of standard primer characters."[21] According to *Library Journal*'s Helen E. Walker, "this hilarious tale" would "quickly become a favorite with first- and second-graders," but all "youngsters . . . will enjoy the humor, rhythm, and illustrations."[22] Like Walker, the *New Yorker*'s Emily Maxwell also felt that the book would appeal to both new and more experienced readers. *The Cat in the Hat,* she wrote, "uses only words familiar to first-grade readers and pretends to be intended to make learning to read palatable, but it is really the sort of book children insist on taking to bed with them."[23]

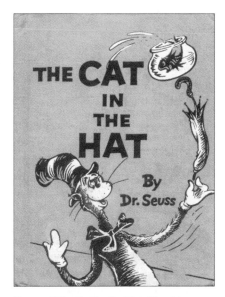

Cover of *The Cat in the Hat,* Houghton Mifflin edition, 1957.

Cover of *The Cat in the Hat,* Random House first edition, 1957.

One contemporary reviewer, however, thought the book neither up to Seuss's usual standard nor appealing to a wide range of readers. The *Horn Book Magazine*'s Heloise P. Mailloux thought that the cover's "For Beginning Readers" would be a turnoff: "This is a fine book for remedial purposes, but self-conscious children often refuse material if it seems meant for younger children." She also claimed that *The Cat*'s limited vocabulary prevented it from having "the absurd excellence of the early Seuss books."[24] In contrast, the *New York Herald Tribune Book Review*'s Margaret S. Libby suggested that the book's limited vocabulary made Seuss a more disciplined and successful poet: "Restricting his vocabulary to a mere 223 words (all in the reading range of a six- or seven-year-old) and shortening his verse has given a certain riotous and extravagant unity, a wild restraint that is pleasing."[25]

By May 1958, Random House had sold over 200,000 copies of *The Cat in the Hat*. By November, it had sold 300,000.[26] And, as E. J. Kahn, Jr., wrote in his *New Yorker* profile of Dr. Seuss, by the end of 1960 *The Cat in the Hat* was about to reach a million copies sold, its $1.95 price bringing "its retail gross to nearly two million dollars—equivalent to the gross on six

Dr. Seuss signing books, c. 1957.

million copies of a thirty-five-cent paperback. Only two works of fiction, *God's Little Acre* and *Peyton Place,* have sold as well as that in paperback form."[27] A year later, *The Cat in the Hat* was already well into its second million in sales.[28]

The baby boom was a major factor in Seuss's success. In 1952, women in the United States gave birth to 3.9 million children. Those children turned five in 1957, the year *The Cat in the Hat* came out. In 1957, the peak year of the baby boom, 29.1 million children were in kindergarten and elementary school—and another 4.3 million children were born. By way of comparison, in 2000, when 4 million children were born, the birth rate was 14.4 per 1,000 women; the birth rates in 1952 and 1957 were, respectively, 25.1 and 25.3.[29] As an article in a 1964 issue of *Business Week* reported, the "60 million children now under 14" represented a huge market for children's books: "The yearly total of titles has doubled since 1954, to nearly 3,000 last year (including 371 new editions). Total juvenile sales have doubled since 1957, from $56 million to an estimated $138 million in 1963."[30] In other words, the baby boom created a boom in children's books.

These developments and the success of *The Cat* made it possible for Seuss to make children's books his profession. Thirty years later, an interviewer asked when he decided to write children's books full-time. Dr. Seuss replied, "When the bumper crop of children born on the G.I. Bill of Rights came along. Up until 1950 you couldn't make a living as a children's book writer. G.I.s had all these kids and they began to buy kids' books like mad—overnight."[31]

Random House and Houghton Mifflin were not the only major publishers to begin producing books for beginning readers. In August 1957, Harper & Brothers got into the primer business, publishing its first I Can Read Book, Else Holmelund Minarik's *Little Bear,* illustrated by Maurice Sendak. This book had, of course, been planned prior to the publication of *The Cat in the Hat.* As children's book historian Leonard S. Marcus writes, legendary Harper's children's book editor Ursula Nordstrom had been thinking of such a series for years and "could not have been more pleased" with the imminent publication of *Little Bear.* But "months prior to publication, Nordstrom's sense of triumph came crashing down . . . when Random House launched its own somewhat similar series with a Dr. Seuss book called *The Cat in the Hat.*"[32]

The runaway success of *The Cat in the Hat* prompted Seuss, Helen Geisel, and Phyllis Cerf to found Beginner Books, a division of Random House designed to publish books that help

Cover of *The Cat in the Hat Comes Back,*
Random House first edition, 1958.

Cover of *The Cat in the Hat Comes Back,*
Random House library edition, 1958.

children learn to read. In the fall of 1958, *The Cat in the Hat Comes Back* and four other titles launched the Beginner Books series, which would soon grow to include books by P. D. Eastman, Robert Lopshire, Roy McKie, Stan and Jan Berenstain, and Bennett Cerf himself. Harper attracted an equally impressive roster of authors for its I Can Read series, including Syd Hoff, Esther Averill, Lillian Hoban, Crockett Johnson, Arnold

Dr. Seuss talking with a toy designer about toys based on his characters, 1959.
(Note the Cat in the Hat toy and book at the back of the picture.)

Lobel, and Gene Zion. In the 1950s, '60s, and '70s, an array of talented people were writing books for novice readers.

Seuss's second such book, *The Cat in the Hat Comes Back,* also attracted strong reviews. The *New York Herald Tribune Book Review* considered the new Cat book "the best of the five" Beginner Books published that fall: "The semi-smooth jingles, the irresistibly funny situations, the exaggerations in text and pictures . . . are all there, no more hampered by a small vocabulary than a bird is hampered in making an attractive song by being able to sing only a few notes."[33] Ellen Lewis Buell wrote in the *New York Times Book Review,* "The new antics of the Cat in the Hat are just as funny and unexpected as in the original story. There are the same hypnotic rhythms, and the same kind of cumulative action, building at jet speed to suspense and surprise."[34]

In November 1958, Seuss traveled by jet and helicopter to promote *The Cat in the Hat Comes Back* and *Yertle the Turtle—* then the two latest Dr. Seuss books. He made appearances and signed books in department stores across the Midwest and Northeast, including Chicago's Marshall Field's, Boston's Jordan Marsh, and Philadelphia's Strawbridge and Clothier. In its four-page article "The One and Only Dr. Seuss and His Wonderful Autographing Tour," *Publishers Weekly* reported that Detroit's J. L. Hudson Company "flew Dr. Seuss from the main store" to its suburban branches "in a helicopter, a device which was well publicized," drawing "hundreds of children to the branch stores."

When Seuss stepped out of the helicopter, crowds of children were there to meet him. "It was as if I were Santa Claus," he said.[35] His appearance brought 2,500 people to the main store. Hudson's Northland branch had to stay open two hours past closing so that all Seuss-seeking customers could get his autograph. At that branch alone, he sold 1,200 books.[36] Cleveland's Higbee Company held a luncheon for Seuss and the children, where they ate "Yertlebergers" and "Cat in the Hat parfaits."[37] All five hundred tickets sold out on the day the store announced the luncheon. During Seuss's visit, Higbee sold over 2,000 of his books. As *Publishers Weekly* reported, "Dr. Seuss had to autograph so fast that there had to be salespeople on hand constantly putting the books before him and taking them away."[38]

Though no doubt pleased to be selling so many books, Seuss felt "very strongly that children shouldn't be forced to buy, and he objects to it very strongly when stores attempt to remove youngsters from the waiting lines if they have not actually spent any money." To accommodate his fans, he "autographed countless cards and slips of paper as well as books."[39]

Seuss divided the rest of his career between the "big books" (as he called them) and the smaller Beginner Books. Meanwhile, sales of the Beginner Books drew new readers to Seuss's big books. After the publication of *The Cat,* sales of earlier books (all of which were big books) rose dramatically, and sales of new big books benefited, too. As E. J. Kahn, Jr., wrote in his 1960 *New Yorker* profile of Dr. Seuss:

> *The King's Stilts,* which was published in 1939, sold 4,648 copies the first year. By 1941, its annual sales were down to 394. In 1958, the last year for which figures are obtainable, they were up to 11,037. *The King's Stilts* has been a more sluggish mover than any other Dr. Seuss book; its cumulative sales have climbed nearly to the 75,000 mark. Another early Dr. Seuss, *Horton Hatches the Egg,* which has had total sales of more than 200,000 and is still briskly hatching profits, sold 5,801 copies in 1940, the year it came out. It, too, fell off—to 1,645 the following year. In 1958, it sold 27,643 copies.[40]

By July 1964, *The Cat in the Hat* had grossed more than $3 million at $1.95 a copy. At that time, *Business Week* estimated Seuss's royalties at $200,000 a year.[41]

Though he published a dozen children's books between 1937 and 1956, it was only in the late 1950s that Dr. Seuss began to rank among the bestselling children's authors. In a November 1958 *New York Times Book Review* list of "Children's Best Sellers" covering the past year's sales, Seuss had three in the top sixteen: A. A. Milne's *The World of Pooh* (1957) was at number one, followed by Seuss's *Yertle the Turtle* (1958) at number two, *The Cat in the Hat Comes Back* (1958) at number seven, and *How the Grinch Stole Christmas!* (1957) at number eight.[42]

In Alice Payne Hackett's *Best Sellers* compendia (*50 Years of Best Sellers, 60 Years of Best Sellers,* etc.), Dr. Seuss appears for the first time in the list that spans 1895 to 1965. This list's top four are L. Frank Baum's *The Wonderful Wizard of Oz* (1900), Evelyn Millis Duvall's *Facts of Life and Love for Teen-Agers* (1950), and two by Gene Stratton-Porter: *Freckles* (1904) and *A Girl of the Limberlost* (1909). Seuss is not far behind, with *The Cat* and its sequel at nine and fourteen, respectively, followed by *One Fish Two Fish Red Fish Blue Fish* (1960) at twenty, *Green Eggs and Ham* (1960) at twenty-two, *Yertle the Turtle* (1958) at thirty-four, *Hop on Pop* (1962) at thirty-six, and *Dr. Seuss's ABC* (1963) at thirty-seven. By contrast, in the 1895 to 1975 list, Dr. Seuss is the undisputed leader, holding the top five spots with, in descending order, *Green Eggs and Ham, One Fish Two Fish Red Fish Blue Fish, Hop on Pop, Dr. Seuss's ABC,* and *The Cat in the Hat. The Wonderful Wizard of Oz* and E. B. White's *Charlotte's Web* (1952) get sixth and seventh place, respectively, and *The Cat in the Hat Comes Back* lands at number eight.

Buoyed by *The Cat* and other Beginner Books, Dr. Seuss had become the most popular children's author in America by the 1970s. He remains so today. According to *Publishers Weekly*'s December 2001 list of the "All-Time Bestselling" hardcover children's books, Dr. Seuss had sold more children's books in America than any other author—more even than J. K. Rowling, whose Harry Potter series places her just behind Seuss as the next top seller in the U.S. Rowling may yet surpass Seuss, but based on the sales figures for the *Publishers Weekly* list (figures that do *not* include every Seuss book), Seuss had sold 71,186,554 books and Rowling had sold 25,651,045. All four of her titles were in the top twenty—and I expect that the two more recent Potter novels would be also. Seuss's bestselling titles were *Green Eggs and Ham,* at number four, *The Cat in the Hat,* nine, *One Fish Two Fish Red Fish Blue Fish,* thirteen, *Hop on Pop,* sixteen, *Oh, the Places You'll Go!,* seventeen, *Dr. Seuss's ABC,* eighteen, *The Cat in the Hat Comes Back,* twenty-six, *Fox in Socks,* thirty-one, *How the Grinch Stole Christmas!,* thirty-five, and *My Book About Me* (illustrated by Roy McKie), forty. Eight of these ten titles are Beginner Books; only *How the Grinch Stole Christmas!* and *Oh, the Places You'll Go!* are not.

The Cat in the Hat *has* gone places. As he sings in his 1971 television special (written by Dr. Seuss and Chuck Jones), "Cat, hat. / In French, *chat, chapeau.* / In Spanish, *el gato* in a *sombrero.* / And I'll tell you

Dr. Seuss and a person dressed as the Cat, c. 1960.

something more. / Now you listen to me *gut.* / In German, I'm a *Katze und es ist meine [sic] Hut!*" Within three years of its publication, *The Cat* had already been published in French, Chinese, Swedish, and Braille.[43] It has since been issued in over a dozen more languages, including Spanish (1967), Hebrew (1971), Portuguese (1972), Dutch (1975), Danish (1979), German (1979), Maori (1983), Italian (1996), Polish (1996), Latin (2000), Japanese (2001), Greek (2003), Yiddish (2003), and Norwegian (2005). *The Cat in the Hat Comes Back* has been published in Braille (1960), Afrikaans (1972), Dutch (1975), Hebrew (1979), Chinese (1992), Italian (2004), and Spanish (2004).[44]

Despite having been translated into many languages, Dr. Seuss has always been more of an American phenomenon than an international one. Almost every American-born person would recognize the name and the poetic style of Dr. Seuss. Herb Cheyette of Dr. Seuss Enterprises estimates

that "one out of every four children born in the United States receives as its first book a Dr. Seuss book."[45] However, Dr. Seuss is not a household name in non-English-speaking countries. One reason may be the difficulty of translating the nonsensical language and wordplay upon which his works depend. How would one translate the mysterious substance "oobleck" (from *Bartholomew and the Oobleck*) or "snarled up in a terrible snerl"

Cover of *The Cat in the Hat* in Italian.

Cover of *The Cat in the Hat* in Latin.

Cover of *The Cat in the Hat* in Chinese.

Cover of *The Cat in the Hat* in Hebrew.

Cover of *The Cat in the Hat* in German.

Cover of *The Cat in the Hat Comes Back* in Chinese.

Cover of *The Cat in the Hat Comes Back* in Hebrew.

(from *If I Ran the Zoo*)? Because *The Cat in the Hat* and its sequel usually avoid invented words, they have presented less difficulty to the translator.

If the problem of translating his slangy American idiom into other languages has curtailed Dr. Seuss's success abroad, we might then expect him to have won over other English-speaking countries. Indeed, Dr. Seuss's work has been popular in Canada, Australia, and New Zealand. But Seuss has taken a long time to catch on in Great Britain, at least among adults.

Reflecting upon the then-recent publication of Dr. Seuss's works in the U.K., Janice H. Dohm of Britain's *The Junior Bookshelf* wrote in 1963, "There is no doubt that Dr. Seuss . . . is the favorite author of American children today. There is some doubt about why and whether [his] books should be so enthusiastically received."[46] For instance, "most of the pictures are downright ugly and the texts are often tiresome and sometimes vulgar."[47] However, Dohm admitted that "after seeing children of so many types light up over that hideous cat, it is impossible to feel that Dr. Seuss is simply a mistake."[48] She concluded by suggesting that Seuss might one day gain critical favor: "Compared with Lear and Carroll he seems madly common, slick, unmemorable, and yet Lear seems no better to some people— might the good doctor prove the all-American Lear?"[49]

Twelve years later, British critical opinion on Dr. Seuss showed signs of changing. In the *Times Educational Supplement,* Myra Barrs, an admirer of his work, wrote that Seuss took so long to become popular in Britain for precisely the reasons that Dohm identified: his books seemed vulgar, ugly, and too American. However, Barrs considered these supposed characteristics to be virtues: noting that Seuss's books "are brash and noisy" and "overpoweringly American," she mused that their "American voice" may be why Dr. Seuss appeals to so many children.[50] In 1997, the American-born children's author-illustrator Ted Dewan wrote in the *Times Educational Supplement* that Seuss is "a natural successor to the likes of Edward Lear" and wondered "why Seuss doesn't sit alongside the giants of children's literature in Britain."[51] The *Times Educational Supplement* endorsed Dewan's analysis, including *The Cat in the Hat* in its list of 101 of the best books for children, published in the same issue.

Americans recognized Dr. Seuss's importance decades before then. As the sales figures indicate, the American phenomenon began shortly after the publication of *The Cat in the Hat.* By May 1958, the *New York Times Book Review*'s David Dempsey wrote that Beginner Books "may well be the biggest thing that has happened to the American classroom since the advent of William Holmes McGuffey's Readers in 1836."[52] In 1959, Clifton Fadiman echoed Dempsey, calling *The Cat in the Hat* "the most influential first-grade reader since McGuffey."[53] Dr. Seuss had become so famous that he appeared on the television quiz program *To Tell the Truth* in 1958. Four panelists tried to guess which of three candidates was Ted Geisel, a.k.a. Dr. Seuss. After all had asked questions of each possible Seuss, only columnist Hy Gardner guessed correctly that Ted Geisel was indeed Dr. Seuss.[54] Though people knew Dr. Seuss's name, they did not know his face.

His name and his Cat gained further national recognition in the 1960s. Next to a photograph of President John F. Kennedy and two members of the American Booksellers Association, a *New York Times* article from January 19, 1962, begins, "Two hundred books, ranging from *A History of the English-Speaking Peoples* to *The Cat in the Hat,* were added today to the White House library by the American Booksellers Association." Noting that one bookseller gave the President a copy of Dare Wright's *The Lonely Doll* "especially for Caroline," the report goes on to say that there were "plenty of other books on the list" that Kennedy's four-year-old daughter "might find interesting," including Carl Sandburg's *Early Moon,* Robert Frost's *You Come Too,* and Dr. Seuss's *The Cat in the Hat.*[55] Later in the decade, the Cat himself entered presidential politics via Robert Coover's satirical novella "The Cat in the Hat for President" (1968), in which he figures as an upstart candidate. His campaign slogan, punning on the Beginner Books' "I CAN READ IT ALL BY MYSELF," is, of course, "I CAN LEAD IT ALL BY MYSELF."[56]

As a political candidate would, the Cat appears in parades and in cartoons. In November 1979, the Cat, with Seuss and his second wife, Audrey S. Geisel, appeared in Detroit on a float in the Thanksgiving Day parade. A Cat in the Hat balloon joined Macy's Thanksgiving Day Parade in November 1994. (In 1997, high winds pushed the Cat balloon into a lamppost, whose light fixture was sheared off, toppling into the crowd and injuring four spectators. The balloon was retired prior to the 1998 parade.) Following the 2000 American presidential election, Ward Sutton's cartoon "The Cat in the Chad" imagined the Cat creating the mess in Florida, where, thanks to the butterfly ballot's confusing design, many retirees accidentally voted for Pat Buchanan instead of Al Gore. Bursting into one elderly couple's "retirement nest," the Cat in the Chad says, "Let's have us some fun! / Let's have a surprise! / Let's mix up the voting! / Let's use

Ted and Audrey in the J. L. Hudson Thanksgiving Day Parade, Detroit, November 1979.

Sam Gross, "He had a hat!" From the *New Yorker,* February 18 and 25, 2002.

butterflies!" In a February 2002 issue of the *New Yorker,* cartoonist Sam Gross suggests that the Cat's mischievous tendencies may get him in trouble with the law. An elderly lady opens her door to see two policemen with a hatless Cat in the Hat, who evidently fits her description of a suspect. The lady looks at the Cat and exclaims, "He had a hat!"

Perhaps the Cat in the cartoon lacked a hat because U.S. Supreme Court Justice Stephen Breyer was borrowing it. On February 28, 2002, he donned the hat and necktie of the Cat, in recognition of Read Across America Day.[57] Since 1997, the National Education Association has sponsored this event around March 2, Dr. Seuss's birthday. The Cat in the Hat serves as the symbol for Read Across America Day, when teachers, parents, celebrities, and public figures put on the Cat's hat and read Dr. Seuss books to schoolchildren. In the summer of 1994, anticipating the Cat's role as official mascot of Read Across America, the New York Public Library included the Cat in a mural above its main branch, where he served as "the ringmaster of

your imagination . . . saying 42nd Street can be magical."[58]

In the American mind, the Cat's hat has come to represent Dr. Seuss in particular and the imagination more generally. In the early 1990s, Cat hats became a hot fashion accessory. According to a March 1991 issue of *Entertainment Weekly,* "floppy toppers" modeled after the Cat's hat had been spotted on the heads of MTV VJ Julie Brown, rocker Lenny Kravitz, singer Bobby Brown, and actresses Diane Keaton and Jamie Lee Curtis. At that February's Grammy Awards, "Seuss hats rivaled seamed stockings for Most Groovy Accessory. L. L. Cool J. is so smitten he has over 25 floppies in red-and-black leather."[59]

In 1999, the Cat's hat and face were on a 33-cent U.S. stamp, captioned "Dr. Seuss' 'The Cat in the Hat.'" The Cat is also at the center of the Dr. Seuss National Memorial in Springfield, Massachusetts. Designed by Lark Grey Dimond-Cates (Audrey Geisel's daughter), the memorial features a statue of Geisel seated at his desk next to the Cat, who rests his right hand on Geisel's chair. The 2004 "Theodor Seuss Geisel" stamp (37 cents) displayed several Seuss characters, including the Cat and the Grinch. The Grinch has enriched the English language ("Grinch" has become a synonym for a grouchy, stingy person), but the Cat remains Seuss's most iconic character. When people want to represent Dr. Seuss, they usually show the Cat in the Hat.

True to his mercurial nature, the Cat is both corporate symbol and sly subversive, both a respected reading teacher and a reckless rascal, both endorsed by public officials and embraced by the

Dr. Seuss and the Cat. Dr. Seuss National Memorial, Springfield, Massachusetts.

counterculture. He is a character of possibility, and the many roles he has assumed suit his adaptable persona. As political impresario Clark says in Coover's 1968 tale of the Cat's presidential campaign, "the Cat is funny. And dramatic. We have a terrible need for the extraordinary. We are weary of war, weary of the misery under our supposed prosperity, weary of dullness and routine, weary of all the old ideas, weary of all the masks we wear, the roles we play, the foolish games we sustain. The Cat cuts through all of this. We laugh. For a moment, we are free."[60]

After the Cat and his return, Seuss went on to create many other memorable characters, such as Sam-I-am, Fox in Socks, and the Lorax. But he continued to bring back the Cat, featuring him in four other books and three animated TV specials. The best known of these was the cartoon version of *The Cat in the Hat* (1971), with the Cat's voice supplied by Allan Sherman, best remembered today for his summer 1963 novelty hit "Hello Mudduh, Hello Fadduh! (A Letter from Camp)." A few years after *The Cat* was published, the Cat appeared in the form of plastic models made by Revell and plush toys made by Impulse. In the 1970s, the Cat's likeness appeared on an inflatable pillow, a plastic guitar, a music box, an alarm clock, a watch, and bedsheets.[61] Beyond the products, the Cat's children and ancestors star in Seuss's *I Can Lick 30 Tigers Today! and Other Stories* (1969). Another relative, Archbishop Katz, was to be the central character in a never-completed religious satire.[62] The Cat in the Hat kept coming back.

The Cat in the Hat, television special, 1971: The Cat enters.

The Cat continues to come back because he is the public face of Dr. Seuss. On Thursday, September 26, 1991, the front page of the *New York Times* announced, "Dr. Seuss, Modern Mother Goose, Dies at 87." He had died in his sleep that Tuesday. Below the *Times* headline were two images, captioned "Dr. Seuss signing books in 1986. At left is his most famous character, the Cat in the Hat."[63] Virtually all obituaries and tributes featured the Cat in the Hat. The *Charlotte Observer*'s Kevin Siers drew the Cat with his hat off and his head bowed, a tear

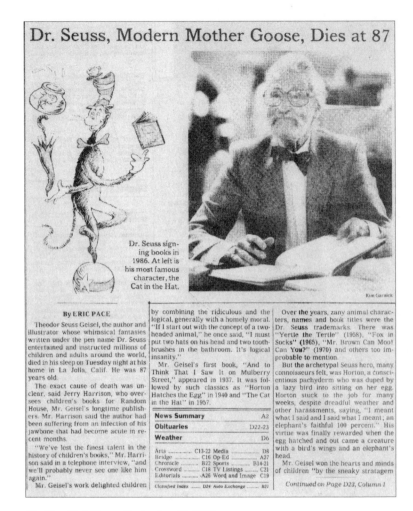

The New York Times, September 26, 1991.

falling from his eye. The *Seattle Times*'s Brian Basset drew Seuss as the Cat, exiting the house on his tidying-up machine, as he does at the end of *The Cat in the Hat*. Quoting from that page of the book, Basset's cartoon concludes with the lines "Then he said, 'That is that.' / And then he was gone / With a tip of his hat."

It may be a cliché to say that Seuss lives on through his work, but . . . he does. The books featuring the Cat continue to sell very well. The Cat's words even appear in *Bartlett's Familiar Quotations*. And in the last dozen or so years, the Cat has been a star of stage, screen, and more. Matt Frewer portrayed him in the TV special *In Search of Dr. Seuss* (1994), David Shiner in the original production of *Seussical* (2000), Mike Myers in the feature film (2003), and Kelsey Grammer on audiobook (also 2003). Seuss and his Cat live on through these interpretations and reinterpretations. I hope that *The Annotated Cat: Under the Hats of Seuss and His Cats* encourages you to participate in this project of interpreting Seuss, too.

When we read, we interpret. *The Annotated Cat* provides a variety of contexts in which we might interpret the books—biographical, historical, political, cultural, formal, aesthetic, and others. Reading *The Cat in the Hat* and *The Cat in the Hat Comes Back* with all of this additional information, we can gain a deeper, more complex appreciation of the books themselves and of the man who wrote them. This, at least, is my goal.

But what would Dr. Seuss have thought of this work? On the one hand, I expect that he would have been pleased to be taken seriously. Because he wrote for children, people often thought he had an easy job. As Miles Corwin noted in a 1983 profile:

> Drunken women at cocktail parties often sidle up to Geisel and slur, "What are you going to do when you grow up?" And their husbands will add, "When I get a few hours on the weekend, I'm going to put together a book like one of yours."
>
> "I tell people of that sort that I also have a hobby I practice on weekends—brain surgery," Geisel says. "Or I'll manage to spill a drink on them. The whole attitude really is very insulting."[64]

He felt insulted because writing good books for children is hard work. As he said:

> Writing children's books is a sweat-and-blood thing. You have to get in there and cut and prune and throw your best passages out, because a writer's best passages, you know, are usually beyond the ken of children—and of adults. Most of them are sloppy writing, and children catch on more quickly when you're doing sloppy writing than adults do. They just walk away. Kids are a much more demanding audience, because they don't have to be polite.[65]

Seuss estimated that he typically produced over 1,000 pages for every sixty-four-page children's book. And while the surviving draft material for each of his books is generally not so voluminous, his papers do show a perfectionist at work, revising and revising again. "I know my stuff looks like it was all rattled off in 28 seconds, but every word is a struggle and every sentence is like the pangs of birth," he once explained.[66]

So I think part of Dr. Seuss would have liked *The Annotated Cat* because it recognizes his hard work and his artistic achievement.

And yet, if glad to be taken seriously, Seuss would have also mocked the idea of being taken seriously. He longed for recognition and, at the same time, secretly felt that he did not deserve his success. As Neil Morgan observes, Seuss had an "endearing insecurity that led him . . . to wonder if what he created was good enough."[67] For example, consider Seuss's reaction in 1984 to receiving a special Pulitzer Prize for his body of work: "I gulped a bit. I stammered. And then I stammered some more. Now, I feel like I've been stammering all day and, maybe, it still could be a hoax."[68]

He was even more skeptical of academic recognition. In 1972, when asked what he thought of doctoral dissertations written on his work, Seuss replied, "I think they're a waste of time." His response is at least partially personal. As he explained:

> I came to that decision back in 1925, when I first learned what happened if you get a Ph.D. in letters. I was at Oxford, and a man named Emile Legouis, who was the greatest authority on Jonathan Swift at the time, lured me to the Sorbonne to do my Ph.D. thesis on Jonathan Swift. Dr. Legouis informed me that everything was known about Swift's life except one crucial period in his life between the age of 17 and 18, and nobody knew whether he had written anything then or not. If I found something that he had written, he told me, I could analyze it for my thesis. But if he hadn't written anything, there would be no doctorate. "After all," he must have figured, "he's a rich American, so it doesn't make much difference anyway." But I spent two years finding that out. That's when I left the halls of European ivy. Ever since, I've been watching people take their degrees in the ever-constricting confines of English literature, and I realize that the confines have been narrowed so far that I'm about the only author left.[69]

Now, the young Ted Geisel did not really spend two years finding out that he did not want to pursue a Ph.D. In a different account that is mostly confirmed by the Morgans in their biography, he remembers listening to Legouis and then "leaving his charming home and walking straight to the American Express Company and booking myself a passage on a cattle boat to Corsica. There I proceeded to paint donkeys for a month."[70] Of course, he may not have painted donkeys, either. As the Mor-

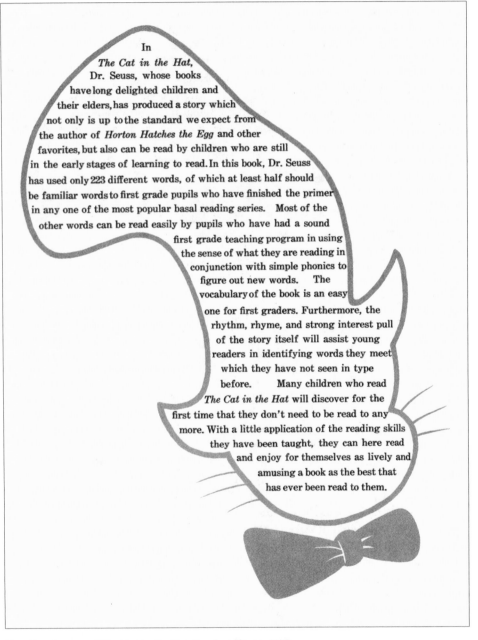

In *The Cat in the Hat*, Dr. Seuss, whose books have long delighted children and their elders, has produced a story which not only is up to the standard we expect from the author of *Horton Hatches the Egg* and other favorites, but also can be read by children who are still in the early stages of learning to read. In this book, Dr. Seuss has used only 223 different words, of which at least half should be familiar words to first grade pupils who have finished the primer in any one of the most popular basal reading series. Most of the other words can be read easily by pupils who have had a sound first grade teaching program in using the sense of what they are reading in conjunction with simple phonics to figure out new words. The vocabulary of the book is an easy one for first graders. Furthermore, the rhythm, rhyme, and strong interest pull of the story itself will assist young readers in identifying words they meet which they have not seen in type before. Many children who read *The Cat in the Hat* will discover for the first time that they don't need to be read to any more. With a little application of the reading skills they have been taught, they can here read and enjoy for themselves as lively and amusing a book as the best that has ever been read to them.

Penultimate page of *The Cat in the Hat*, Random House, 1957.

gans note, "Ted was already honing his skill for exaggeration."[71] Whatever the reason for his decision to leave graduate work in English, the point of his story was to convey his skepticism toward both academia and the idea that his own work would be worthy of close study.

Despite his dismissal of postgraduate study, he remained interested in education. The back jacket flap of the first edition of *The Cat in the Hat* begins its profile of the author as follows: "From earliest youth, Dr. Seuss wanted to be an educator. He started preparing at Dartmouth, then at Oxford University in England. His plan was to teach English literature." But, the profile continues, "somehow things got sidetracked," and Seuss instead found a market for his "very unusual doodlings" in magazines, advertisements, and books. "Dr. Seuss had already gone to the top in all these fields," the profile explains. "But in this pioneering venture, *The Cat in the Hat,* he finally returned to his first love—education."

In interviews, Seuss also referred to his long-deferred pedagogical ambitions. Just after the publication of *The Cat in the Hat,* he announced plans to create more primers, adding, "That is where I am realizing my latent desire to be a professor."[72] Five years later, when asked about his favorites among his books, he replied, "I'd say that the most useful of the books is *The Cat in the Hat.* That had a different purpose, to help reading, and it goes back to my old ambition to be an educator."[73]

Seuss poked fun at professors but also once wanted to be a professor. He made light of people taking his work seriously but also saved his papers, donating them to the University of California . . . thereby allowing scholars to take his work seriously. Seuss's ambivalent response to his own work brings to mind Groucho Marx's famous comment, "I don't care to belong to any club that will accept me as a member."

The "Annotated Club" presently includes Lewis Carroll (Martin Gardner's *Annotated Alice*), L. Frank Baum (Michael Patrick Hearn's *Annotated Wizard of Oz*), Mark Twain (Hearn's *Annotated Huckleberry Finn*), Charles Dickens (Hearn's *Annotated Christmas Carol*), E. B. White (Peter F. Neumeyer's *Annotated Charlotte's Web*), L. M. Montgomery (Wendy E. Barry, Margaret Anne Doody, and Mary E. Doody Jones's *Annotated Anne of Green Gables*), J. R. R. Tolkien (Douglas A. Anderson's *Annotated Hobbit*), the Brothers Grimm (Maria Tatar's

DR. SEUSS

From earliest youth, Dr. Seuss wanted to be an educator. He started preparing at Dartmouth, then at Oxford University in England. His plan was to teach English literature. Surely, he thought, after proper training, some Ivy Hall would call him to fill a dignified chair.

No Ivy Hall called. Somehow things got sidetracked. And maybe that was just as well. The notebooks of this would-be professor had very unusual doodlings in the margins . . . assorted weird animals. Flying dinosaurs, and such. While he was still a graduate student, the fame of this nonsense began to spread.

Soon, newspapers wanted it. Magazines wanted it. Advertisers found it would sell their products. Book publishers quickly realized that every child in the country would some day be his fan.

Dr. Seuss had already gone to the top in all these fields. But in this pioneering venture, *The Cat in the Hat*, he finally returned to his first love—education.

The wonderful rhymed nonsense of this book has one specific purpose . . . to make young beginning readers more eager and anxious to read.

Inside back flap of dust jacket, *The Cat in the Hat*, Random House, 1957.

Annotated Brothers Grimm and *Annotated Classic Fairy Tales*), and Charles Perrault and Hans Christian Andersen (*Annotated Classic Fairy Tales*). I hope that Dr. Seuss would have been proud to belong to this club.

And I hope that *The Annotated Cat* shows people that it is fun to take Seuss's work seriously. As is true of all great children's books, *The Cat in the Hat* and *The Cat in the Hat Comes Back* operate on many levels. Yes, they teach us to read. But they also teach us about poetry, politics, ethics, comics, history, and con artistry—not to mention spot removal and indoor kite-flying. There's so much going on in these books because Seuss respected children's intelligence. Treating children with respect was key to his philosophy of writing for them. As he told the Associated Press's Dennis Georgatos in 1985, "I think I can communicate with kids because I don't try to communicate with kids. Ninety percent of the children's books patronize the child and say there's a difference between you and me, so you listen to this story. I, for some reason or another, don't do that. I treat the child as an equal."[74] Ludwig Bemelmans, creator of the Madeline books, made a similar observation when he said, "Dr. Seuss treats the child as an adult, and I think a children's book, to be good, must not be made for an inferior creature, for the diaper brigade. Because children are very, very, very alert, you know?"[75]

Seuss recognized this. He understood that the members of his audience were not lesser people simply because they knew less vocabulary. This insight enabled him to write books that children want to read. Outlining his plan for the Beginner Books a little over a year after *The Cat in the Hat* was published, Seuss explained, "We don't expect to revolutionize teaching methods, but we do hope to make learning new words more fun than it is at present."[76]

Fun is the secret. As the Cat says, "It is fun to have fun / But you have to know how." Seuss knew how. Juggling words, creating rhymes and pictures that stimulate the imagination, Seuss showed all of us that reading is a great way to have fun.

—Philip Nel, January 2007

of the Cat in the Hat, which she hung above her desk at the Geisel home in La Jolla, California. Cerf inscribed it, THIS CAT STARTED A PUBLISHING HOUSE. NO OTHER CAT CAN MAKE THIS CLAIM.[1]

In creating the Beginner Books series, Seuss hoped to get children excited about learning to read. As he told an interviewer in 1964, "My aim is to help kids to be able to say that reading is something that is fun to do."[2] The slogan I CAN READ IT ALL BY MYSELF echoes the "aha!" feeling that characterized his own discovery of reading. Asked "What's the first reading experience you can recall?" Seuss replied, "I became conscious of reading with the help of the Springfield, Mass., *Daily News.* I remember coming to life one day when I picked up a copy of the paper and found myself reading. It was the first time I understood what it meant to read."[3] Seuss came to life when he discovered he was reading all by himself; the Beginner Books' motto conveys this sense of excitement.

The Cat in the Hat Comes Back was the first Dr. Seuss book published with the I CAN READ IT ALL BY MYSELF logo on its cover. These words were then added to subsequent printings of *The Cat in the Hat*. The first Seuss book to feature the current Beginner Books logo on its initial printing was his third Beginner Book, *Green Eggs and Ham* (1960). This new logo was added to later printings of the earlier books.

Book collectors take note: in addition to having FOR BEGINNING READERS on its jacket, a first edition of *The Cat in the Hat* has several other distinguishing features. As Helen Younger, Marc Younger, and Dan Hirsch point out in their *First Editions of Dr. Seuss Books* (2002), one distinctive mark is the $2.00 price. In the top-right corner of the dust jacket's front flap—above the words "I can spell CAT"—is the price code signifying $2.00, "200/200" (later editions, such as the one pictured here, have the price code signifying $1.95, "195/195"). The spine of the jacket has "THE CAT IN THE HAT" in white, "Dr. Seuss" in red, and "RANDOM HOUSE" in black. Below "RANDOM HOUSE," later editions include "B-1"—marking the book as the first in the Beginner Books series. However, first editions do not mention Beginner Books. They do have educators' endorsements on the back of the jacket, and they also use matte (as opposed to shiny) paper for the printed cover beneath the jacket.[4] The early jacket reproduced here is not from a first edition, but it likely dates from 1958.

I Can Read It All by Myself (cover logo)
The success of *The Cat in the Hat* inspired Theodor Seuss Geisel (Dr. Seuss), his first wife, Helen Palmer Geisel (1898–1967), and Phyllis Cerf (b. 1911) to launch the Beginner Books line of reading primers for Random House. Cerf, who worked out of the Random House offices in New York, made Helen a needlepoint

THE ANNOTATED CAT

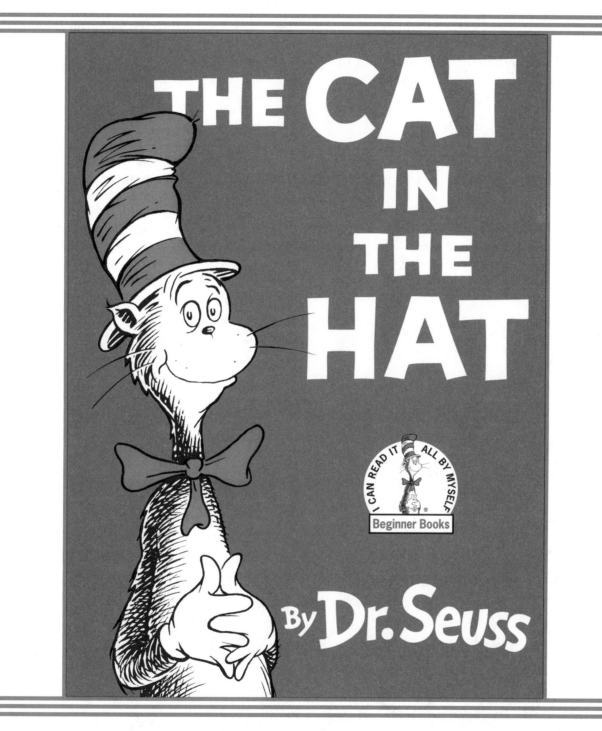

THE CAT IN THE HAT front cover

The Cat in the Hat (endpapers)

In her 1979 profile of Dr. Seuss, poet Karla Kuskin observed that Seuss's characters "have two family characteristics: slightly batty, oval eyes and a smile you might find on the Mona Lisa after her first martini"[5]—a description that, according to Judith and Neil Morgan, Seuss "happily quoted."[6] The Cat on the right, with one eyelid partly lowered, neatly evokes Kuskin's phrase.

Also on the right-hand endpaper, the Cat has five fingers on his left hand. With the possible exception of page 10 of *The Cat in the Hat,* the right-hand endpaper marks the only time in either *The Cat in the Hat* or *The Cat in the Hat Comes Back* that the Cat's hand has five fingers. Usually, the Cat has three fingers—one on either side of his hand, and a thick central finger (that resembles three fingers lumped together). Less frequently, he has four fingers on both hands or a different number of fingers on each hand. In the Cat's later appearances (the animated TV special, *I Can Read with My Eyes Shut!, The Cat's Quizzer,* and so on), the number of fingers per hand remains inconsistent, but within the three-to-four-finger range: that is, depending on the page (or frame), he has either three or four fingers per hand, and sometimes four on one and three on the other.

Why the discrepancies? Arguably, the varying number of digits could be attributed to the fact that a cat's paw has four prominent digits (a fifth is tucked around the side of the paw): fewer than five fingers per Cat's hand may more closely correspond with the four digits per cat's paw. However, the number is not consistently four. Further, what the Cat has at the ends of his arms more closely resemble hands than paws—indeed, since he walks upright, his front "legs" are clearly arms. As explained on page 44, Seuss drew expressively, adding or subtracting details to create a comic or emotional effect. As a result, elements like the Cat's size and the number of fingers vacillate.

Hand-colored prototype for endpapers in *The Cat in the Hat Songbook.*

THE CAT IN THE HAT endpapers

The Cat in the Hat (title)

Precisely how Seuss decided on the Cat in the Hat as his book's central character is a matter of debate. Throughout his life, Seuss told reporters stories that blended fact with fiction. As far back as 1934 (when he was famous for his Flit ads and magazine cartoons), Seuss told interviewer Bob Warren, "Let's see, you want an interview, a sort of life story as it were." Warren nodded. Seuss asked, "Truth or fiction?" Warren replied, "A little bit of both ought to do quite well." So Seuss conducted this and all interviews by telling stories that entertain but are not wholly accurate.[7]

This much is certain: Seuss wrote *The Cat in the Hat* because he was worried that children were not learning to read. John Hersey's (1914–1993) "Why Do Students Bog Down on First R?" (*Life,* 1954) and Rudolf Flesch's (1911–1986) *Why Johnny Can't Read—and What You Can Do About It* (1955) both said that boring primers like *Fun with Dick and Jane* were a major cause of children's failing to read. Hersey even suggested that Seuss write a better primer. William Spaulding (1898–1979), whom Seuss had worked with during the Second World War and who was director, at the time, of Houghton Mifflin's education division, said to him: "Write me a story that first-graders can't put down!" According to the Morgans and Robert Cahn, he stipulated that Seuss limit the book's vocabulary to no more than 225 different words, choosing those words from a list of 348.[8]

The precise numbers are not certain: depending on the interview, Seuss could use 200 to 250 words from a list of 300 to 400 (see the interviews by Beyette, Cahn, Carlinsky, Clark, Cott, Dangaard, Freeman [1964 and 1969], Frutig, Hacker, Hopkins [1978], Kitch, Kupferberg, and Lingeman). There are 236 different words in *The Cat in the Hat*. (In her *Dr. Seuss* [1988], Ruth K. MacDonald comes close to this number: she counts 237.)[9]

How Seuss got the idea for the Cat is equally uncertain. His favorite story—or, at least, the one he told most often—is that the title was inspired by his frustration with the word list. As he told Dan Carlinsky in 1979, "I read the list three times and almost went out of my head. I said, I'll read it once more and if I can find two words that rhyme that'll be the title of my book. (This is genius at work.) I found 'cat' and 'hat' and I said, The title will be *The Cat in the Hat*."[10]

However, more persuasive evidence suggests that the image preceded the words. His earliest accounts of creating the story all center around a sketch of the Cat. Seuss gave Robert Cahn the following explanation, which appeared in the *Saturday Evening Post* of July 6, 1957: "All I needed, I figured, was to find a whale of an exciting subject which would make the average six-year-old want to read like crazy. . . . None of the dull old stuff: Dick has a ball. Dick likes the ball. The ball is red, red, red, red."[11] Cahn paraphrases Seuss's idea for "a book about scaling the peaks of Everest at sixty degrees below zero." Houghton Mifflin thought the idea "exciting" but said, "However, you can't use the word 'scaling,' you can't use the word 'peaks,' you can't use 'Everest,' you can't use 'sixty,' and you can't use 'degrees.'" He then tried a story about a bird but discovered the word "bird" was not on the list; he briefly toyed with calling his story *The Wing Thing* but abandoned the idea. Six months later, Seuss was looking at "page after page of scrawls . . . piled in his den. He had accumulated stories which moved along in fine style but got nowhere. One story about a King Cat and a Queen Cat was halfway finished before he realized that the word 'queen' was not on the list." When "he was almost ready to give up, there emerged from a jumble of sketches a raffish cat wearing a battered stovepipe hat." Seuss "checked his list—both hat and cat were on it."[12] His tale about being inspired by a sketch of the Cat also appears in articles by Donald Freeman from 1964 and 1969.

On November 17, 1957, Seuss published two different versions of how he came to write *The Cat in the Hat*—"How Orlo Got His Book," in the *New York Times Book Review,* and "My Hassle with the First Grade Language," in the *Chicago Tribune* (both are reproduced at the back of this book). The "Hassle" version details his efforts to write the Everest story and the story about a King Cat and a Queen Cat. The "Orlo" version recounts his attempts to write *The Wing Thing* and describes his idea for a story titled *The Queen Zebra,* promptly abandoned upon learning that neither "queen" nor "zebra" was on the word list. He compares the experience of writing *The Cat in the Hat* to trying "to make apple stroodle without stroodles."

Asked how his books begin, Seuss replied, "Mine always start as a doodle. I may doodle a couple of animals. If they bite each other, it's going to be a good book. If you doodle enough, the characters begin to take over themselves—after a year and a half or so."[13] Judith and Neil Morgan's biography *Dr. Seuss & Mr. Geisel* (1995) offers more support for the idea that the image came before the words. Seuss told them that he got the idea for the Cat while riding with William Spaulding in an elevator at

Continued on page 26

THE CAT IN THE HAT title page

Continued from page 24

Houghton Mifflin in Boston. The elevator operator, Annie Williams, was "a small, stooped woman wearing 'a leather half-glove and a secret smile'"[14]—a sly smile and white gloves are two of the Cat's most recognizable features. Neil Morgan, well aware of Seuss's tendency to invent stories about himself, reports that drawing came much easier to Seuss than writing did—a claim that also places the image first. As he writes in Edward Connery Lathem's *Theodor Seuss Geisel: Reminiscences & Tributes* (1996):

> One day as Judith and I were interviewing Ted for the biography we were writing, we asked him to explain the creative process. Drawing was easy, he said, for him; the sweat came with writing. He said: "I stay with a line until the meter is right and the rhyme is right, even if it takes five hours. Sometimes I go counter to the clock."
>
> Ted at that point went silent and looked as if he were dazed. Finally, he said, "I don't understand what I just said, do you?" We said, "No." He said, "Well, then, that's it; that's the creative process." The subject was closed.[15]

Seuss's claim that his books start with doodles seems to confirm the idea that the picture came first, but we may never know the precise origin of the Cat. Consider, for example, Seuss's fanciful response to the question of where he gets his ideas:

> This is the most asked question of any successful author. Most authors will not disclose their source for fear that other, less successful authors will chisel in on their territory. However, I am willing to take that chance. I get all my ideas in Switzerland near the Forka Pass. There is a little town called Gletch, and two thousand feet up above Gletch there is a smaller hamlet called Uber Gletch. I go there on the fourth of August every summer to get my cuckoo clock repaired. While the cuckoo is in the hospital, I wander around and talk to the people in the streets. They are very strange people, and I get my ideas from them.[16]

The sun did not shine. (page 1)

At some point after 1985 (and, quite possibly, much more recently than that), Random House began printing *The Cat in the Hat* without the blue in the raised initial letter on this page. Instead, the hand-drawn "T" became simply a black outline with white inside. The missing blue appears to be a printing error. In Dr. Seuss's books, most initial letters are not hand-drawn, but when they are hand-drawn, they are always filled in.

Helen Younger, an expert on Seuss editions, reported that first editions, early reprint editions, and the Houghton Mifflin edition all include the blue "T." Seussologist Charles D. Cohen noted the presence of a blue "T" in a Macy's promotional edition (1995), Random House's 40th anniversary edition (1997), and the U.K. edition of *The Complete Cat in the Hat* (2002). All English-language copies Cohen has seen included a blue "T," and nearly all foreign editions began with a blue first letter. Two that lack the blue were a 2003 Greek edition (which left the letter unfilled) and the 1967 French/English edition (which did not have an enlarged first letter).

Finally, Random House's Cathy Goldsmith, Seuss's art director from 1980 to 1991, reports that Seuss never said anything about the color of the "T," which leads her to conclude he never saw a copy of the book with the omission.

Based on all of the above information, we have restored the blue here, and Random House has committed to including it in future editions.

The sun did not shine.
It was too wet to play.
So we sat in the house
All that cold, cold, wet day.

THE CAT IN THE HAT page 1

Too wet to go out
And too cold to play ball.
So we sat in the house.
We did nothing at all.

I sat there with Sally.
We sat there, we two.
And I said, "How I wish
We had something to do."

But all we could do was to
Sit!
    Sit!
        Sit!
            Sit!
And we did not like it.
Not one little bit.

NO BLUE

I sat there with Sally. (page 2)
In naming his character Sally, Seuss may be referring to the Dick and Jane primers: as Ruth K. MacDonald notes, "Oddly enough, Sally is the name of the younger sister of Dick and Jane." She asks, "Was Seuss poking fun?"[17]

It is quite possible that he was poking fun. In the May 24, 1954, issue of *Life* magazine, Hersey accused "bland, idealized" primers like Dick and Jane of contributing to illiteracy in America. To replace these "pallid primers," Hersey called upon "the wonderfully imaginative geniuses among children's illustrators" to come up with something new, and he specifically named Howard Pyle, Walt Disney, and Dr. Seuss.[18] His article reproduced three two-page spreads from the Dick and Jane books, including "See It Go" from *Fun with Dick and Jane* by William S. Gray (1885–1960) and May Hill Arbuthnot (1884–1969). Adapted from Louise Neyhart's (1905–1998) "The Runaway

Kite," "See It Go" features Dick, Jane, and Sally. Since Hersey's article helped inspire Seuss to write *The Cat in the Hat,* he may well have had Dick, Jane, *and* Sally in mind as he wrote.

Certainly, when discussing *The Cat in the Hat,* he frequently referred to Dick and Jane. In a November 1964 *McCall's* interview, Seuss said that with *The Cat in the Hat,* he wanted to write a book that did not include any of the "old dull stuff like 'Dick has a ball. Dick likes the ball. The ball is red, red, red.'"[19] In other words, just as the Cat arrives to rescue Sally and her brother from boredom, Seuss wrote *The Cat in the Hat* to rescue children from boring primers. Of *The Cat in the Hat,* Seuss said, "It's the book I'm proudest of because it had something to do with the death of the Dick and Jane primers."[20] Or, as Ellen Goodman wrote in a 1966 *Detroit Free Press* article, *The Cat in the Hat* "worked like a karate chop on the weary little world of Dick, Jane and Spot."[21] (Random House would later adopt this quotation as a back-cover blurb for *The Cat in the Hat* and other Beginner Books.)

Dick, Jane, and Sally also have a ball, toy boat, and umbrella, but they never combine them in the exuberant, chaotic manner that the Cat does on pages 16–17 and 18–19 of *The Cat in the Hat (CITH).* It is as if Seuss takes some of the elements from the Dick and Jane books (he is limited by his word list, just as Dick and Jane's authors were) and juggles them, showing what fun one can have with a limited list of ingredients. Dick, Jane, Sally, Spot (their dog), and Puff (their cat) do have fun and get into mild scrapes, but, as Hersey writes, the children remain "abnormally courteous, unnaturally clean boys and girls."[22] In *The Cat in the Hat,* the children are polite, but Seuss removes

Continued on page 30

I sat there with Sally.
We sat there, we two.
And I said, "How I wish
We had something to do!"

Too wet to go out
And too cold to play ball.
So we sat in the house.
We did nothing at all.

So all we could do was to
Sit!
    Sit!
        Sit!
            Sit!
And we did not like it.
Not one little bit.

THE CAT IN THE HAT pages 2–3

See It Go

"Look," said Dick.

"See it go.

See it go up."

Jane said, "Oh, look!

See it go.

See it go up."

"Up, up," said Sally.

"Go up, up, up."

6

7

Continued from page 28

the parents, replaces the fluffy Puff with the wily Cat, and invites anarchy into the reading primer. Hersey called Seuss's book a "gift to the art of reading" and a "harum-scarum masterpiece."[23]

Either unaware of or unperturbed by Seuss's criticism of her Dick and Jane books, Arbuthnot considered *The Cat in the Hat* "one of Dr. Seuss's best." In *Children's Reading in the Home* (1969), Arbuthnot called the book "a preposterous, nonsensical fantasy" with a conclusion that "brings every young reader back to a rereading of this completely satisfying nightmare."[24]

We sat there, we two. (page 2)
In March 1958, the average family had 2.3 children. This, at least, is the statistic for families with "related children under 18" and "own children under 18," according to the U.S. Census Bureau's Current Population Reports for March 1958. So, in portraying two children, Seuss reflects the average family size.[25]

He also reflects his own family's size. Ted Geisel grew up with one sister, Margaretha (Marnie) Geisel (1902–1945). (Another sister died in infancy.) Perhaps this fact lies behind the several brother-and-sister pairs in his stories, such as Peter T. Hooper and his sister in *Scrambled Eggs Super!* (1953), the two cats in "The Glunk That Got Thunk" from *I Can Lick 30 Tigers*

Today! and Other Stories (1969), and Ziggy and Zizzy Zozzfozzel in *The Cat's Quizzer* (1976). Most of Seuss's books feature lone male protagonists. But when he does include a sibling, the character is often female.

"We had something to do!" (page 2)
Seuss's original colored-pencil-and-crayon sketches include a clock on the wall, perhaps to enhance the sense of boredom (when one has nothing to do, time passes slowly). The position of the clock's hands indicates that it is exactly either 1 p.m. or 2 p.m.—the sketch is not precise enough to indicate which hour.

Too wet to go out (page 2)
In the bottom left-hand corner of the page, Seuss represents toys the children might use outside: bicycle, tennis racket, balls for either tennis (suggested by the racket) or baseball (suggested by "too cold to play ball" and by the presence of a baseball bat in Seuss's original colored-pencil sketches), and the red-striped ball with the star. This is the same ball on which the Cat will balance, using the fishbowl (first seen on *CITH* page 3) as part of his act. Though the toys and fish hint at the activity to come, here they contribute to the sense of stasis and boredom. The toys lie unused; the fish sleeps.

Everything about the artwork contributes to this feeling of listlessness. As Molly Bang (b. 1943) says in her *Picture This: How Pictures Work* (1991), "Smooth, flat, horizontal shapes give us a sense of stability and calm, vertical shapes are more exciting and more active, and diagonal shapes are dynamic because they imply motion or tension."[26] Seuss's emphasis here is on the horizontal, underscoring the "stability and calm" that the children find so dull. The eye follows the main diagonal line on page 2 up to the horizontal on page 3, coming to rest at the fish's table. Although the vertical lines of the window and of the fish's table do reach upward, the horizontal top and bottom lines contain them. If, as Bang argues, we "feel more scared looking at pointed shapes" and "we feel more secure or comforted looking at rounded shapes or curves," then the curves of the fishbowl, chairs, and children's heads put the reader at ease.[27]

In contrast, compare this scene with the chaotic ones on *CITH* pages 40–41 and 44–45, where virtually all lines are diagonal, and sharp-cornered kites threaten the furniture.

And too cold to play ball. (page 2)
Where the book emphasizes the fact that the room contains *outdoor* toys, the animated television special (1971) displays *indoor*

toys instead. With a storyboard by Chuck Jones (1912–2002) and lyrics and teleplay by Seuss, the TV version of *The Cat in the Hat* follows the line "nothing at all" with a song in which the narrator asks, "How can you have fun / Just sitting doing nothing when there's nothing to be done?" During this song, the fish looks at all the toys with which the boy and Sally could be playing: train set, dollhouse, easel, Tinkertoys, crayons, books, puzzle, toy crane, marbles, toy stove, doll in a carriage, and tea service on a table at which a doll and a teddy bear are seated. At the end of the song, the fish scowls at the children as if to say, "There's *plenty* to be done here." So, if the book views the children's boredom with sympathy (one cannot play indoors with outdoor toys), the cartoon suggests that their boredom is their own fault (they have an abundance of indoor toys).

So all we could do was to (page 3)

The Cat in the Hat is written mostly in anapestic dimeter, while sometimes preceding an anapestic foot with an iamb. An iamb is an unstressed syllable followed by a stressed syllable; an anapest is two unstressed syllables followed by a stressed syllable; and "dimeter" means that such a pattern occurs twice in a line. On *CITH* page 2, "Too wet to go out" is an iamb with an anapest; the remaining three lines of that stanza are in anapestic dimeter. If we read pages 3 and 5 aloud, ignoring both line breaks and punctuation, we would hear this metrical pattern

continue. However, if we read these pages as verse (taking both line breaks and punctuation into account), then all the lines on page 3 depart from this pattern: "So all we could do was to" begins with an unstressed syllable and then switches to dactylic dimeter—a pattern of one stressed syllable followed by two unstressed syllables.

The departure from the book's metrical pattern breaks the rhythm, creating a slight pause at this scene as the reader takes in the children's boredom. This brief suspension of movement makes the "BUMP!" on the next spread that much more dramatic because we go

from stasis (on page 3) to sudden interruption (on pages 4–5). The final line of page 5 resumes anapestic dimeter, reestablishing the book's forward momentum. As Seuss once observed, "You also establish a rhythm, and that tends to make kids want to go on. If you break a rhythm a child feels unfulfilled."[28] Here, Seuss creates that unfulfilling sense by breaking the rhythm, then exploits this tension with the "BUMP!" and finally resumes the rhythm (on page 5) to make readers want to go on.

Not one little bit. (page 3)

The colored-pencil sketches indicate that Seuss originally had a two-page spread between what are now pages 3 and 4. On the page before page 1, he has written:

> Merge
> 1, 2 + 3, + 4 + 5
> + 6 + 7
> losing one
> spread.

Then he has crossed this out—presumably because he merged the pages and lost the extra spread. At the top of page 2, he has written, "Old 4 + 5 eliminated" and crossed this out. Curiously, at the top of the final page 4 of the sketches, Seuss has crossed out "2 + 3 eliminated." So which spread was eliminated? No discarded spread survives, but it seems that the original spread for pages 4–5 disappeared (and not the original pages 2–3) because the numbers on pages 1, 2, and 3 remain unchanged but those on pages 4 and 5 have been altered. For instance, at the top left of page 4, the number 6 has been crossed out and the number 4 written to its right. At the top right of page 5, beneath the number 5, you can see the top-right corner of the number 7. This renumbering pattern continues up to the spread for pages 24–25—that is, each page number has been reduced by two.

At that point, Seuss either made a mistake in his numbering or omitted an additional two-page spread between pages 25 and 26. Pages 26–45 usually have two crossed-out page numbers, one four greater and the other two greater than the final page number. From pages 46 through 49, the numbers remain unchanged. On pages 50 through 53, Seuss decreased the numbers by two and then changed them back again. On all subsequent pages, the numbers remain the same—though it is worth noting that Seuss has made two copies (or retained two copies) of the final four two-page spreads.

Something went BUMP! (page 5)

In the far-left top margin of the colored-pencil sketches, Seuss has written, "TILT." Why? Presumably because, in the sketches, the chairs are not tilted but upright. Seuss initially relied upon the children's facial expressions to convey the fright they must feel: the faces are larger, and we see them closer to full-on (instead of in profile). In the revised version, the tilted chairs contribute to the emotional effect.

How that bump made us jump! (page 5)

Of his philosophy of writing for children, Seuss said, "I try to make every page get to a right-hand page" and then "to make it a cliff-hanger where you want to have to find out what happens on the next page."[29] This spread exemplifies the cliff-hanger approach. The two children and the fish all look rightward, toward the source of the noise, and—as Ruth K. MacDonald observes—the "BUMP!" sound appears "to emanate from even farther to the right, off the right-hand side of the right page,"[30] encouraging the reader to turn the page.

And then
Something went BUMP!
How that bump made us jump!

THE CAT IN THE HAT pages 4–5

86

7

We looked!
Then
And we saw him step in on the mat!
We looked!
And we saw him!
The Cat in the Hat!
And he said to us,
"Why do you sit there like that?"

"I know it is wet
And the sun is not sunny.
But we can have
Lots of good fun that is funny!"

The Cat in the Hat! (page 6)

According to a Gallup poll from January 1956, 54 percent of Americans had pets in their households. Of that group, 67 percent had at least one dog, 41 percent at least one cat, 22 percent at least one bird, and only 7 percent any fish.

At the time he wrote *The Cat in the Hat,* Seuss did not have a cat. He and Helen did have cats at one point, probably early in their marriage. In his 1960 *New Yorker* profile, E. J. Kahn, Jr., writes, "At the moment, the Geisels, who once kept twenty-five or thirty cats, have only one pet—an aging, wheezy Irish setter."[31] Dogs seem to have been Ted Geisel's preferred pet. When he was a little boy, his mother gave him a stuffed dog, which he named Theophrastus. As his biographers report, Geisel kept his stuffed Theophrastus "close to him throughout his life, often within sight from his drawing board."[32] He also adopted the name as one of his pseudonyms, Dr. Theophrastus

Seuss, which first appeared on his "Boids and Beasties" cartoon published in *Judge* on November 19, 1927. And he had dogs of the non-stuffed variety. As a boy, Ted Geisel had a bulldog named Rex; as adults, he and Helen had Irish setters. As the Morgans note, after the Geisels moved to California in 1943, a "neighbor bred Irish setters and a succession of them became a constant in the Geisels' life."[33]

But cats are a recurring theme in Seuss's work. As Charles D. Cohen notes in his *The Seuss, the Whole Seuss, and Nothing but the Seuss* (2004), "Throughout the 1930s and 1940s, a cat appeared in the background of Dr. Seuss illustrations the way that Hitchcock appeared in his films—not in every one but often enough to be noticed."[34] Each of the "seven black-gowned magicians" from *The 500 Hats of Bartholomew Cubbins* (1938) has "a lean black cat." *The King's Stilts* (1939) is Seuss's first book in which cats play a prominent role in the story. As King Birtram explains, "Everything in Binn depends on our Patrol Cats. They are more important than our army, our navy, and our fire department too, for they keep the Nizzards away from the Dike Trees, and the Dike Trees keep the ocean back out of our land." (If left unchecked, Nizzards—"a kind of giant blackbird with a sharp and pointed beak"—would eat the roots of the trees that protect the island kingdom of Binn.) Unlike the Cat in the Hat, these cats walk on all fours.

Locating the first Seussian cats who walk upright, Cohen points to three characters who, visually, must be the Cat's direct ancestors: (1) a clarinet-playing cat in Seuss's illustrations for "What Swing Really Does to People," an article by Benny Goodman from the May 14, 1938, issue of *Liberty;* (2) a hat-wearing cat who chants along with King Derwin's magicians in Seuss's

Continued on page 36

THE ANNOTATED CAT

We looked!

Then we saw him step in on the mat!

We looked!

And we saw him!

The Cat in the Hat!

And he said to us,

"Why do you sit there like that?"

"I know it is wet

And the sun is not sunny.

But we can have

Lots of good fun that is funny!"

THE CAT IN THE HAT pages 6–7

Continued from page 34

Bartholomew and the Oobleck (1949); and (3) the "carefree Ormie" in Seuss's sketches for some 1949 advertisements for the Ford Motor Company.[35]

For the Cat's literary ancestors, Cohen points to the title character of George Herriman's (1880–1944) "Krazy Kat" (1913–1944), a favorite comic strip of Seuss's. The personality of Seuss's Cat is much closer to Ignatz Mouse, the upstart who

enjoys hurling bricks at Krazy Kat. However, Cohen points to some visual continuities between Cat and Kat: "What Ted seems to have kept of Krazy Kat was the image of a bipedal cat wearing a bow tie. Even before Krazy appeared in color starting in June 1935, movie posters from the 1920s show Krazy's bow tie to be *red*."[36] Cohen also suggests Howard R. Garis's (1873–1962) *Uncle Wiggily*, a top-hatted rabbit, as an influence on the Cat. The character, who first showed up in stories published in the *Newark News* in 1910, appeared in over fifty books, starting with *Uncle Wiggily's Adventures* (1912). According to Cohen,

Uncle Wiggily "reinforced the characteristic of walking erect and wearing a red bow tie and added the element of a crutch or cane, which Ted transformed into the Cat's umbrella. On the covers of many books, such as *Uncle Wiggily's Automobile* (1913) and *Uncle Wiggily at the Seashore* (1915), Wiggily also wears a top hat."[37] Cohen considers Ub Iwerks's (1901–1971) animated cartoon *Dick Whittington's Cat* (1936) another potential influence because, in Iwerks's rendition, the cat wears a hat and gloves—just as Seuss's Cat does.[38] But Cohen considers Felix the Cat to be the "feline predecessor whose personality most resembles the Cat in the Hat."[39] As Cohen explains, in the movie *Felix Minds the Kid* (1922), "Felix ends up in a home alone with a child and proves to be the world's worst babysitter. At one point, he uses a white ball, decorated with one thick, dark band, in a balancing routine, as Ted's Cat would do 35 years later."[40]

Other antecedents of Seuss's Cat appear earlier in children's literature. The title character of Charles Perrault's (1628–1703) "Master Cat, or Puss in Boots" (1697) walks upright and wears a hat in the pictures for many versions of the tale, including those illustrated by Gustave Doré (1832–1883), whose *Contes de Perrault* was published in 1862, and by George Cruikshank (1792–1878), whose *Puss in Boots* appeared in 1864. In Cruikshank's illustrations, Puss also carries a cane. Puss is good at "playing clever tricks,"[41] and Seuss's Cat knows a "lot of good tricks." More importantly, both Puss and Cat are wily, resourceful, and successful con artists. Puss defies social conventions, managing to arrange a

marriage between his master (a miller's son) and a princess. As we will see, the Cat also manages to break societal rules and get away with it.

Seuss was certainly familiar with Perrault's tale. In July 1949, at the University of Utah, he delivered a series of talks on children's literature. During his discussion of fables, myths, and epics, Seuss mentioned "Puss in Boots" as an example of a turning point in the history of fairy tales, during the period in which "cheerfulness creeps in" to children's literature.

In those same lectures, Seuss listed George Cruikshank, Edward Lear (1812–1888), and John Tenniel (1820–1914) among the "first great juvenile illustrators." Cruikshank gave us the Puss in Boots (with hat and cane) mentioned above; Lear drew many cats, his best known in "The Owl and the Pussycat" (1871); Tenniel illustrated the Cheshire Cat in Lewis Carroll's (1832–1898) *Alice's Adventures in Wonderland* (1865). Seuss's Cat has little in common with Lear's pussycat but shares the Cheshire Cat's sense of mischief. Carroll's Cat is good at finding arguments to support his implausible claims; similarly, Seuss's Cat anticipates the children's objections and, for a time, gets them to accept his idea of fun.

An intriguing possibility that Seuss never mentioned is Harry S. Miller's song "The Cat Came Back" (1893), about a yellow cat that keeps returning to Mister Johnson's home and, subsequently, to several other locations. As the refrain says, the "cat came back for it wouldn't stay away." Whether "The Cat Came Back" had any influence on *The Cat in the Hat* or *The Cat in the Hat Comes Back* is impossible to know, but the song remained popular enough to inspire Cordell Barker's animated cartoon in 1988.

"Why do you sit there like that?" (page 6)

Although the Cat in the Hat will later speak in anapestic dimeter, his first line reverses that meter—dactylic dimeter (plus one additional unstressed syllable). That is, instead of two unstressed syllables followed by a stressed syllable, the Cat's dialogue has a stressed syllable followed by two unstressed syllables. Since he will soon reverse the order of the house, his first line very aptly reverses the rhythm of the verse.

"Lots of good fun that is funny!" (page 7)

In Seuss's colored-pencil sketches, the Cat is much smaller—so much so that he is nearly the size of the children. His smaller size suggests both that he is childish and that, initially, he poses little threat to the children.

"I know some good games we could play," (page 8)
In the animated cartoon version, the fish interrupts throughout this speech, but his ineffectual interruptions appear mostly comic. He's unable to get in much more than "Now, you listen here, Cat" or "Listen, Cat in the Hat" because the Cat is busy charming the children and ignoring the fish. At the end of the speech, the fish shouts, "Out of this house! / I'm warning you: Get!" The Cat finally turns to the fish and says, "Who's that? / I believe that we haven't yet met." The fish replies, "The name is Krinklebein. Carlos K. Krinklebein." Daws Butler (1916–1988), who provided the fish's voice, emphasized the comedy in the fish's indignant response to the Cat. Butler was also the voice of Hanna-Barbera's Yogi Bear and Huckleberry Hound and Jay Ward's Cap'n Crunch.

"I will show them to you." (page 8)
In the original sketches (pencil and crayon, with pasted-in typescript), Seuss's Cat is a little less bold. Instead of simply announcing what he "will" show, he says that he "can" show or asks them to "let" him show—as if he is seeking the children's consent. In the sketches, the first version of this line is "I can show them to you." Seuss crossed out "I can" and replaced it with "Let me." He then crossed that out and penciled in "I will."

In the final version, Seuss relies on illustrations (instead of words) to convey the Cat's pretense of politeness. In the sketches, the Cat's hat is on his head, and he gestures with his right arm. In the final version, however, Seuss erased the original hat and changed the position of the arm so that the Cat is tipping his hat. A related change occurs in the position of the Cat's umbrella. Initially, the umbrella pointed down; in the finished book, the Cat jauntily balances the umbrella on his fingertip, pointing it up over his shoulder. Tipping his hat and holding his umbrella as if it were a cane, the Cat acts the role of the urbane gentleman (or gentlecat).

"Will not mind at all if I do." (page 8)
As the fish points out on *CITH* page 11, Mother would indeed mind. Once again, in the original sketches, the Cat gives the children time to object. Instead of "Your mother / Will not mind at all if I do," Seuss typed, "Do you (think) that your mother / Would mind if I do?" He then removed the question. After the first line, he handwrote, "Your mother would." He crossed out the conditional "would" and wrote "will." After the second line, he added "mind at all" before replacing it with "Not mind at all if I do." With the change from the Cat's asking permission to the

Cat's granting himself permission, the final version shows the Cat as more confident and more manipulative.

Then Sally and I (page 8)
An earlier name for Sally was Janet. On the colored-pencil sketches, Seuss has typed, "And Janet and I." Pasted over that phrase is "Then Sally and I."

Our mother was out of the house / For the day. (page 8)
Some contemporary critics have wondered what sort of mother would leave her children home alone for the day. As Louis Menand (b. 1952) writes, "What private demons or desires compelled this mother to leave two young children at home all day, with the front door unlocked, under the supervision of a fish? Terrible as the cat is, the woman is lucky that her children do not fall prey to some more insidious intruder."[42] At the time of its publication, however, no reviewers expressed anxiety over the mother being out of the house for the day.

So where was Mother? Although Seuss provides no explanation for her daylong absence, Mother may have been at work: in 1958, one mother in seven was employed full-time outside of the home, and 53 percent of these working moms had children under twelve years old; 58 percent of these children under twelve were in the home, being looked after by either a relative or a nonrelative.[43] Perhaps reviewers thought the book's childcare arrangement fairly normal because the fish acts as a kind of relative, keeping an eye on Sally and her brother. Children being left home alone would have been more unusual: only 8 percent—or about one in thirteen—of children under twelve (whose mothers worked) were responsible for their own care.[44] However, as Liza Mundy observes in an essay that uses *The Cat in the Hat* as an occasion to reflect upon motherhood, "A mom could be absent, decades ago, because at any given moment she could assume that lots of other moms in the neighborhood were not."[45] The 1971 TV special confirms this idea. As Mother returns home (near the end of the story), the fish monitors her progress through the neighborhood, identifying each house by its married female occupant: "She's passing Mrs. Blumberg's house!" and "She's passing Mrs. Thompson's house!" he exclaims. That both women are married allows us to infer that they may also be mothers. The TV version also discloses, near the end, precisely where Mother went: she has been grocery shopping. As the fish announces Mother's approach to the still-

Continued on page 40

"I know some good games we could play,"
Said the cat.
"I know some new tricks,"
Said the Cat in the Hat.
"A lot of good tricks.
I will show them to you.
Your mother
Will not mind at all if I do."

Then Sally and I
Did not know what to say.
Our mother was out of the house
For the day.

THE CAT IN THE HAT pages 8–9

Continued from page 38

being-tidied-up house, he says, "Now she's taking her groceries out of the car." Of course, the book and the cartoon adaptation differ in many ways, and the book does not say whether she was shopping, at work, or somewhere else.

How long is she gone? The animated cartoon suggests that Mother is away for a shorter period of time and ultimately explains where she went. In the book, she is gone "for the day." In the cartoon, she says before she leaves, "I'll be back at, uh, ah, 3:30 sharp." Although she seems unsure if she'll be back at 3:30, she does at least measure her absence in hours and minutes, instead of a full day. The published book lacks such specific temporal cues, but page 2 of Seuss's colored-pencil sketches includes a clock reading either 1 p.m. or 2 p.m. So, in Seuss's original conception, the mother apparently is gone for only part of the day.

Irrespective of the occasion for the mother's absence, absent parents are a common feature of children's books. Lewis Carroll's *Alice's Adventures in Wonderland,* L. Frank Baum's (1856–1919) *Wonderful Wizard of Oz* (1900), Erich Kästner's (1899–1974) *Emil and the Detectives* (1930), Astrid Lindgren's (1907–2002) *Pippi Longstocking* (1945), and Maurice Sendak's (b. 1928) *Where the Wild Things Are* (1963)—to name but a few—all feature children having adventures without their parents. Alice is in a dream, the orphaned Dorothy has been whisked off to Oz, Emil takes the train to Berlin alone, Pippi's papa is at sea, and Max travels solo to the land of the wild things. Indeed, the absence of adult supervision creates the occasion for these characters to have adventures. As Mundy notes, after reading Menand's essay, she and her friends began "recalling all the interesting things that did in fact occur when our mothers happened to be elsewhere."[46]

"He should not be here." (page 11)

Seuss called the fish "my version of Cotton Mather,"[47] and he probably did not intend that as a compliment. Mather (1663–1728), who advised the prosecutors in the Salem witchcraft trials, was pastor of Boston's Old North Church and a famous moralist. In "The Duties of Children to Their Parents" (1699), Mather wrote, "*Undutiful Children,* for the Contempt they cast upon their Parents, are often *Cursed* by God, with a *Mischief* brought upon all their Affairs. A Strange *Disaster* uses to follow *Undutiful Children,* much *Evil pursues* that kind of *Sinner;* there is a secret *Vengeance* of God, perplexing their Affairs; through that *Vengeance* of God, None of their Affairs do

prosper with them" (emphasis Mather's).[48] Appropriately, Louis Menand calls the fish "a tin-pot Puritan."[49]

In the animated version, the fish introduces himself as Carlos K. Krinklebein, a name that sounds more Jewish than Christian. Although his name does not directly link him to Mather, its etymology suggests that he's a bit of a snob. According to the *Oxford English Dictionary,* "krinkle" means both "to wrinkle" and "to cringe"; "bein" can denote someone who is well-off. His name, then, describes an old, well-to-do character given to cringing, an impression confirmed by vocal artist Daws Butler, who gave the fish the voice of an uptight killjoy. Later in the cartoon adaptation, Thing One and Thing Two reinforce this perception when they sing, "There's always some fish, some sour-belly fish / Whose only one wish is to flatten the fun." They also call him a "crochety one" and a "blotchety one."

Since Thing One and Thing Two's ideas of "fun" would frighten most homeowners, it is not surprising that critics tend to focus on the fish's role as superego. Jonathan Cott (b. 1942) considers the fish a combination of Mather and a "superego."[50] Or, as Betty Mensch (b. 1943) and Alan Freeman (1943–1995) write, "Drawing on old Christian symbolism (the fish was an ancient sign of Christianity), Dr. Seuss portrays the fish as a kind of ever-nagging superego, the embodiment of utterly conventionalized morality."[51] Several other critics have made the superego comparison, notably Francelia Butler (1989), Anna Quindlen (1991), and Louis Menand (2002). And, while Ruth K. MacDonald does not label the fish "superego," she does say that "the fish represents the mother."[52]

If we were to extend this psychological interpretation of the book, then the Cat, Thing One, and Thing Two seem to spring from the id—pleasure-seeking, impulsive, chaotic. The children serve as the ego, trying to mediate between the fish (superego), on the one hand, and the Cat and his Things (id), on the other. Quindlen's piece, which calls the Cat "pure id," appears to endorse this interpretation, but Mensch and Freeman suggest that the Cat is part id and part ego: "The cat seems to act as a kind of mediator: However irreverent, he complies with social norms at least enough to avoid dreaded punishment (he *does* clean up his mess), while at the same time retaining his utter commitment to having fun. Unlike the accommodationist ego of Freudian imagery, however, the cat is more liberator than integrator, too much a fierce deconstructor of norms to be content with mere balancing."[53]

But our fish said, "No! No!
Make that cat go away!
Tell that Cat in the Hat
You do NOT want to play.
He should not be here.
He should not be about.
He should not be here
When your mother is out!"

THE CAT IN THE HAT pages 10–11

"My tricks are not bad," (page 12)

As the children soon discover, the Cat will unleash "all kinds of bad tricks" (*CITH* page 45). Like many of Seuss's famous characters, the Cat is a classic American con artist. Seuss portrays some of his con men as swindlers: the Grinch (1957), the Once-ler (from *The Lorax*, 1971), and Sylvester McMonkey McBean (below, in *The Sneetches and Other Stories*, 1961) are all dishonest salesmen, tricking people into doing things or buying things they shouldn't. Where those characters operate in the tradition of William Faulkner's (1897–1962) Flem Snopes, the Cat acts more in the style of the title characters from L. Frank Baum's *The Wonderful Wizard of Oz* and Meredith Wilson's (1902–1984) *The Music Man* (1957): they are confidence men whose imagination injects excitement into the lives of others. Professor Harold Hill brings joy into River City, the Wizard of Oz helps Dorothy's friends become who they want to be, and the Cat shows that it "is fun to have fun / But you have to know how."

"Up-up-up with a fish!" (page 12)

In the 1971 TV special, the "Up-up-up with a fish" game is completely different—if equally precarious for the fish. After saying "He should not be here / When your mother is out!" the fish retreats into his bowl and blows bubbles up at the Cat. The Cat replies, "My dear Mr. Krinklebein, / My tricks are quite safe." As he speaks, he gathers the bubbles, placing them one on top of the next to create a bubble-spring. "I invite you to join in the fun, if you wish," he says, placing the fishbowl on the spring, "with a game that I call Up-up-up with a fish!" The fishbowl shoots up toward the ceiling, teetering dangerously on the stack of bubbles. "Put me down! / Put me down, / You fool Cat!" the fish shouts (contrast with *CITH* page 13), and the Cat pops one bubble at a time, bringing the fish jerkily back to the tabletop.

"Now! Now! Have no fear.
Have no fear!" said the cat.
"My tricks are not bad,"
Said the Cat in the Hat.
"Why, we can have
Lots of good fun, if you wish,
With a game that I call
UP-UP-UP with a fish!"

"Put me down!" said the fish.
"This is no fun at all!
Put me down!" said the fish.
"I do NOT wish to fall!"

THE CAT IN THE HAT pages 12–13

"And a cup on my hat!" (page 14)

In what appears to be the earliest interview given after the publication of *The Cat in the Hat,* Dr. Seuss referred to the juggling scenes as very useful for introducing vocabulary. Dorothy Barclay, the author of the piece, paraphrases Seuss instead of quoting him, but you can hear his voice: "Writing a book with strict limitations on the words to be used . . . was somewhat akin to making a mosaic, Dr. Seuss reported in a recent interview. He just kept moving them around in his brain until they began to form patterns. The juggling scene was helpful for bringing in a raft of required nouns—'cup,' 'milk,' 'cake,' 'rake,' 'toy,' 'fan'—that otherwise would not have fitted into the design."[54]

This juggling of words also looks back to *If I Ran the Circus* (1956), where a Juggling Jott (at left) juggles twenty-two question marks. As Kevin Shortsleeve writes, "Seuss books are bursting with carnivalesque imagery. The Cat in the Hat himself . . . acts very much like a traditional clown and happens also to be a juggler."[55]

Said the cat . . . (page 14)

In the far-right margin of the colored-pencil sketches for page 15, Seuss has written in pencil, "Cat smaller—for growth pattern," indicating that he will make the Cat slightly larger on subsequent pages—as he does do in the final version. The effect of this "growth pattern" is to enhance the comic exaggeration: as the juggling act grows increasingly elaborate, the Cat's size and confidence both increase. In a 1975 interview with Edward Connery Lathem, Seuss discussed this artistic technique when describing the difficulty of animating his characters: "I make it hard for [anyone to bring my books over to] TV. If you look through my *Cat in the Hat* book [you'll see that] I haven't drawn two [pictures of the Cat] the same. If I want to exaggerate—to lengthen an arm to balance a page—I do it. [The animators] almost died when I went up there [and turned the Cat over to them]."[56] (The bracketed words in the quotation are Lathem's. As he revised the article for publication, he wrote his editorial suggestions in brackets and Seuss either accepted or modified them. The parts of the interview dealing with Seuss's early life appeared in the April 1976 issue of the *Dartmouth Alumni Magazine.* Other portions, such as this quotation, were never published.)

"Have no fear!" said the cat.

"I will not let you fall.

I will hold you up high

As I stand on a ball.

With a book on one hand!

And a cup on my hat!

But that is not ALL I can do!"

Said the cat . . .

THE CAT IN THE HAT pages 14–15

"But that is not all!" (page 16)

The year after John Hersey's *Life* article (see page 6), Rudolf Flesch's *Why Johnny Can't Read* (1955) also faulted "those series of horrible, stupid, emasculated, pointless, tasteless little readers" like the Dick and Jane books for failing to teach children to read.[57] The thrust of Flesch's critique is that the educational system, then using the whole-word method, needed to return to phonics. According to Flesch, teaching children to recognize words instead of the sounds that make up each word is like asking them to "learn to read English as if it were Chinese. One word after another after another after another. If we want to read materials with a vocabulary of 10,000 words, then we

have to memorize 10,000 words; if we want to go to the 20,000 word range, we have to learn, one by one, 20,000 words; and so on."[58] Instead, he says, we should use phonics because "if a child isn't taught the sounds of the letters, then he has absolutely nothing to go by when he tries to read a word. All he can do is guess."[59] Learning to read, Flesch says, is not a matter of guessing. Rather, "learning to read means learning to sound out words. . . . Phonics is the key."[60]

Flesch liked Seuss's work not only because it was much more fun than the Dick and Jane books but because of the sound and rhythm of Seuss's language. For example, the end rhymes ("cat" and "hat," "fish" and "dish," "ball" and "all") and internal rhymes ("cup" and "up," "look" and "books") aid the young reader in pronouncing unknown words. Seuss recognized this himself. As he said, "Rhyming more or less makes kids pronounce words correctly." Speaking of his book *One Fish Two Fish Red Fish Blue Fish* (1960), Seuss said that "if a youngster is sounding out the words, what a help when 'sing' is related to 'thing' and 'Ying.' 'It's fun to sing / if you sing with a Ying / My Ying can sing like anything.'"[61] As Ruth K. MacDonald puts it, rhyme "permits the reader to find a clue for the pronunciation of a new word, or an ambiguous word, in the word with which it must rhyme. . . . With the device of rhyme, the author avoids many problems of introducing unfamiliar vocabulary, and shows the reader one of the mysteries of language: that with a simple change of a consonant, the entire meaning of a word changes."[62] According to at least one contemporary report, this method succeeded. In the February 1958 issue of *The Reading Teacher*, Mary Elisabeth Coleman writes, "*The Cat in the Hat* by Dr. Seuss justifies its publicity. A second-grade reader reports, 'I can get most of the new words because there usually is a rhyming word.'"[63]

Two years after *The Cat in the Hat*'s publication, Flesch wrote of Seuss's language, "What exactly is it that makes this stuff immortal? I don't know. There is something about it— a swing to the language, a deep understanding of the playful mind of a child, an indefinable something that makes Dr. Seuss a genius pure and simple."

Dr. Seuss has written a book that Johnny can read!

Which is why this new kind of first reader has taken the country by storm!

THE CAT IN THE HAT

$2.00. RANDOM HOUSE

"Look at me!

Look at me now!" said the cat.

"With a cup and a cake

On the top of my hat!

I can hold up TWO books!

I can hold up the fish!

And a little toy ship!

And some milk on a dish!

And look!

I can hop up and down on the ball!

But that is not all!

Oh, no.

That is not all . . .

THE CAT IN THE HAT pages 16–17

"It is fun to have fun" (page 18)

Don L. F. Nilsen points out that both "It is fun to have fun" and "we can have / Lots of good fun that is funny!" (*CITH* page 7) are examples of polyptoton, in which a word is repeated in a sentence, but with a different function.[64] In the first example, "fun" figures as both adjective and noun; in the second, "fun" is a noun and "funny" is an adjective. This device recurs in Seuss's work, as in "I can fan with the fan" (on this page) and "And NOW comes an act of Enormous Enormance! / No former performer's performed this performance!" (from *If I Ran the Circus,* 1956). As Ruth K. MacDonald observes, through his use of polyptoton, "Seuss introduces the child reader into the playfulness that language can have when it is tinkered with, and sanctions this playfulness by his expert use of it."[65]

"But that is not all." (page 18)

The Cat on the cover and endpapers is the character's most reproduced image, but this scene's Cat and the Cat on *CITH* page 15 must be tied for second place. The Cat's attempt to balance himself (and much more) atop the ball has become an iconic representation of him, appearing frequently in articles and political satire. This page's image was first reproduced in Rochelle Girson's profile of Dr. Seuss (*Saturday Review,* May 11, 1957) and emerged again in

the *Saturday Evening Post* (July 6, 1957), *McCall's* (November 1964), and Ruth K. MacDonald's *Dr. Seuss* (1988). A redrawn version appears in the March 4, 1979, issue of the *Magazine of the Boston Herald American.* The page 15 illustration appears on the cover of *Early Years* (April 1973) and in obituaries for and tributes to Seuss: the *New York Times* (September 26, 1991), *Publishers Weekly* (October 25, 1991), and the *Dartmouth Review* (November 13, 1991). Judith Frutig's "Dr. Seuss's Green-Eggs-and-Ham World" (*Christian Science Monitor,* May 12, 1978) uses the image from *CITH* page 17.

In political satire, the scene's first appearance is probably in Robert Coover's (b. 1932) send-up of presidential campaigns, "The Cat in the Hat for President" (1968). At a convention, when

accepting his nomination for president of the United States, the Cat "arrived on roller skates, holding up a cake on a rake. On, or in, the cake sat a goat wearing a coat, an umbrella balanced on its nose. On the top of the umbrella wobbled a fishbowl with a fish inside that was crying: 'Stop it! Stop it! / I will fall! / I do not like this! / Not at all!'"[66] In Coover's tale, the Cat's candidacy demonstrates people's willingness to embrace a new and exciting candidate even if he may not be suitable for the job. As Party Chairman Mr. Brown notes, "The Cat was entertaining maybe, exciting, liberating, even prodigious—but he was also, obscurely, a threat. Dangerous, yes, he was. He seemed to be in control of himself, but who could follow him without great personal peril?"[67]

In December 1998, while many Republicans were attempting to impeach President Bill Clinton and the president himself was ordering air strikes on suspected weapons sites in Iraq, Pulitzer Prize–winning cartoonist Signe Wilkinson evoked this specific illustration of the Cat in the Hat in her caricature of Clinton. In her cartoon, Clinton balances on a ball, trying to hold up more items than is possible: "I can hold up a thong / And the dress with the stain! / I can send off a bomb / On this cool fighter plane! / I can make up a speech / While you try to impeach! / But that is not all! / Oh, no. / That is not all! . . ." The cartoon implied that Clinton was failing in his attempts to balance American foreign policy with his own looming impeachment. On the eve of the 2004 presidential election, *MAD* magazine's writer Desmond Devlin and artist Mort Drucker portrayed George W. Bush as the Cat on a ball—the earth—carelessly juggling. Devlin wrote, "As you listen to President George W. Bush and his administration, you may notice a sort of bizarre logic emerge, a magical childlike reality in which the only rules are the ones they make up themselves." As evidence, he cited the 2004 State of the Union, in which the president claimed, "I will send you a budget that funds the war, protects the homeland, and meets important domestic needs, while limiting the growth in discretionary spending to less than 4 percent. . . . By doing so, we can cut the deficit in half over the next five years."[68]

"Look at me!

Look at me!

Look at me NOW!

It is fun to have fun

But you have to know how.

I can hold up the cup

And the milk and the cake!

I can hold up these books!

And the fish on a rake!

I can hold the toy ship

And a little toy man!

And look! With my tail

I can hold a red fan!

I can fan with the fan

As I hop on the ball!

But that is not all.

Oh, no.

That is not all. . . ."

THE CAT IN THE HAT pages 18–19

That is what the cat said...

THEN HE FELL ON HIS HEAD!

He came down with a PLUMP!

He ~~fell off~~ came down from of the ball.

And Sally and I,

We saw all the things fall!

He came down with a bump (page 21)

In his workshops at the University of Utah in July 1949, Seuss spoke of children's humor. In his notes, under the heading "HUMOR. What's funny to a child," he has written the following list:

Sounds
Surprise
Grotesque, Incongruous
Falling down (the mighty falling)
Absurdity
Horseplay

The citation he provides—"Arbuthnot 42"—indicates that these ideas come from page 42 of *Children and Books* (1947) by May Hill Arbuthnot. Although he would later criticize her Dick and Jane books, he seems to agree with some of her ideas about humor in children's literature. In a chapter on Mother Goose, she identifies all of the above as features of a child's sense of humor. She writes, "What does he laugh at? It is hard to say; we can only watch and listen. Sometimes he laughs at the sound; often he laughs at the grotesque or the incongruous. Surprise tickles him, absurd antics amuse him, and broad horseplay

Continued on page 52

That is what the cat said . . .
Then he fell on his head!
He came down with a bump
From up there on the ball.
And Sally and I,
We saw ALL the things fall!

THE CAT IN THE HAT pages 20–21

Continued from page 50

delights him." Noting that there "are plenty of examples from *Mother Goose,*" Arbuthnot provides several, including "Humpty Dumpty has a fall (falls always bring a laugh)."[69]

This scene contains many of the humorous elements listed: surprise, falling down, absurdity, and sound. Sounds are a key part of Seuss's humor. In *Scrambled Eggs Super!* (1953), Peter T. Hooper rides "on the top / Of a Ham-ikka-Schnim-ikka-Schnam-ikka Schnopp." The title character of *Mr. Brown Can Moo! Can You?* (1970) repeats the word "GRUM" to imitate "a hippopotamus / chewing gum." Here, the Cat has entered with a "BUMP!" (*CITH* page 5) and now comes down with a "bump." The Things' kites will go "Bump! Thump! Thump! Bump!" (page 40). The boy's net will come down with a "PLOP" (page 52). Seuss was sufficiently interested in getting the right sound that he revised until he liked what he heard: the "bump" on this page began as "PLUMP!" (see next annotation); both "Bump! Thump! Thump! Bump!" and "PLOP" began differently, too (see pages 70–71 and 82–83).

From up there on the ball. (page 21)

"He came down with a bump / From up there on the ball" began as "He came down with a PLUMP! / He fell off of the ball." Seuss first changed it to "He came down with a PLUMP! / He came down from the ball" before settling on this version. Although it loses the onomatopoetic "PLUMP" (because it wasn't on the word list?), the revised "He came down with a bump" is a more dramatic way of bringing the Cat to earth. It conveys the sound of the fall ("bump") and contrasts where he was ("up there") to where he is ("down"). The rhythms of the poetry propel the reader forward, and the alliterative "b" sounds in "bump" and "ball" make the verse more fun to say. Seuss was a master of the art of revision. As he once said, "To produce a 60-page book, I may easily write more than 1,000 pages before I'm satisfied. The most important thing about me, I feel, is that I work like hell—write, rewrite, reject, re-reject, and polish incessantly."[70]

For his dedication to revision, Seuss credited Saxe Commins, his original editor at Random House—and the editor of Ernest Hemingway and Eugene O'Neill. "He convinced me," Seuss said, "that I had as much responsibility to take time and work hard as they did. He helped me realize that a paragraph in a children's book is equivalent to a chapter in an adult book."[71]

We saw ALL the things fall! (page 21)

In the colored-pencil sketches, the Cat's antics pose a greater threat to the safety of the children. In the sketch for this page, the children appear in the foreground (instead of the background) and are backing into the corner of the page—as if to avoid the shower of objects raining down. The cake looks as if it may crash onto their heads. In the published version, though they look anxious, they are more out of harm's way.

"Not one little bit!" (page 22)

On the page opposite the first page of the colored-pencil sketches, Seuss has written in pencil:

> Check + place strongly
> 1) REFRAINS
> 2) One little bit
> 3) When our mother was out
> 4) Another good game that I know
> 5) Tip of his hat

Although he has also crossed out everything on this page, these phrases do in fact serve as refrains throughout the book. "One little bit" appears here and on *CITH* pages 3 and 39. Variations of "mother was out" occur four times—the original phrase on page 8, "mother is out" on page 11, and "mother is not [here]" on pages 25 and 35. Similarly, "good games" is on page 8, and "good game" is on pages 22 and 27. The Cat tips his hat on pages 9, 30, and 59; the words "tip of his hat" are on pages 31 and 58.

And our fish came down, too.
He fell into a pot!
He said, "Do I like this?
Oh, no! I do not.
This is not a good game,"
Said our fish as he lit.
"No, I do not like it,
Not one little bit!"

THE CAT IN THE HAT pages 22–23

Said the fish to the cat. (page 25)

The Cat and the Grinch—whose stories were both published in 1957—may be the characters with whom Dr. Seuss most closely identified. For a December 1957 *Redbook* article on the Grinch, he drew a portrait of himself looking into the mirror and the Grinch looking back. Seuss, whose license plate read GRINCH, also described the Grinch as a "nasty anti-Christmas character that was really myself."[72] For a July 1957 *Saturday Evening Post* profile, he drew a portrait of himself as the Cat in the Hat. And as Michael Frith (b. 1941) said, "The Cat in the Hat and Ted

Geisel were inseparable and the same. I think there's no question about it. This is someone who delighted in the chaos of life, who delighted in the seeming insanity of the world around him."[73] Tellingly, when asked whether he associated himself with any of his characters, Seuss replied, "Yes. Especially the devious ones."[74]

Ted Geisel certainly shared the Cat's subversive sense of humor. Throughout his life, he enjoyed playing practical jokes. During a dinner party in the 1930s, he and his friend Hugh Troy (whose pranks are now legendary) "slipped into the kitchen and hid a large, dime-store pearl in an oyster." When it was "served to the head of a Wall Street firm," the pearl was discovered, and "there was serious discussion as to whether the finder or the hostess owned it. They politely pushed the pearl back and forth" until Helen Geisel explained that it was a joke.[75]

At a charity gala at a San Diego Neiman Marcus store in 1986, Seuss, who was "not in a party mood," wandered away from the festivities. As the Morgans report, "Friends finally found him in the women's shoe department, happily changing prices on every box of Ferragamos and Bruno Maglis in sight."[76]

Although he did share the Cat's sense of mischief, Seuss also once remarked, "If I were invited to a dinner party with my characters, I wouldn't show up."[77] And to a child who asked if he had ever acted like any of his characters, Seuss replied, "No, because I don't want to get put in jail."[78]

Said the fish in the pot. (page 25)

Of the many experiences that helped Seuss write *The Cat in the Hat* and other Beginner Books, his work during the Second World War is frequently overlooked. The first time Seuss used such limited vocabulary to tell a story was not *The Cat in the Hat* but *Private SNAFU*. In January 1943, Theodor Seuss Geisel left New York for Hollywood, where he became a captain in the U.S. Army's Information and Education Division—Fort Fox.[79] Major Frank Capra (1897–1991), the Oscar-winning director, headed the division. Philip D. Eastman (1909–1986)—who, as P. D. Eastman, would later write Beginner Books like *Go, Dog. Go!* (1961)—served in the same unit.[80] Capra placed Geisel in charge of the animation branch and assigned him to make educational films that would run in the *Army-Navy Screen Magazine,* a biweekly newsreel shown to the troops.[81] Geisel and Eastman teamed up with civilian directors Chuck Jones and Friz Freleng (1905–1995), vocal impressionist Mel Blanc (1908–1989), composer Carl Stalling (1891–1974), and the other creative minds behind Bugs Bunny, Daffy Duck, and Porky Pig. Together, they created Private SNAFU. Teaching by negative example, Private SNAFU embodied his name, an acronym for "Situation Normal All Fouled Up" (a different word can be substituted for "Fouled"). He shirks his duties and wanders into booby traps, and in one episode, his loose lips literally sink his ship.

Since many U.S. troops were not well educated or even literate, these cartoons had to get their message across in plain English. As Technical Fairy, First Class—a masculine Tinker Bell with five-o'clock shadow—tells SNAFU at the end of the "Gripes" episode (July 1943), "The moral, SNAFU, is the harder you woik, the sooner we're gonna beat Hitler, that joik." This sentence has the same metrical emphasis as "'You SHOULD NOT be here / When our mother is not. / You get out of this house!' / Said the fish in the pot." The presence of these anapests suggests that in writing the *SNAFU* cartoons, Seuss developed skills he would use in writing the Beginner Books series. In this sense, *Private SNAFU* is an uncle (or father) of the 236-word *The Cat in the Hat*.

"Now look what you did!"
Said the fish to the cat.
"Now look at this house!
Look at this! Look at that!
You sank our toy ship,
Sank it deep in the cake.
You shook up our house
And you bent our new rake.
You SHOULD NOT be here
When our mother is not.
You get out of this house!"
Said the fish in the pot.

THE CAT IN THE HAT pages 24–25

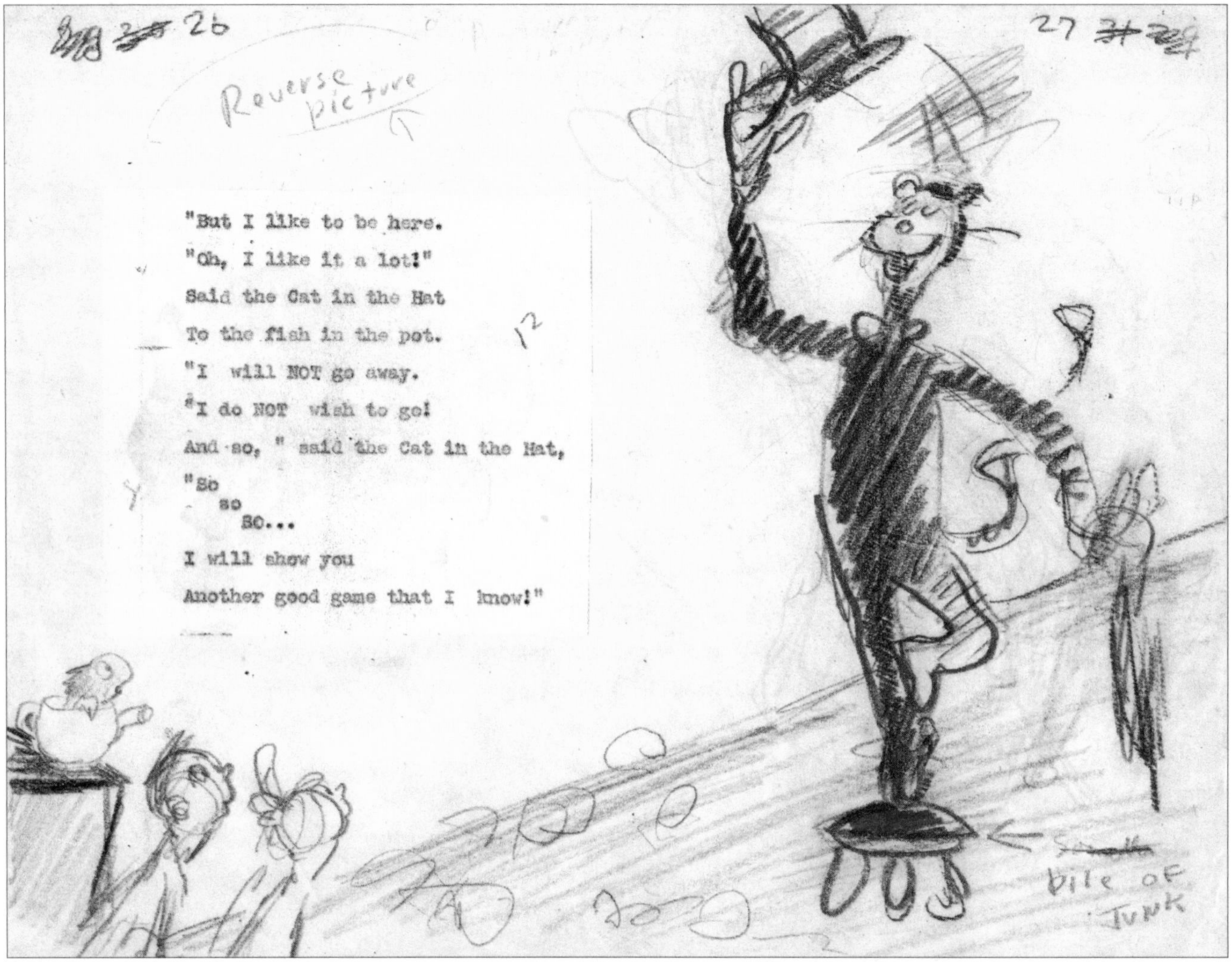

Reverse picture

"But I like to be here.

"Oh, I like it a lot!"

Said the Cat in the Hat

To the fish in the pot.

"I will NOT go away.

"I do NOT wish to go!

And so, " said the Cat in the Hat,

"So

so

so...

I will show you

Another good game that I know!"

pile of junk

"But I like to be here." (page 27)

The differences between this spread and its version in the colored-pencil sketches show that Seuss worked hard not only on the words but also on the pictures. He originally had this picture reversed, with the Cat on the right and the children and fish on the left. Perhaps with an eye to visual continuity, he switched the order so that the Cat has remained on the left in every spread since pages 20–21. Placing the Cat on the left here creates a more dramatic shift on page 29, when the Cat enters at right, carrying the big red box for his next "good game."

"Oh, I like it a lot!" (page 27)

In the animated version, after the end of the "UP-UP-UP with a fish" game, the fish tells the Cat to leave. However, the Cat pre-tends to ask permission to stay. Instead of the cheerful expression that accompanies the speech in the book, the Cat puts on a sad, sympathetic look and says, "It's up to you kids, / Whatever you say. / If you think me untrustworthy, / Send me away." Sally says, "Well, he is getting the house sort of messy and dirty, and Mother—." The boy adds, "Yeah, Mother. Back home at 3:30." His hat drooping, the now frowning Cat says, "A vote of no confidence. / I most humbly bow to the voice of the majority. / Good-bye, now. Off to Siberia." And he walks out the door. He waits a beat and then bursts back in. "Ha!" he shouts. "Somebody stole my moss-covered, three-handled family grudunza. Nobody's going to leave this room until I find it!" He points an accusing

Continued on page 58

"But I like to be here.
Oh, I like it a lot!"
Said the Cat in the Hat
To the fish in the pot.
"I will NOT go away.
I do NOT wish to go!
And so," said the Cat in the Hat,
"So

    so

        so . . .

I will show you
Another good game that I know!"

THE CAT IN THE HAT pages 26–27

Continued from page 56

finger at the fish. The search for the grudunza gives the Cat a reason to stay and fills much of the rest of the cartoon.

In early versions of the TV script, the moss-covered, three-handled family grudunza is a "Hooto-Footo-Booto-Bah," allowing the Cat to sing "Somebody Stole My Hoo-to Foo-to Boo-to Bah!" from *The Cat in the Hat Songbook* (1967).

To the fish in the pot. (page 27)

Seuss's meter creates a parallel between the book's principal opposing forces, "the Cat in the Hat" and "the fish in the pot." Beginning with *CITH* page 25, the phrase "the fish in the pot" appears three times (also see *CITH* pages 35 and 39), echoing "the Cat in the Hat" and neatly encapsulating the imbalance of power between the two. The pot confines the fish, leaving him at the mercy of the Cat—"his natural predator," as Betty Mensch and Alan Freeman point out.[82] The hat does not confine the Cat at all: it aids him in his balancing act (*CITH* pages 15–19) and

produces smaller cats in *The Cat in the Hat Comes Back*.

An early draft of the script for the television special plays up the predator-prey relationship in a scene at the dinner table. Since the Cat knocked him out with a mallet ("a very small tranquilizer," the Cat calls it), the fish is sound asleep. The Things refuse to help the Cat find his Hooto-Footo-Booto-Bah (the early version of the grudunza) unless they are fed. They race to the table, which "is set for [a] dinner party." The children initially try to stop the Things, but soon everyone gets caught up in singing "The Super-Supper March"

(from *The Cat in the Hat Songbook*). According to Seuss's stage directions:

> Scene ends in madness. Kids and Things and Cat wildly throwing food about as they sit at table.
>
> Camera moves in on Cat who is drinking out of a succession of glasses. He picks up fish bowl, starts to drink.
>
> Fish wakes up, groggily. Fish and Cat in eye to eye confrontation.

The fish shouts at the Cat, "I know you consider me / a sour bellied carp. . . . / But their mother gets back here / at three-thirty sharp!" Seuss evidently thought this confrontation dramatically compelling because the script next announces, "End of Act 1. INTO COMMERCIAL."

"Another good game that I know!" (page 27)

Of the 236 different words in *The Cat in the Hat,* only one has three syllables—"another," which appears here and on *CITH* page 57. The fourteen two-syllable words are "Sally," "mother," "mother's," "something," "nothing," "playthings," "little," "after," "about," "always," "away," "any," "sunny," and "funny."

Came back in with a box. (page 28)

In the television special, the Things emerge from under the Cat's hat, and the hat has the magical properties displayed in *The Cat in the Hat Comes Back*. Like a car full of circus clowns, the hat holds far more than its small space could possibly contain. In the cartoon, the Cat removes his hat to reveal an identical hat and a small purple box. As the box grows larger in his hand, he says, "In this box are my helpmates, Thing One and Thing Two." Placing the box on the floor, he adds, "From this box will emerge Thing Two and Thing One. / And they can find anything under the sun."

And then he ran out.

And, then, fast as a fox,

The Cat in the Hat

Came back in with a box.

A big red wood box.

It was shut with a hook.

"Now look at this trick,"

Said the cat.

"Take a look!"

THE CAT IN THE HAT pages 28–29

With a tip of his hat. (page 31)

Tipping his hat as he prepares to introduce the Things, the Cat behaves as their impresario. His role as showman and the Things' roles as performers are much more apparent in the early drafts for the TV script of *The Cat in the Hat* and in the "bone pile" (discarded material) for the TV special *The Grinch Grinches the Cat in the Hat* (1982).

In the *Cat* script, there is a "drum roll" as the Cat announces, "Ladees and Gentlemen . . . Presenting: Thing Two and Thing One!" The Things do not emerge. There is a "Louder drum roll." The Cat says again, "Ladees and Gentlemen . . . Presenting: Thing Two and Thing One!" Again, the Things do not emerge. The Cat says to the children, "Why, I do believe they're frightened of you! / Make friends. Shake hands with Thing One and Thing Two." The children "cringe," so the Cat demonstrates. "Say how-dee-doo. Like this," he says, putting his hand in the box. Next, there "is a snarl and a snap." The Cat cries,

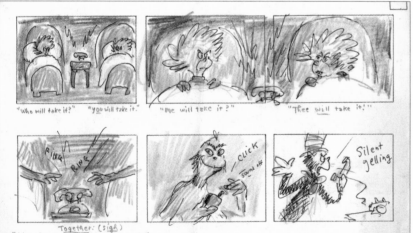

"OUCH!" and orders the Things, "Come out and find my Hooto-Footo-Booto-Bah!" They refuse. From the box, Thing Two says, "We're reluctant. We're recalcitrant. We're on strike." Stepping out of the box, Thing One adds, "We're overworked." Thing Two steps out next to him and says, "We're underfed." They refuse to find the Cat's Hooto-Footo-Booto-Bah unless they are fed. If their claims are true, then the Cat is a rather unreliable impresario.

The discarded portions of *The Grinch Grinches the Cat in the Hat* also suggest that the Things may be performers with the Cat as their agent. Here, the Things—who are absent from the final script—have their own nightclub act. The Cat phones the Things, who are sleeping in twin beds. They debate which of them should answer the phone. When they decide to answer it together, the Grinch's "Vacu-Sound-Sweeper" interferes with the audio and only "a small Blupp sound comes out

Continued on page 62

THE ANNOTATED CAT

Then he got up on top
With a tip of his hat.
"I call this game FUN-IN-A-BOX,"
Said the cat.
"In this box are two things
I will show to you now.
You will like these two things,"
Said the cat with a bow.

THE CAT IN THE HAT pages 30–31

Continued from page 60

of the receiver." Not knowing what to make of this, they go back to bed. Later, the phone wakes them up again, they look at the clock, and Thing Two says, "We gotta go on in 15 minutes!" He runs out the door. Thing One picks up the phone and, disguising his voice, says, "This is a recording. Thing One and Thing Two will return your call later. They are making their nightly appearance at the Casa Casatta." He runs out the door. They do appear at the nightclub, on the "center floor," where "they go into their Amazing Adagio." The Things perform with "great acrobatic skill" until the Grinch intervenes. As the stage directions explain, "The Grinch, by remote control [from his tower], sends in Dark Rays whenever one of them is in the air and the other one doesn't know where to go to catch him." Their act "ends up as a fiasco."

"You will like these two things," (page 31)

In calling these two characters "things," Seuss creates opportunities for puns. In the television special, the fish shouts, "Out! And take those Things with you! Out!" Pretending to misunderstand what the fish means by "Things," the Cat replies, "Take the things? But whoever heard of a house without things in it?"

On this page, Seuss offers a more subtle pun on the narrator's original wish. On the second page of the book, the boy complains of doing "nothing at all" and says, "How I wish / We had something to do!" In the very next two-page spread, "Something went BUMP!" (*CITH* page 5), and here the Cat promises to show the children "two things"—Thing One and Thing Two. Doing no*thing* at all, the boy wished for some*thing* to do, and the Cat— a some*thing*—arrived, bringing with him two *things*. In addition to playing with the word "thing," Seuss perhaps also suggests that the boy should be careful what he wishes for. He asked for something; he got two things and a cat. That said, the Cat does return to "pick up all my play*things*" (emphasis mine) at the end of the book. His efforts in clearing away the evidence dilute the tale's cautionary elements.

"You will see something new." (page 33)

This line and the two lines following are in the sixteenth edition of *Bartlett's Familiar Quotations* (1992). *Bartlett's* includes a quotation from one other Dr. Seuss book: "I meant what I said / And I said what I meant. . . . / An elephant's faithful / One hundred per cent!" from *Horton Hatches the Egg*.

Then, out of the box (page 33)

If "FUN-IN-A-BOX" (*CITH* page 31) at first brings to mind a very large jack-in-the-box, this scene also echoes the story of Pandora's box. In classical mythology, Zeus creates the first woman, names her Pandora, and sends her to Prometheus and his brother Epimetheus. Wary of gifts from the gods, Prometheus declines and advises his brother to do likewise. But Epimetheus accepts Pandora, and she comes to live with him. In his house is a jar or a box (depending on the version of the story) containing all manner of ills, such as envy, revenge, and various afflictions. Curious to discover the contents, Pandora opens the box, unleashing these evils into a world that has until then been free of them.[83] Here, the Cat opens the box, unleashing Thing One and Thing Two, who proceed to wreak havoc in a house that has been tidy. The last item in Pandora's box is hope. Although the Cat's box may not deliver hope, it does bring the promise of fun and excitement—along with a large measure of chaos.

Whether or not Seuss consciously alludes to Zeus, he was certainly aware of Pandora's box. In the July 1949 workshops at the University of Utah, Seuss mentioned the story in his discussion of myths. He said that although the "significance and theology" of many myths would have been "lost on kids," he thought that some—such as Pandora's box—would work well. Because "kids go for the imagination and the grandeur," he said, they would enjoy "Bellerophon taming the winged horse," "Icarus falling into the sea," "Hermes flying with his winged sandals," "life under the sea with Neptune," "Thor and his hammer," "Jason and the golden fleece," and "Pandora's box."

"I will pick up the hook.

You will see something new.

Two things. And I call them

Thing One and Thing Two.

These Things will not bite you.

They want to have fun."

Then, out of the box

Came Thing Two and Thing One!

And they ran to us fast.

They said, "How do you do?

Would you like to shake hands

With Thing One and Thing Two?"

THE CAT IN THE HAT pages 32–33

Did not know what to do. (page 34)

Both Sally and her brother seem equally at a loss for words, but the boy later finds his voice (*CITH* pages 45, 50, and 52) and she remains silent throughout the book. In contrast, the animated special portrays the children as equally capable of speaking up: either both do not know what to say or both speak. At this moment in the cartoon, both are silent; earlier, when the Cat said it was up to them whether he would stay, both children expressed reservations.

Pamelyn Ferdin (b. 1959), who provides Sally's voice in the TV *Cat in the Hat,* portrayed several outspoken characters: she was the voice of Lucy Van Pelt in several *Charlie Brown* TV specials from the late 1960s and early 1970s, and the voice of Fern Arable in the 1973 animated adaptation of E. B. White's *Charlotte's Web.* She later became an animal rights activist, founding the Los Angeles chapter of the Animal Defense League in 1997. In 2003, she was sentenced to thirty days in prison for displaying a bull hook (a two-foot wooden pole with a hook at its end, used for training elephants) at a protest against Circus Vargas's treatment of elephants. At the time, she explained that she brought the bull hook because of "freedom of speech" and added that "100 feet away the bull hook was being used in a violent way by an elephant handler, and I was arrested and he wasn't."[84]

Like Ferdin and Sally in the animated *Cat,* the Sally of *The Cat in the Hat Comes Back* is much more willing to speak up for herself. See page 104.

With Thing One and Thing Two. (page 34)

Thing One and Thing Two do not shake hands or pretend to be "tame" (see *CITH* pages 34–37) in the animated cartoon. The moment the Cat opens the box, both Things burst out and head straight for the fish, as Thing One—voiced by Thurl Ravenscroft—sings, "Fish! Fish! There's always one. / Some long-faced, sourbelly son-of-a-gun!" Within seconds, he is spinning the fish's bowl on a cane above his head.

Ravenscroft (1914–2005) is the singing voice of the Grinch (Boris Karloff does the speaking part) in *How the Grinch Stole Christmas!* (1966) and a Wickersham Brother in *Horton Hears a Who!* (1970). If in these Seuss cartoons Ravenscroft played a mischievous or sneaky character, he also portrayed many more genial types, such as Tony the Tiger in Kellogg's Frosted Flakes commercials. According to Brian E. Jacob's comprehensive Web site *All Things Thurl,* Ravenscroft's recording career included singing backup for Spike Jones, the Andrews Sisters, and Elvis

Presley, among many others. He also recorded hundreds of Disney records, as well as narrations for rides in the Disney theme parks.

But our fish said, "No! No!" (page 34)

In the television cartoon, the fish's first words to the Things are even more severe. After being spun atop a cane (by Thing One) and caught (by the boy), the fish hops over to the telephone and dials. "FBI? FBI? Listen, listen," he says. "I am a fish residing at 2322 Magnolia Boulevard. And I want to report a Cat in a Hat." Hearing no response, he shouts, "FBI! FBI!" and slaps the receiver. More urgently, he says, "Somebody please answer! Where is everybody?" A Thing pops out of the receiver and replies in a female operator's voice, "Sorry. That line is temporarily out of order."

And Sally and I
Did not know what to do.
So we had to shake hands
With Thing One and Thing Two.
We shook their two hands.
But our fish said, "No! No!
Those Things should not be
In this house! Make them go!

"They should not be here
When your mother is not!
Put them out! Put them out!"
Said the fish in the pot.

THE CAT IN THE HAT pages 34–35

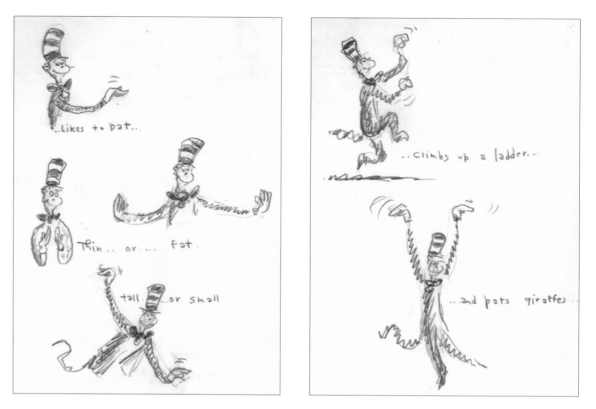

And he gave them a pat. (page 37)

In writing "My Uncle Terwilliger Likes to Pat" for *The Cat in the Hat Songbook,* Seuss may have considered a song about the Cat (and not Uncle Terwilliger) liking to pat animals. Or he may have simply drawn illustrations of the Cat doing all the pats that Uncle Terwilliger likes to do—patting a "poodle with his left hand," a "camel with his right hand," and a "frog with his left big toe!" In the original manuscript for *The Cat in the Hat Songbook,* Uncle Terwilliger also "climbs up a ladder and pats giraffes"; this is not in the final version published in the *Songbook,* however.

THE ANNOTATED CAT

"Have no fear, little fish,"
Said the Cat in the Hat.
"These Things are good Things."
And he gave them a pat.
"They are tame. Oh, so tame!
They have come here to play.
They will give you some fun
On this wet, wet, wet day."

THE CAT IN THE HAT pages 36–37

"They should not fly kites" (page 39)

The house contains kites, framed pictures, books, balls, a toy boat, and many other items, all of which suggest that Sally, her brother, Mother, and the fish are living comfortable middle-class lives. The TV special discloses their address—2322 Magnolia Boulevard—and the first drafts of the television script provide a few more clues about the family's background. Mother drives a "red Volkswagen," and they *do* have a father who lives with them (a detail confirmed in the sequel, when the Cat gets the spot on Dad's shoes and bed). In one draft, Thing Two says that the father is "a Yale man." Late in another draft, the Things "emerge from closet with Blue football sweater with big white 'Y.'" The boy says, "Don't touch *that*! That's my Daddy's Yale sweater." Thing One replies, "His Daddy's Yale sweater!" Thing Two repeats, "His Daddy's Yale sweater!" Both Things "get into the sweater as if it were a cloth vaudeville horse. They gallop around in it." They sing, "It's always fair wet-ter / when good fel-

lows get toget-ter / In a fine old Yale sweater. . . . / Bulldog. Bulldog. Rah! Rah! Rah! / Eli Yale."

Including the father's Yale degree also provides occasion to poke fun at the rituals of higher education. In the earliest version of the TV script, the fish tells us that he "went to Caltech," where he studied "Mathematooshus." As he says, "very few fish can make such a claim." In the TV special, the Cat gets a version of these lines. He "went to Cat Tech," where he studied "Calculatus Eliminatus." And he adds, "What other cats do you know who can make such a claim?" "Calculatus Eliminatus," supposedly the scientific method of finding an object, is a spoof of research methods: the Cat and the children mark each place where the family grudunza is *not,* covering the house in meaningless shorthand like

"K300," "57B," "842J," and "F607." In the script, "Mathematooshus" is a parody of both math problems and academic jargon. As proof that the fish can "figure figures just as easy as can be," he offers an absurd mathematical problem and an equally absurd answer (all in lyrics borrowed from *The Cat in the Hat Songbook*'s "I Can Figure Figures"): "Twenty thousand turtles times ten tin tops / Plus fifteen billion buttons / minus seven lollipops. / Divide by two bananas. / That makes eleventeen / French fried noodles and a green string bean." When the Cat prompts him to continue, the fish speaks in nonsensical scientific language: "Now for a little biangularization. We take the uneven integrals, platitudinize the interstitial absolutes . . ." Seuss's parody of the Caltech (Cat Tech) education suggests that we might view the Yale sweater as merely comic and not as a criticism of the New Haven university. Though a graduate of Dartmouth (Ted Geisel was class of 1925), perhaps he is not poking fun at a rival Ivy League institution.

Seuss also claimed that he was not mocking the Harvard Club when, on the final page of *Thidwick the Big-Hearted Moose* (1948), he had the pesky animals "stuffed" and mounted on the club's wall. As he told Mike Salzhauer in an interview published in 1981, he put the animals there because "I had to end the damn book. And I saw the best way to end it would be to put the animals on some wall and I had recently had lunch at the Harvard Club, which had about eight million animals—mostly shot by Teddy Roosevelt—hanging all over the walls. So, it seemed a logical place to put it in. . . . No animosity to the Harvard Club at all."[85]

"Now, here is a game that they like,"
Said the cat.
"They like to fly kites,"
Said the Cat in the Hat.

"No! Not in the house!"
Said the fish in the pot.
"They should not fly kites
In a house! They should not.
Oh, the things they will bump!
Oh, the things they will hit!
Oh, I do not like it!
Not one little bit!"

THE CAT IN THE HAT pages 38–39

Then Sally and I
Saw them run down the hall.
And we saw those two Things
Bump their kites on the wall!
Bump! Bump! Bump! Thump!
Down the wall in the hall.
And Sally and I
Did not know what to do.
There was no way to stop them,
Thing One and Thing Two!

Saw them run down the hall. (page 40)
In the first draft of the script for the *Cat in the Hat* TV special, the fish identifies the portrait on the wall as Uncle Terwilliger. The Cat then asks whether Uncle Terwilliger has any "lamentable habits." The fish replies, "None of your business!" The Cat says, "O-ho! Family scandal! Pretty shocking . . . eh?" The fish, "pointing to door," says, "Get moving. Get going!" The Cat refuses: "Won't go till you tell about Uncle Terwilliger." So the fish sings "My Uncle Terwilliger Waltzes with Bears," a song included in *The Cat in the Hat Songbook*. Bears materialize and begin waltzing with Uncle Terwilliger (who leaves the picture frame) and with the Things, the Cat, Sally, and her brother.

We saw those two Things (page 40)
As a child, Seuss enjoyed reading Wilhelm Busch's (1832–1908) *Max and Moritz* (1865) and certainly would have known Rudolph Dirks's (1877–1968) *The Katzenjammer Kids,* which debuted in 1897 and was based on Busch's mischievous children.[86] With their innate destructiveness, love of pranks, and knack for creating chaos, Busch's Max and Moritz—and Dirks's Hans and Fritz—are ancestors of Seuss's Thing One and Thing Two. Fortunately for Sally and her brother, the Things are a bit less destructive, if equally wild. The Things' kites upset vases, pictures, and lamps, but the Katzenjammers—whose name means "the howling of cats," a German term for "hangover"—actually blow things up (in one strip, they sink a ship). The equally dangerous Max and Moritz fill their teacher's pipe with gunpowder, put beetles in their uncle's bed, and cause the deaths of three hens and a rooster.

The panels on page 72 are from a Katzenjammer strip titled "An Off Day on Board the *Prosit!*" The strip appeared in the *New York Journal* in 1906 or 1907, and was reprinted in the book *The Komical Katzenjammers* (1908)—published the year Ted Geisel turned four. This episode finds the Katzenjammer Kids dunking a cat in dough and then placing the professor's top hat on the cat's head—note its resemblance to the Cat's hat. Meanwhile, Anna has left to tell the captain of the kids' mischief. In panels four through six, first the captain and then the ship's chef kicks them in the britches. In the seventh panel, the professor finds his hat. In the next four panels, the professor kicks them in the britches and their mother spanks them. In the final panel, Hans and Fritz head off to seek revenge on Anna.

Bump! Thump! Thump! Bump! (page 40)
The typescript for the colored-pencil sketches has "Bump! Bump! Bump! Thump!" Changing the line to "Bump! Thump! Thump! Bump!" gave the published version a poetic symmetry absent from the draft.

Continued on page 72

Then Sally and I
Saw them run down the hall.
We saw those two Things
Bump their kites on the wall!
Bump! Thump! Thump! Bump!
Down the wall in the hall.

THE CAT IN THE HAT pages 40–41

Continued from page 70

Down the wall in the hall. (page 40)

In the original sketches, Seuss added four more lines to the text:

> And Sally and I
> Did not know what to do.
> There was no way to stop them,
> Thing One and Thing Two!

As he always did at the sketch stage, Seuss added up the number of lines of text. Instead of a single number, he wrote "10 or 8," indicating that he was considering cutting two of these four lines. In the end, he cut all four.

Perhaps Seuss decided that the illustrations did an ample job of emphasizing the children's helplessness, and so removed lines like "There was no way to stop them" from the final ver-

sion. Or he may have thought that four more lines—though they would fit on this page—might crowd the illustration. Most likely, he followed his usual methods of revision. As he remarked in 1974, "My stuff is full of sweat. To get four lines I'll write 200. I'm not saying those final four lines are good, either, but they're as good as I can make them. It's what you leave out that makes a book good."[87]

On the head of her bed! (page 42)

As in most TV situation comedies from the 1950s, the parents have separate beds. Mother's bed (Seuss does call it "her bed") has a pink headboard. On page 28 of *The Cat in the Hat Comes Back,* Seuss takes us into "Dad's bedroom" and shows us his bed, which has a light blue headboard. Unlike their sitcom counterparts, Mother and Dad have separate bed*rooms,* too. Curiously, Mother's bed is a single (one pillow) and Dad's bed is a double.

THE ANNOTATED CAT

Thing Two and Thing One!
They ran up! They ran down!
On the string of one kite
We saw Mother's new gown!
Her gown with the dots
That are pink, white and red.
Then we saw one kite bump
On the head of her bed!

THE CAT IN THE HAT pages 42–43

Then those Things ran about
With big bumps, jumps and kicks
And with hops and big thumps
And all kinds of bad tricks.
And I said,
"I do NOT like the way that they play!
If Mother could see this,
Oh, what would she say!"

And I said, (page 45)

In the colored-pencil sketches, Seuss has the boy peeking out behind the corner and the Cat's head roughly where the boy is in the published book. Next to the Cat, he has written, "← out?" He followed his instinct and removed the Cat. In placing the boy here, Seuss not only sets him apart from Sally but signals the more active role that he will soon play (see *CITH* page 50). On all previous pages, the boy is either right next to Sally or doing the same thing as she is (such as shaking hands with the Things, *CITH* pages 34–35). Here, he is standing right in the thick of it, his body facing Sally but his gaze directed at one of the Things. Within but separate from the melee, the boy is free to act. Tangled in the kite's string, Sally is not free to act—indeed, she looks as if she's having the wind knocked out of her.

"If Mother could see this," (page 45)

In both Cat books, as events spiral further and further out of control, the level of anxiety increases for any reader who identifies with the children. As Selma G. Lanes (b. 1929) writes in *Down the Rabbit Hole: Adventures & Misadventures in the Realm of Children's Literature* (1971), "The anxiety in Seuss's books always arises from the flouting of authority, parental or societal. It is central to the Seuss formula that the action of all his books takes place either (1) in the absence of grown-ups, or (2) in the imagination. [In] *The Cat in the Hat* [the cat] performs his forbidden games when 'Our mother was out of the house for the day' and [he does so in] *The Cat in the Hat Comes Back* only 'when our mother went down to the town for the day.'"[88] Lanes also provides a perceptive analysis of how Seuss uses anxiety to create suspense: "Seuss cannily manages to magnify and multiply the sense of suspense in his stories . . . by a clever and relentless piling on of gratuitous anxiety until the child is fairly ready to cry 'uncle' and settle for any resolution, however mundane, that will end his at once marvelous, exquisite and finally unbearable tension. The process is not unlike the blowing up of a balloon: bigger, bigger, bigger, and finally, when the bursting point is reached, Seuss simply releases his grip and all tension, like trapped air, is freed."[89] Seuss liked Lanes's analysis and praised her for not allowing her "voluminous research to bog down the spirit of [her] writing."[90]

A possible influence on Seuss's spiraling-out-of-control narratives is Peter Newell (1862–1924), whose *The Hole Book* (1908) was a childhood favorite of Seuss's.[91] *The Hole Book* begins, "Tom Potts was fooling with a gun / (Such follies should not be), / When—bang! the pesky thing went off / Most unexpectedly!" The bullet makes a hole through a "fine French clock," the wall behind the clock, and the page itself. Except for the book's last page, each page from this point onward has a hole punched through it. Causing comic chaos, the bullet goes through a boiler, a rope on a swing, a fence, a gas tank, a portrait, an aquarium, and many other items, until one wonders whether it will ever stop. On the final page, "Mis' Newlywed had made a cake, / With icings good and stout— / The bullet struck its armor belt, / And meekly flattened out." Newell wrote and illustrated two other books in which one item sails through the pages, creating more and more chaos as it goes: *The Rocket Book* (1912), about a firework that shoots up through each floor (and ceiling) of an apartment building, and *The Slant Book* (1910), about a runaway baby carriage.

Then those Things ran about

With big bumps, jumps and kicks

And with hops and big thumps

And all kinds of bad tricks.

And I said,

"I do NOT like the way that they play!

If Mother could see this,

Oh, what would she say!"

THE CAT IN THE HAT pages 44–45

46-47

Then our fish said, "Oh, LOOK!"
And our fish shook with fear.
"Your mother is on her way home!
Look! I see her!
Oh, what will she do to us?
What will she say?
Oh, she will not like it
To find us this way!"

"Do you hear?" (page 47)

Instead of "Do you hear?" the typescript on the colored-pencil sketches has the fish saying, "Look! I see her!" The change to "Do you hear?" gives the fish a more parental tone. "Look! I see her!" more closely aligns him with the children; "Do you hear?" sounds more authoritative, as if he is advising the children to take action.

Perhaps more significant, the original illustration shows much more through the window. The mother's foot and hem are there, but so is a row of identical houses (Sally and her brother may not be the *only* bored children on this day). So, in addition to placing his perspective closer to that of the children, the fish's "Look! I see her!" directs attention to the mother specifically, distinguishing her from everything else that is visible outside.

Then our fish said, "LOOK! LOOK!"

And our fish shook with fear.

"Your mother is on her way home!

Do you hear?

Oh, what will she do to us?

What will she say?

Oh, she will not like it

To find us this way!"

THE CAT IN THE HAT pages 46–47

"You will have to get rid of" (page 48)

The fish's repeated desire—here made more urgent by Mother's imminent arrival—to stop the giant, cartoonish Cat and his Things from wrecking the household might be considered in the context of the debate surrounding comic books and juvenile delinquency. In 1948, psychiatrist Fredric Wertham (1895–1981) argued that violent, immoral comics were leading children toward delinquency. The issue received national attention from then into the 1950s, culminating in 1954 with the publication of Wertham's *Seduction of the Innocent* and Senate hearings on comic books. Wertham wrote, "I have come to the conclusion that this chronic stimulation, temptation and seduction by comic books . . . are contributing factors to many children's maladjustment."[92] He worried that "children are left entirely unprotected" from comic books.[93] Wertham's writing and then the Senate hearings prompted the comic-book industry to adopt a "Comics Code" governing the content of its works. The code and the increasing popularity of television drove many comics publishers out of business.

There's no way to prove that Seuss had Wertham and the code in the back of his mind. In 1954, one public librarian seeking to "combat 'blood-and-horror' comic books" actually placed Seuss's books on "a recommended list of books" that children might read instead.[94] Similarly, in 1957, few contemporary reviewers indicated that they saw any subtext concerning Wertham or his allies. Indeed, only two reviews even hinted at any connection between *The Cat* and the comics. The *New York Times Book Review*'s Ellen Lewis Buell called *The Cat in the Hat* "fine, furious slapstick," a phrase that applies equally well to film and to comic books.[95] The *New Yorker*'s Emily Maxwell, who also praised the book, noted its "very lowbrow cartoons," which suggests that she saw a connection to comic books.[96]

Even though contemporary reviewers may not have dwelt on the connections between Seuss's books and comic books, both *The Cat in the Hat* and *The Cat in the Hat Comes Back* feature a character drawn in a cartoony style who creates havoc in the lives of otherwise well-behaved children. And Seuss, who wrote the short-lived *Hejji* comic strip for some of William Randolph Hearst's newspapers (including the *New York Journal American* and the *Chicago Herald & Examiner*) from April through June 1935, was certainly aware of the comic-book controversy. Though he did object to literature of poor quality, he does not appear to have been on the side of Wertham and the would-be censors. Indeed, during an address entitled "Mrs. Mulvaney and the Billion Dollar Bunny" (given during his 1949 workshops at the University of Utah), he made a none-too-veiled reference to this debate when he distinguished between well-written books, which he placed atop "Mount Parnassus," and lesser-quality (if aggressively marketed) ones, which he located on "Bunkum Hill" and "Mount Hokum." Considering why children read books from Bunkum Hill and Mount Hokum, Seuss asked, "Why DO our children go to those mountains for their reading?" He responded, "You just can't explain that away by saying that they're attracted by the depravity. Our children aren't morons. They're not morally depraved. I don't think so and neither do you." The phrase "morally depraved" seems to have been an allusion to Wertham and his supporters.

Instead of dismissing such literature as dangerous, he suggested that writers of children's books might learn from it. Seuss said that "if you want to capture the wandering attention of our children . . . if you want to win that attention and hold it . . . maybe you could profit a bit by finding out a few things that they know over there. Things that, quite obviously, we don't know over here. Such as the fact that they don't insult a child's intelligence." Rather than condescending by saying, "Gather round me, kiddie-widdies, and I'll tell you a story-wory," the writers on Bunkum Hill "say (very ungrammatically, perhaps) 'Look here, Bub. You and me we're citizens of this world together, so let's sit down man to man and discuss these Hyper-hydra-hetra-tetra-helio-copiter caps.'" His language here is clearly that of a comic book. The strength of such books, according to Seuss, is that these writers "approach the child as an equal. Approaching him this way, they get his attention. And once they have it, they don't lose it." Seuss felt those writers who aspired to Mount Parnassus could learn from the writers on Bunkum Hill—presumably, the comic-book writers.

Elsewhere in his Utah lectures, Seuss addressed comic books by name. He noted that "the comic books pander to—take advantage of—" a child's basic needs. In other words, he said, comic books "write to the market. I'm *not* suggesting *you* write to the market—especially not the way they do. But you must know the psychology of that market." Although he had some reservations about the style of comic books and the motives of their authors, he credited these writers with understanding how children thought and what they liked.

So, if we interpret Seuss's cartoonish Cat as a manifestation of the "threat" posed by comic books, Seuss does not consider the threat to be very great. The Cat does make a mess, but

Continued on page 80

"So, DO something! Fast!" said the fish.

"Do you hear!

I saw her. Your mother!

Your mother is near!

So, as fast as you can,

Think of something to do!

You will have to get rid of

Thing One and Thing Two!"

THE CAT IN THE HAT pages 48–49

Continued from page 78

he cleans up after himself and he does not corrupt the children, who often have anxious expressions on their faces. By the end of *The Cat in the Hat,* the boy is asking the Cat to leave; throughout *The Cat in the Hat Comes Back,* both Sally and her brother are doing so. Rather than being led astray by the Cat, the children oppose him—and, without adult intervention, the Cat has left the house by each book's conclusion. In other words, children can protect themselves from comic books.

I went after my net. (page 50)

Seuss's books frequently express faith that children can set things right. As Henry Jenkins writes in "'No Matter How Small': The Democratic Imagination of Dr. Seuss" (2003), "Seuss trusts the child to find his or her way to what is 'fair' and 'just.'"[97] In *The Lorax,* the Once-ler entrusts a boy—identified only as "you"—with the last of the Truffula Seeds, telling him to plant trees and restore the despoiled environment so that "the Lorax / and all of his friends / may come back." In *Bartholomew and the Oobleck,* Bartholomew must intervene to save the country from total immersion in goo: only after he shames King Derwin into apologizing does the oobleck cease. And in the live-action feature film *The 5000 Fingers of Dr. T* (1953, screenplay cowritten by Seuss and Allan Scott), Bart Collins sings a song that advances this idea. After failing to enlist an adult ally in support of his campaign to oust the megalomaniacal Dr. T, Bart (played by Tommy Rettig, who later starred as Jeff on TV's *Lassie*) sings:

> Now just because we're kids,
> > because we're sort of small,
> Because we're closer to the ground,
> And you are bigger pound by pound,
> You have no right, you have no right
> To push and shove us little kids around.

At this moment in *The Cat in the Hat,* the boy acts in precisely this spirit. Deciding that the Cat will not push him around anymore, he goes for his net and races to stop the Things from creating more chaos. As the next spread shows us, he succeeds.

"I can get those Things yet!" (page 50)

As a possible antecedent for the Things, Charles Cohen suggests

"Wild Tones" live in Radios…they're the Bad Tones that escape from the back of your speaker.

the Wild Tones from Seuss's advertisements for Stromberg-Carlson radios in 1937. As he says, they "bear a bushy resemblance to the equally untamable" Things One and Two. Just as the Wild Tones "made such a ruckus and ruined radio broadcasts," so Thing One and Thing Two "wreaked havoc on an entire household."[98]

So, as fast as I could,
I went after my net.
And I said, "With my net
I can get them I bet.
I bet, with my net,
I can get those Things yet!"

THE CAT IN THE HAT pages 50–51

Then I let down my net.
It came down with a KLOP!
And I had them! At last!
The two Things had to stop.
Then I said to the cat,
"Now you do as I say.
"You pack up these Things
And you take them away!"

"Oh dear!" said the cat.
"You did not like our game..?
Oh dear!
What a shame!
What a shame!
What a shame!"

It came down with a PLOP! (page 52)

In the colored-pencil sketches, Seuss has written, "It came down with a KLOP!" The sound effect on *CITH* page 53 was also originally "KLOP"—a red "K" is clearly visible beneath the "P."

In the 1989 German edition, *Der Kater mit Hut,* the word is spelled with an extra "P"—"PLOPP." The Hebrew edition's word is pronounced *PLOPE.* In Spanish, it's PAF. In Latin, it's SSSS. And the Italian edition, *Il Gatto col cappello,* spells the word exactly the same as the American edition: "PLOP."

And I had them! At last! (page 52)

In the animated television special, the boy does not need to capture the Things. As soon as the fish announces Mother's arrival, they head straight back for their box. If, in the book, only the child's intervention can rid the house of Cat and Things, in the TV adaptation, the child does not need to act: the mere mention of the children's mother provides sufficient motivation for the Things to skedaddle. In the book, both Things and Cat appear to have no sense of the rules; in the animated television special, however, they have known the rules all along.

"And you take them away!" (page 52)

In the animated television special, after the fish delivers a version of this line, the Cat is so provoking that, exasperated, the fish tells him that he's not a cat and what's on his head is not a hat. This claim provides the impetus for the final musical number, in which the Cat sings, "In English, cat, hat. / In French, *chat, chapeau.* / It really is quite obvious, / Don't you know?" As the song goes on, we also learn the words for "cat" and "hat" in many other languages, such as German, Spanish, and Russian.

"Oh dear!" said the cat. (page 53)

On this two-page spread and the next, the Cat's bow tie and Sally's ribbon are nearly opposites of each other. Here, his droops, telegraphing his sadness; hers is buoyant, signaling her joy. On the next two-page spread, his still droops, and hers is slightly less perky than before (as she wonders how they will pick up the mess). Throughout the book, Sally's bow and the Cat's bow tie link them visually. Sometimes her bow and his tie look similar (as on *CITH* pages 12–13 and 36–37). More often (and more appropriately, given her opposition to the Cat), Sally's bow is either at an angle to his bow tie or an upside-down mirror image of it (see *CITH* pages 6–7, 14–15, 20–21, 52–53, and 54–55). Whether or not Seuss intentionally created this visual motif, it's worth noting because Seuss frequently expresses emotion through inanimate objects like trees and clothes. When a scene or character is cheerful, trees and bows are extra springy; when a situation is sad, they droop.

Then I let down my net.

It came down with a PLOP!

And I had them! At last!

Those two Things had to stop.

Then I said to the cat,

"Now you do as I say.

You pack up those Things

And you take them away!"

"Oh dear!" said the cat.

"You did not like our game . . .

Oh dear.

What a shame!

What a shame!

What a shame!"

THE CAT IN THE HAT pages 52–53

Within the illustration (typewritten text):

"That is good," said the fish.
"He has gone away. Yes.
But your mother will come.
She will find this big mess!
And this mess is SO big
And SO deep and SO tall,
We can not pick it up.
There is no way at all!"

Then he shut up the things
In the box with the hook.
And the cat went away
With a sad kind of look.

percent of the light "through to a printing plate (smooth zinc usually), prepared with a photo-sensitive emulsion. The light that struck the plate fixed the emulsion in place. The plate was then wiped clean, and wherever we had emulsion, we had printing."[99]

Seuss's instructions to the printers also underscore how particular he was. On page 55 of the sketches, he wrote "40%" not only on the seat of the chair, but also on its back and on each of its four legs. On the tissue overlay for page 46, he wrote on the curtain, "100% Red," and added an arrow pointing to the dress. Leaving no detail to chance, he added, in parentheses, "Leave stocking white."

With a sad kind of look. (page 54)
In the colored-pencil sketches, Seuss has written in the far-left margin, close to the Cat's face, "Cat more distant + smaller." As explained on page 44, Seuss uses size to convey the Cat's sense of confidence and power. Here, the Cat feels sad and powerless.

"She will find this big mess!" (page 55)
The finished pen-and-ink drawing (reproduced above with its colored-pencil-marked tissue overlay) offers a glimpse into the offset-lithography printing process used in 1957. The inks available would have been black, special red, and special blue. As rare-book librarian Michael Joseph explains, to make 40 percent red (which appears pink), "one screen would be used to produce 40 percent of the full color." Using this screen, the press would "print solid red over 40 percent of the area, in the form of dots scaled to 40 percent. The white page color showing between the dots works with the red dots to produce the effect of pink." The mechanics of the printing worked like this: Once made, the screen was exposed to a light source, permitting 40

"And so deep and so tall," (page 55)
To overcome the "tough job" of writing with a limited number of words, Seuss said that the "trick is to imply with your illustrations what you're not allowed to say in words."[100] These pages exemplify how his illustrations exceed and amplify the text. To convey the size and scope of this mess, Seuss brings in items from previous pages and adds new ones. Though not named on this page, the ball, book, toy ship, cake, kites, rake, dress, fan, pot, and one of the cups appear previously in both words and pictures. Items that appear only as illustrations include one vase (with two flowers) and the lamp shade, framed pictures, chair, bowl, hairbrush, perfume bottle, saucer (on which the cup sits), platter (on which the cake sits), and boxes (or are they tables?). For the first time in *The Cat in the Hat,* Seuss includes a telephone, footstool, and second cup and saucer. The accumulation of these images mires the children (and the fish) in the largest mess displayed in the book and increases the fear—expressed by the fish—that "We can not pick it up. / There is no way at all!"

"That is good," said the fish.
"He has gone away. Yes.
But your mother will come.
She will find this big mess!
And this mess is so big
And so deep and so tall,
We can not pick it up.
There is no way at all!"

Then he shut up the Things
In the box with the hook.
And the cat went away
With a sad kind of look.

THE CAT IN THE HAT pages 54–55

"I always pick up all my playthings" (page 57)

In the colored-pencil sketches, Seuss has the Cat saying, "I ALWAYS pick up all my play-things," which is identical to the text here except for the all-caps "ALWAYS" and the hyphen in "play-things." What is notable is that Seuss was wondering either about including the word "always" or about whether the word should be in capital letters. At the top of the page, he has written in pen, "?Always?" and from this word, he has drawn a pen line down the right-hand margin, ending in an arrow pointing to "I ALWAYS pick up all my play-things."

"Good trick that I know!" (page 57)

During a 1964 visit to a New Zealand schoolroom, Seuss was interviewed for a TV news program. The reporter asked, "How does his tidying-up machine work?" Eyeing his audience of six-year-olds, Seuss replied with mock seriousness, "Well, sometimes it doesn't work at all. This is a steam contraption. There's a dipolator in here that runs the whole thing—which ties on to the cantabulous, which is down near the end here. The cantabulous and the dipolator sometimes don't throing—which gets us into a terrible situation." As he spoke, Seuss demonstrated "throinging." Holding up both hands, fingers spread apart, he fit the fingers of one hand in between the fingers of the other, as if each hand were a gear.[101]

The work of Rube Goldberg (1883–1970) is the likely influence for this machine, which Seuss calls a "Pick-Up Machine" in the first draft of the TV script. Goldberg's strip

The Inventions of Professor Lucifer G. Butts (1907–1948) features elaborately impractical labor-saving devices that, in their sheer outlandishness, convey a bemused skepticism toward technology. These cartoons are the direct antecedents to the many inventions that appear in Seuss's books, such as the Bad-Animal-Catching-Machine of *If I Ran the Zoo* (1950), the Utterly Sputter of *The Butter Battle Book* (1984), and the invention you see here. Seuss was fond enough of Goldberg's inventions to spoof them in a *Judge* cartoon from May 19, 1928.

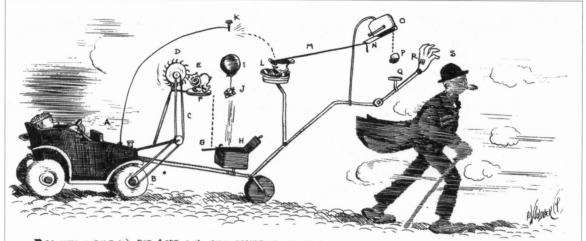

BUY AUTOMOBILE (A) FOR $275 AND HIRE CHAUFFEUR TO DRIVE IN BACK OF YOU ON WINDY DAY—MOTION OF BELT (B), ATTACHED TO FRONT WHEEL, IS COMMUNICATED TO BELT (C) WHICH TURNS TICKLER (D)—PICKLE-SPANIEL (E) LAUGHS UNTIL HE CHOKES AND FALLS OFF PLATFORM (F) HITTING CATCH (G) AND OPENING BOX (H)—BALLOON (I), WITH SUSPENDED PIECE OF CHEESE (J) RISES AND BURSTS ON PIN (K)—CHEESE DROPS INTO SHOE (L)—STRENGTH OF CHEESE CAUSES SHOE TO WALK AWAY PULLING SHOE-LACE (M) AND SLIDING COVER (N) OFF BOX (O) RELEASING TEN-POUND BISCUIT (P)—BISCUIT HITS SURFACE (Q) CAUSING ARM HOLDING IRON HAND (R) TO COME DOWN WITH A JOLT, AND HAND PRESSES HAT (S) ON HEAD SO TIGHT IT HAS TO BE BLASTED OFF WITH DYNAMITE UPON YOUR RETURN HOME.

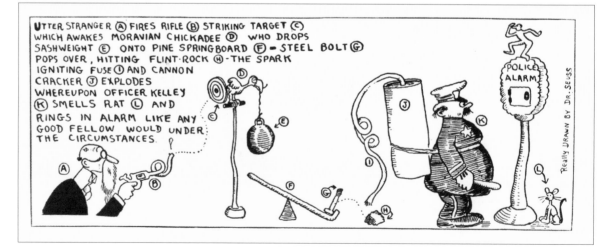

UTTER STRANGER (A) FIRES RIFLE (B) STRIKING TARGET (C) WHICH AWAKES MORAVIAN CHICKADEE (D) WHO DROPS SASHWEIGHT (E) ONTO PINE SPRINGBOARD (F)—STEEL BOLT (G) POPS OVER, HITTING FLINT-ROCK (H)—THE SPARK IGNITING FUSE (I) AND CANNON CRACKER (J) EXPLODES WHEREUPON OFFICER KELLEY (K) SMELLS RAT (L) AND RINGS IN ALARM LIKE ANY GOOD FELLOW WOULD UNDER THE CIRCUMSTANCES.

POLICE ALARM

Really drawn by Dr. Seuss

And THEN!
Who was back in the house?
Why, the cat!
"Have no fear of this mess,"
Said the Cat in the Hat.
"I always pick up all my playthings
And SO . . .
I will show you another
Good trick that I know!"

THE CAT IN THE HAT pages 56–57

Then we saw him pick up (page 58)
Seuss felt that this scene helped to contain some of the Cat's rebellious tendencies. As he told Jonathan Cott, "*The Cat in the Hat* is a revolt against authority, but it's ameliorated by the fact that the Cat cleans everything up at the end. It's revolutionary in that it goes as far as Kerensky and then stops. It doesn't go quite as far as Lenin."[102]

In 1917, after Czar Nicholas II (1868–1918) abdicated, Aleksandr Kerensky (1881–1970) became first a member and then the leader of Russia's provisional government. Although he advocated some popular reforms (such as abolishing capital punishment and introducing freedom of the press), he also supported Russia's continued involvement in the extremely unpopular First World War. Public discontent with the latter policy created an opportunity for Vladimir I. Lenin (1870–1924), who opposed the war and favored redistributing the wealth—more radical positions than Kerensky held. Under Lenin's leadership, the Bolsheviks won, and the Soviet Union was founded.

The Cat, then, is more like Kerensky because he's not as radical as Lenin. The Cat, too, introduces some reforms (such as changing the rules for indoor fun) but does not ultimately advocate a complete household revolution. When Seuss said the Cat was more like Kerensky than Lenin, Cott responded, "Like many of your books, *The Cat in the Hat* is quite anarchistic." Seuss replied, "It's impractical the way anarchy is, but it works within the confines of a book."[103] Seuss's apparent approval of the fact that the Cat's "impractical" revolt is confined to the book confirms the sense that the Cat's cleaning up is meant to ameliorate his earlier, radically disruptive behavior.

All the things that were down. (page 58)
A Dick and Jane primer concludes with a vocabulary list. Here, Seuss cleverly works the list into the plot. The words "up," "things," "down," "cake," "rake," "gown," "milk," "books," "fan," "cup," "ship," "away," "then," "gone," and "hat" all return to remind readers what they have learned. In the typescript on the colored-pencil sketches, Seuss managed to work in one more word—"kites." In that version, the line "He picked up the cake" was "The cake. And the kites." With the exception of "were," "strings," and "picked," every single word on this page has appeared at least once earlier in the story. "String" has appeared before, so its plural (which rhymes with the oft-repeated

"things") should be easily recognizable. Similarly, "pick" has appeared three times before (and appears a fourth time in the first line here); readers ought to make sense of the added "ed."

He picked up the cake, (page 58)
The changes between the draft and final pages often reveal Seuss cutting down on nonstandard English. For instance, in the colored-pencil sketches, this final list is entirely in sentence fragments: "The cake. And the kites. / And the rake. And the gown. / And the milk. And the strings." In the published version, Seuss uses commas: "He picked up the cake, / And the rake, and the gown, / And the milk, and the strings," and so on.

And the ship, and the fish. (page 58)
Since this 1,623-word book uses only 236 different words, many words get used multiple times. The word "the," which appears twelve times on this page, is repeated the most—ninety-seven uses in all. "And," which also appears twelve times here, comes in at second place with sixty-nine occurrences. "I" is in third, with fifty-nine instances.

And then he was gone (page 58)
When Theodor Seuss Geisel died in September 1991, cartoonists paid tribute. Brian Basset (b. 1957) reproduced this scene in his cartoon, drawing Dr. Seuss as the Cat in the Hat.

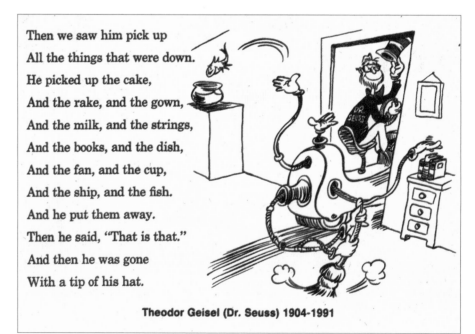

Then we saw him pick up
All the things that were down.
He picked up the cake,
And the rake, and the gown,
And the milk, and the strings,
And the books, and the dish,
And the fan, and the cup,
And the ship, and the fish.
And he put them away.
Then he said, "That is that."
And then he was gone
With a tip of his hat.

Theodor Geisel (Dr. Seuss) 1904-1991

Then we saw him pick up
All the things that were down.
He picked up the cake,
And the rake, and the gown,
And the milk, and the strings,
And the books, and the dish,
And the fan, and the cup,
And the ship, and the fish.
And he put them away.
Then he said, "That is that."
And then he was gone
With a tip of his hat.

THE CAT IN THE HAT pages 58–59

Then our mother came in (page 60)

Mother's entrance in this spread directly echoes the Cat's (*CITH* pages 6–7), and both entrances are at least similar to the Things' (pages 28–29): at left, window, children, table, and fish; at right, door with someone coming through it. That all enter through the same door suggests that the Cat and the Things are not mere fantasy but are as real as the mother. Where Maurice Sendak's *Where the Wild Things Are* (1963) or Crockett Johnson's (1906–1975) *A Picture for Harold's Room* (1960) might use a separate setting as a narrative frame to contain a fantastic excursion, Seuss offers no such boundary. In Sendak's book, Max returns to "his very own room," where he finds his "still hot" supper "waiting for him." The final illustration contains any residual wildness: the plant is in the pot, the moon is surrounded by the window. Johnson's title character returns to his room and, in contrast to the wall-sized drawing through which he departed, he creates a small, framed picture on the wall. As real as the travels of Harold and Max may have seemed at the time, each tale's conclusion confirms that the adventures were imaginary. In contrast, the adventures of Sally and her brother seem quite real: they never leave and return, but remain where they are. *The Cat in the Hat*'s final illustration leaves open the same door through which the Cat entered. In the animated version, Seuss makes the reality of the Cat more explicit. Not only does Mother appear to see the Cat (see next annotation), but the Cat himself suggests that he might return. As he leaves, he sings, "Sweep out the laughter. / There's no more time for laughter— / At least, not until after / I come back." His final words are "And you know? / I just may."

What would YOU do / If your mother asked YOU? (page 61)

This open ending, a method later used to great effect in *The Butter Battle Book,* was likely inspired by Frank R. Stockton's (1834–1902) "The Lady, or the Tiger?" (1882), which Seuss read as a child. "I thought that was the best children's book I'd ever read," he told interviewer Kathleen Smith.[104] Read by both children and adults, Stockton's short story introduces a "semi-barbaric king" who administers justice "by the decrees of an impartial and incorruptible chance." The accused is placed in an amphitheater, where he must pick one of two doors. Behind one is a tiger; behind the other, a lady. If he opens one, a hungry tiger will devour him "as a punishment for his guilt." If he opens the other, he will marry a fair lady (irrespective of his own marital status) "as a reward of his innocence." A handsome young man has had an affair with the king's daughter. Upon discovering their love, the king imprisons the man for daring "to love the daughter of the king." When the man enters the arena, he sees the king's daughter, seated with members of the court near the twin doors. She knows the secret of the doors. The princess, torn between jealousy (if she cannot have him, then neither can another) and despair (he is her beloved), has spent "days and nights of anxious deliberation" and has arrived at a decision. The man's anxious glance asks her, "Which?" and she makes a "slight, quick movement toward the right." No one else sees her because everyone's attention is fixed on the man. The man opens the door on the right. Stockton concludes his story with "Which came out of the opened door,—the lady, or the tiger?"[105] Stockton never answered the question of his oft-reprinted story, though many others tried. "The Lady, or the Tiger?" became a popular parlor game, required reading for high school students, and even a one-act play by Shel Silverstein (1930–1999).

Seuss poses a similar conundrum here. Should Sally and her brother tell their mother a lie that she will believe or the truth, which she will doubt? Should they say, for example, "Oh, nothing much," or should they disclose their adventures with the Cat, Thing One, and Thing Two? After receiving hundreds of queries about "The Lady, or the Tiger?" Stockton finally replied, "If you decide which it was—the lady, or the tiger—you find out what kind of a person you are yourself."[106] Perhaps the same could be said of Seuss's question: our answers tell us more about ourselves than about his story.

Alison Lurie (b. 1926) and Ruth K. MacDonald both agree that the implied answer is "Don't tell Mother." As MacDonald puts it, "It is clear to the reader at the end, when the boy narrator asks, 'What would YOU do' about the mother's questions, that keeping quiet is the answer."[107] The "likely answer from a child's perspective," she says, "is that the children had better simply leave their mother in the dark and give a child's typical answer to the question, 'What did you do all day?' 'Nothing.'"[108] And Alison Lurie writes, "When their mother returns and asks what they've been doing, there is a strong suggestion that they might not tell her."[109] Betty Mensch and Alan Freeman suggest that the point of the ending is to pose a moral question. They write, "That question poses once again the dilemma of virtue's relation to authority. This question is profoundly disturbing to children, for good reason. To choose conventional morality in alliance with authority is to surrender all possibility of existential realization. To be for no other reason than that they tell you to be is

Continued on page 92

Then our mother came in
And she said to us two,
"Did you have any fun?
Tell me. What did you do?"

And Sally and I did not know
What to say.
Should we tell her
The things that went on there that day?

Should we tell her about it?
Now, what SHOULD we do?
Well . . .
What would YOU do
If your mother asked YOU?

THE CAT IN THE HAT pages 60–61

Continued from page 90

not to be at all. On the other hand, children rightly understand the reality of power in the world: Individualized, direct confrontation with authority will surely fail. The child who would defiantly celebrate the Cat's visit is doomed to awesome punishment, yet the child who contritely tells the truth forestalls punishment at the price of self-respect. The other choice is to abandon the search for virtue altogether, making a pact with powerful satanic forces in an orgy of joyful self-gratification that will ultimately lead to empty despair."[110] Although I do not express the idea in quite the same way, I have also suggested that the point of the question is to provoke readers into solving the puzzle themselves.[111]

As a means of soliciting the reader's involvement, Seuss often used an open ending. *The Butter Battle Book*—Seuss's satire of the nuclear arms race—ends with a Yook and a Zook standing on the wall that divides their countries, each poised to drop a Seussian version of a nuclear bomb on the other side. The Yook's grandson asks, "Who's going to drop it? / Will *you* . . . ? Or will *he* . . . ?" The reply: "'Be patient,' said Grandpa. 'We'll see. / We will see . . .'" With that, *The Butter Battle Book* ends, leaving the reader to reckon with the problem posed. In several interviews at the time, Seuss mentioned Stockton's tale, remarking that he had "always wanted to do a book with an ending like that. A nonending. This is it."[112] *Butter Battle* may be his most confrontational "nonending," but it is not his first. Although *The Lorax* does not end with a question, it concludes by inviting "you" to plant trees so that "the Lorax / and all of his friends / may come back." Other books, if lacking questions as provocative as those that conclude *The Cat* or *Butter Battle,* do end with questions. *On Beyond Zebra!* (1955) ends with a new alphabetic character and asks, "What do YOU think we should call this one, anyhow?" *Mr. Brown Can Moo! Can You?* offers a list of what noises its title character can make, adding, "Mr. Brown can do it. How about YOU?"

The television version of *The Cat in the Hat* does *not* end with the book's question. As in the book, the mother enters—although the cartoon does not show her at all (not even her leg and ankle). She says, "Hi, kids! Hope you had fun today. Well, you kids will never believe this, but I could almost swear I saw a Cat—a Cat in a Hat, mind you—going down the street with a moss-covered three-handled family grudunza." The two children look at each other. The animators create the effect of the camera pulling back from outside the window, where we see them looking out. With their house in the background, the top of the Cat's hat bobs along the bottom third of the screen—as if he is walking along the street. The implications of this difference are twofold. First, the mother sees the Cat in the Hat, although she doubts her senses: so if the children *were* to tell her about their day, she would be more likely to believe them. Second, the absence of the question removes the need to think any further about the story. The book ends with a subject for debate, but the cartoon simply ends.

The Cat in the Hat (back cover)
In 1957, the back cover looked like this:

Which cover would YOU use if your editor asked YOU?

The Beginner Book Story

In 1957, Theodor Geisel, known to the world as Dr. Seuss, wrote a book called *The Cat in the Hat*.

It was fun to read aloud, easy to read alone, and impossible to put down.

From this magically right beginning came the concept of Beginner Books, exacting blends of words and pictures that encourage children to read—all by themselves. Hailed by elementary educators and remedial reading specialists, these enormously popular books are now used in schools and libraries throughout the English-speaking world.

Beginner Books®
The right reading readiness
every child needs.™

US $8.99 / $11.99 CAN
ISBN 978-0-394-80001-1
50899

9 780394 800011

Random House
www.randomhouse.com/kids
www.seussville.com

THE CAT IN THE HAT back cover

The Cat in the Hat Comes Back (early cover)
The original jacket takes the Cat in the Hat from page 6 of *The Cat in the Hat Comes Back* and turns the page a few minutes clockwise, so that he appears to be walking on level ground, toward a hill (instead of up a hill, as he is on page 6). Collectors of Seuss's books will also note the motion lines behind the Cat, the blue title (with shadowing) above, and the original Beginner Books logo in front. Oh, and a *white* tie. (Oops.) In subsequent printings, the tie gained its customary red color.

When it did, the background became solid blue, the hill changed to level ground, the motion lines vanished, and the Beginner Books logo turned clockwise so that it was perfectly straight (instead of at an angle). In 1960, the Cat in the Hat emerged from the endpapers of the first book to become a part of the Beginner Books logo, replacing the small child behind the large book.

THE CAT IN THE HAT COMES BACK front cover

The Cat in the Hat Comes Back (endpapers)

In going over the following marked-up pages in which the color application is obviously bad, please look for something else which I suspect, but I am not sure of.

see art   I suspect that something has happened to the entire _Sharpness_   black plate.

Like it did when you discovered that the Yertle plates were foul. And had them made over.

There seems to be a muck, however slight, in the basic black plate. The crispness that we all thought I had in the original pictures doesn't seem to be there any longer.

Maybe this is my imagination. Maybe I wasn't as crisp as I thought I was.

But the black lines seem to have got terribly muddy.

In addition to the Cat's white bow tie, the first printing contained several other errors. As Seuss's note to his publisher points out, the "color application" was "obviously bad," with colors bleeding outside of the lines; to make sure that this was corrected in the next printing, Seuss went through the entire book, circling areas where a color had seeped into a place where it should not have been. And, he said, "the black lines seem to have got terribly muddy," losing their former "crispness." He did acknowledge that he might have been at fault: "Maybe this is my imagination. Maybe I wasn't as crisp as I thought I was." The earlier pen-and-ink version reveals both that he was *not* as crisp as he was in *The Cat in the Hat* and that the black lines did become more "muddy" during the printing process. His attention to the deficiencies of the first printing underscores Seuss's perfectionism, a trait that led him to be intensely critical of his own work.

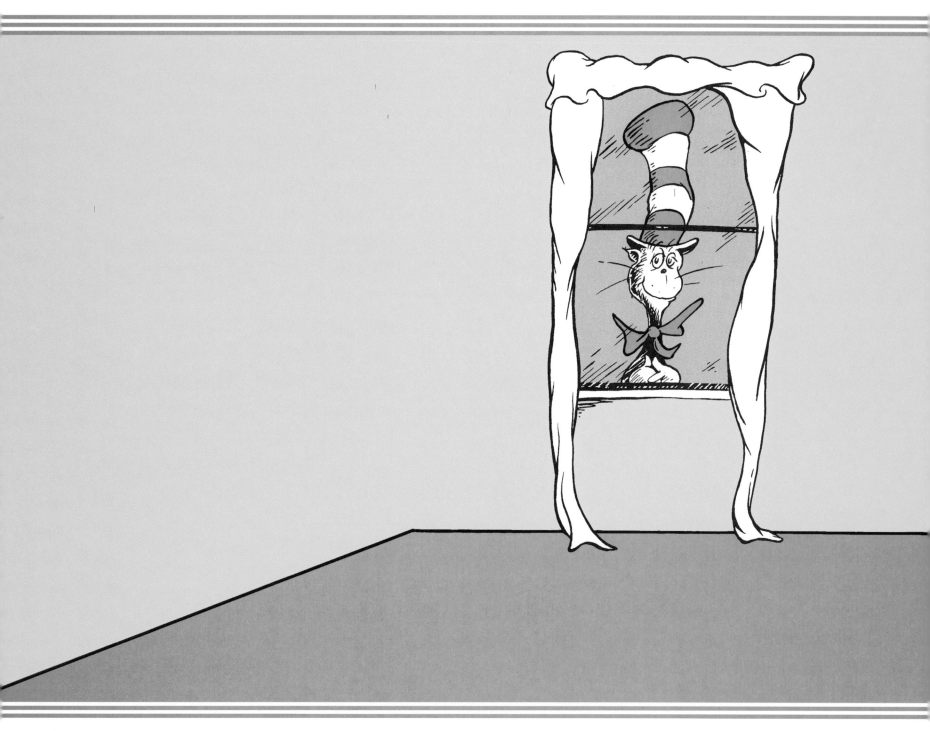

THE CAT IN THE HAT COMES BACK endpapers

The Cat in the Hat Comes Back (title page)

After the success of *The Cat in the Hat,* Seuss, Helen Geisel, and Phyllis Cerf began the Beginner Books line for Random House (see pages 10–11). As Cerf said at the time, "We want to publish books that take up where textbooks leave off. We want to produce books that any child in the first grade not only *can* read but will *want* to read."[1] The series' first five books, all published in the fall of 1958, were *The Cat in the Hat Comes Back,* Mike McClintock's (1906–1967) *A Fly Went By* (illustrated by Fritz Siebel, 1913–1991), P. D. Eastman's *Sam and the Firefly,* Marion Holland's (1908–1989) *A Big Ball of String,* and Benjamin Elkin's (1911–1995) *The Big Jump and Other Stories* (illustrated by Katherine Evans, 1901–1964).

Writing *The Cat in the Hat Comes Back* was challenging. As Seuss said at the time, "Writing a book using only 348 words is a tough job—I ought to know because I threw away six of my own manuscripts before I was able to do a sequel to *The Cat in the Hat.*"[2] However, Seuss managed to write the book more quickly than he did the first. Perhaps using more than *The Cat*

in the Hat's 236 words helped him. *The Cat in the Hat Comes Back* has 290 words. (This figure includes each letter of the alphabet as one word, since each is used as a word to name one of the Little Cats; the word "dollar," written as "$"; the number "10"; and the abbreviation "T.V." If one were to remove the individual letters of the alphabet on the grounds that a letter is usually *not* a word, then one should subtract 24—not 26, because "A" and "I" are both words and are both used—to arrive at 266.)

It is also possible that the faster pace at which Seuss composed prompted him to consider the work as being of lesser quality than the original. As he told Edward Connery Lathem, "Like all other sequels, it wasn't as good as the first. But it has sold almost as well as the first!"[3]

The amount of surviving draft material does not permit an accurate measure of the pace of his creative process, but Seuss either produced less or saved less draft material when writing the book. Unlike those for *The Cat in the Hat,* no colored-pencil sketches survive for *The Cat in the Hat Comes Back.* And unlike the finished drawings for *The Cat in the Hat,* those for this book frequently bear evidence of Liquid Paper (or a similar product).

Note that an exclamation point appears only on the title page of *The Cat in the Hat Comes Back,* and not on the cover itself. Discrepancies between Seuss's covers and title pages are rare but not unheard of. *On Beyond Zebra!* (1955) and *How the Grinch Stole Christmas!* (1957) each have an exclamation point on the cover but not on the title page.

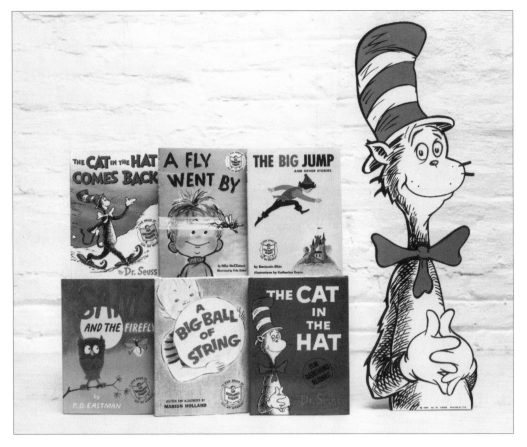

THE CAT IN THE HAT COMES BACK!

By Dr. Seuss

Beginner Books
A DIVISION OF RANDOM HOUSE, INC.

THE CAT IN THE HAT COMES BACK title page

There was work to be done. (page 3)

In many ways, this book is the opposite of its predecessor. By invoking the earlier book's opening, this page throws their differences into relief. The second book begins, as Ruth K. MacDonald notes, "with a view of the same house in inclement weather . . . with the same bird in the same tree suffering in the same way from the precipitation."[4] Such similarities end here. Given the leaves on the trees and bushes on pages 1 and 46 of

The Cat in the Hat, its season is at least late spring, if not summer. The snow tells us that *The Cat in the Hat Comes Back*'s season is winter, or (if the first book takes place in summer) roughly six months later. All of the first book takes place inside the house, while half of the second book takes place outside the house. *The Cat in the Hat* introduces two inert children with leisure time; in contrast, its sequel shows those same two children working hard, with "no time for play." The first book's twenty-three-word opening offers an excuse for sitting by the window: "It was too wet to play" and so "we sat in the house / All that cold, cold, wet day." The second book's twenty-four-word opening provides an imperative, a call to action: "This was no time for games. / There was work to be done." An impediment to play in both books, weather causes boredom in *The Cat in the Hat* but makes work in *The Cat in the Hat Comes Back*. Similarly, the children are much more passive in the first book, waiting until the final pages to take action against the Cat. In the second book, the children oppose the Cat almost immediately; correctly suspecting him of being "up to no good" (page 9 of *The Cat in the Hat Comes Back* [*CITHCB*]), the boy starts after him and reprimands him (page 10). As MacDonald notes, the children's failure to prevent the Cat's mischief in the second book results not from inaction (as it does in the first book) "but because the Cat beats them to it."[5]

The sun did not shine.
It was too wet to play.
So we sat in the house
All that cold, cold, wet day.

This was no time for play.
This was no time for fun.
This was no time for games.
There was work to be done.

THE CAT IN THE HAT COMES BACK page 3

All that snow had to go. (page 4)

When Ted Geisel was eleven years old, what the *Springfield Daily Republican* described as an "old-fashioned December blizzard" came to town. Within twenty-four hours, Springfield received nearly two feet of snow, with snowdrifts up to five and six feet deep. The *Daily Republican* records 22.10 inches falling between 7 a.m. on Monday, December 13, 1915, and 7 a.m. on Tuesday the 14th. According to Wednesday's paper, "When Springfield awoke yesterday [Tuesday] morning it found itself pretty well snowbound": schools were closed; trains and trolleys were delayed, stuck, or derailed. Residents spent Tuesday, a clear day (just as in *The Cat in the Hat Comes Back*), "digging themselves out from under Monday night's tremendous and blustery fall of snow." It took eighteen plows and five hundred men to clear the railway lines.[6] In creating this scene of "Sally and me" shoveling, Dr. Seuss very likely drew upon memories of this blizzard, the largest snowstorm in his boyhood.

"Somebody, SOMEBODY" (page 5)

Of the 290 different words in *The Cat in the Hat Comes Back*, only four have three syllables: "somebody," "somebodies," "W" (the twenty-third Little Cat's name), and "anything." The twenty-six two-syllable words are "Sally," "mother," "Mother's," "water," "working," "eating," "something," "before," "little," "into," "clever," "ever," "never," "over," "about," "after," "again," "alone," "away," "today," "very," "happy," "hurry," "bedroom," "T.V.," and "dollar" (written as "$").

All that deep,
Deep, deep snow,
All that snow had to go.

When our mother went
Down to the town for the day,
She said, "Somebody has to
Clean all this away.
Somebody, SOMEBODY
Has to, you see."
Then she picked out two Somebodies.
Sally and me.

THE CAT IN THE HAT COMES BACK pages 4–5

But the CAT IN THE HAT! (page 6)
R.E.M.'s "The Sidewinder Sleeps Tonite" (*Automatic for the People,* 1992) makes reference to this moment during the bridge between the third verse and final chorus: "The Cat in the Hat came back, wrecked [*sic*] a lot of havoc on the way, always had a smile and a reason to pretend." The first popular song to allude to Seuss's children's books may have been Bobby Russell's "Little Green Apples," which was a number-two hit for O. C. Smith in 1968 and won the Grammy for Song of the Year: "And if that's not lovin' me, / then all I've got to say, / God didn't make little green apples, / and it don't rain in Indianapolis in the summertime. / There's no such thing as Dr. Seuss, / Disneyland, and Mother Goose is no nursery rhyme." The Dr. Seuss book to inspire the most song lyrics is probably *Green Eggs and Ham,* which figures in the Beastie Boys' "Egg Man" (*Paul's Boutique,* 1989), Moxy Früvous's "Green Eggs and Ham" (*Moxy Früvous,* 1992), and 3rd Bass's "Pop Goes the Weasel" and "Green Eggs and Swine" (both from *Derelicts of Dialect,* 1991).

"Oh-oh!" Sally said. (page 7)
Sally, completely silent during *The Cat in the Hat,* here is the first child to speak up against the Cat. Alison Lurie's "The Cabinet of Dr. Seuss" (1990) faults Seuss's books for their "almost total lack of female protagonists," noting that "little girls"—such as Sally—"play silent, secondary roles" and that the few prominent female characters (such as Mayzie in *Horton Hatches the Egg*) are presented in an unflattering light.[7] Though Sally is less central than her brother in both Cat books, she is more actively involved in this one, protesting that the spot will never come off the dress (on *CITHCB* page 19) and joining her brother in demanding that the Cat take his Little Cats away (pages 46 and 47).

Seuss responded to Lurie's charge by pointing out that most of his characters were animals, "and if she can identify their sex, I'll remember her in my will."[8] For a detailed discussion of sex and gender in Seuss's work, see my *Dr. Seuss: American Icon* (2004), pages 101–17. See also page 64 of *The Annotated Cat.*

"Don't you talk to that cat." (page 7)
Ruth K. MacDonald suggests that "Sally takes on the mother's role here, with speech that sounds peremptory and proscriptive. She warns her brother—'Don't you talk to that cat . . . / You know what he did the last time he was here'—with a sort of smug 'I told you so' attitude."[9] The only words spoken by the mother are "Did you have any fun? / Tell me. What did you do?" (at the end of *The Cat in the Hat*) and "Somebody has to / Clean all this away. / Somebody, SOMEBODY / Has to, you see" (*CITHCB* page 5). Sally's "peremptory and proscriptive" speech more closely echoes the mother's words in the second book than those in the first. Her words also bring to mind the voice of the fish, whose first speech begins, "No! No! / Make that cat go away! / Tell that Cat in the Hat / You do NOT want to play." In the absence of both mother *and* fish, perhaps Sally must take on a more parental role.

"Don't you let him come near." (page 7)
For *The Cat in the Hat,* Seuss stuck to the word lists (see page 24 of annotations). In *The Cat in the Hat Comes Back,* he begins to depart from them. As Ruth K. MacDonald notes, "Voom" (which appears on *CITHCB* pages 57–59) is "a minor deviation from the prescribed lists of limited vocabulary used in the earlier book."[10] And the vocabulary "is more conversational than in the earlier book, with contractions, such as 'don't' and 'can't,' and certain childlike exclamations—'Oh, boy!' for instance." As MacDonald says, "on the whole, the vocabulary much more resembles children's speech, and is much less high-flown and literary in effect."[11] Although Seuss always limited his vocabulary for Beginner Books, he eventually tossed out the word lists altogether. When asked in 1973, "How do you feel about the impact your books have had on schools?" Seuss answered, "I'm happy, because I think I'm helping to drive word lists out of existence."[12]

Well . . .
There we were.
We were working like that
And then who should come up
But the CAT IN THE HAT!

"Oh-oh!" Sally said.
"Don't you talk to that cat.
That cat is a bad one,
That Cat in the Hat.
He plays lots of bad tricks.
Don't you let him come near.
You know what he did
The last time he was here."

THE CAT IN THE HAT COMES BACK pages 6–7

He was up to no good! (page 9)

Naming Hilaire Belloc (1870–1953) as someone "whose writings I liked a lot," Seuss speculated that there might have been "some influence" from Belloc on his own work.[13] The claim here that the Cat is "up to no good" and the repeated requests for him to stop misbehaving in both this book and *The Cat in the Hat* offer a distant echo of Belloc's comic-didactic verse for children. Conveying his sense that children tend to behave badly, Belloc introduces *The Bad Child's Book of Beasts* (1896) with this address to the reader:

> I call you bad, my little child,
> Upon the title page,
> Because a manner rude and wild
> Is common at your age.

The Moral of this priceless work
(If rightly understood)
Will make you—from a little Turk—
Unnaturally good.

As the fish does in *The Cat in the Hat,* the boy in this book asks the Cat to amend his wild behavior. On the next two-page spread, he says, "What a bad thing to do!" On the spread after that, he insists, "There is work to be done. / I have no time for tricks." The Cat does not heed him.

In some of Belloc's works, heedless children receive their comeuppance, as in the story of "Franklin Hyde, Who Caroused in Dirt and Was Corrected by His Uncle" from *Cautionary Tales*

Continued on page 108

"Play tricks?" laughed the cat.
"Oh, my my! No, no, no!
I just want to go in
To get out of the snow.
Keep your mind on your work.
You just stay there, you two.
I will go in the house
And find something to do."

Then that cat went right in!
He was up to no good!
So I ran in after
As fast as I could!

THE CAT IN THE HAT COMES BACK pages 8–9

Continued from page 106

for Children (1907). Seuss's Cat plays with a pink spot instead of mud and, unlike Belloc's Franklin Hyde, gets away with messy behavior. Granting the Cat license to misbehave, Seuss's books may more closely resemble the Belloc verses that eschew morals, as in "C Stands for Cobra" from *A Moral Alphabet* (1899): "This creature, though disgusting and appalling, / Conveys no Moral worth recalling."[14]

So I ran in after (page 9)

As evidenced by the remaining traces of pencil lines faintly visible at the top of the preceding spread, the final pen-and-ink drawings offer an example of some late revisions. Originally, the boy's face was farther ahead, and his left arm was slightly lower. Sally's left arm was also slightly lower, and the blobs of snow were closer to landing on her head. Placing greater distance between boy and Cat increases the dramatic tension: the farther the boy is from the Cat, the more difficult it will be to catch up with him. Similarly, moving the snow farther from Sally's hat very subtly amplifies the drama. In the earlier version, the snow will certainly land on her head: because she is the inevitable target, there's no suspense. In the final version, there's still time (albeit not much) for her to move: if she reacts quickly and races after her brother, the snow will not strike her.

On page 9, the pencil drawings had more "motion clouds" behind the Cat, and his hat was slightly higher. Perhaps Seuss decided he had enough motion clouds, or perhaps he did not want to distract from the sweeping *S* the Cat's skis make (a glimpse of the alphabet theme that develops later in the book?). Presumably, he placed the hat lower because it would have been cropped out of the picture if left where it was.

Do you know where I found him? (page 10)

As children's literature scholar Jill P. May points out, the influence of traditional folklore emerges most clearly in Seuss's early works—especially in *The 500 Hats of Bartholomew Cubbins*.[15] However, the Cat's outrageous behavior, conveyed in conversational narrative style, makes this story sound like a tall tale, too. The narrator seems here almost to be daring us to doubt his story. The illustrations confirm the apparent truth of his observations, but the text reads like an exaggerated yarn about a larger-than-life cat. The Cat does not create the Grand Canyon (like Paul Bunyan) or ride a tornado (like Pecos Bill), but he does alter the landscape (see especially *CITHCB* pages 50 through 61). And he does apparently impossible things: when the "mother is near," his tidying-up machine instantly transforms the house from chaos to cleanliness. He produces two Things from a box and twenty-six Little Cats from under his hat.

Do you know where I found him?

You know where he was?

He was eating a cake in the tub!

Yes he was!

The hot water was on

And the cold water, too.

And I said to the cat,

"What a bad thing to do!"

"But I like to eat cake

In a tub," laughed the cat.

"You should try it some time,"

Laughed the cat as he sat.

THE CAT IN THE HAT COMES BACK pages 10–11

"There is work to be done." (page 12)

The repeated claim that there is "work to be done" (see also *CITHCB* page 3) reflects Theodor Seuss Geisel's work ethic. As he told Jack Webb in 1974, "I've made it a rule to sit at my desk for eight hours even if nothing comes. I've seen so many writers and artists become bums, especially in a resort town like this [La Jolla, California]. They go to the beach in the morning and when they come back they don't feel like working. So I work eight hours straight. When the work is going well, I'll go at it hammer and tongs for a month, then take six or seven weeks off. Even then I'll be working, though, filling up notebooks with ideas."[16] He offered variations on this comment in several other interviews.[17] Seuss also once said, "I come up with my ideas by sitting down and sweating. That's where you have to discipline yourself."[18] Michael Frith's description of Ted Geisel at work provides a comparably industrious portrait: "To watch him at work is to watch a man in perpetual motion: his hand plunges into one of the myriad pots of colored pencils that surround him, selects one, sketches fiercely and whips the drawing off its pad. In two strides he is at the wall, push-pins plunge, and picture affixed, he considers it for an intense moment with eyebrows cocked in concentration. Then he is back at the desk, trying variation after variation until he has the one that satisfies him."[19]

This sense of needing to work hard would have been compounded by the fact that he had less time to compose *The Cat in the Hat Comes Back*. The first Cat book—inspired by Hersey's 1954 article—was published in March 1957. By May 1957, he was thinking about writing more primers but hadn't yet named a sequel to *The Cat in the Hat* as his next project.[20] By late 1957 or early 1958, he was evaluating manuscripts for the Beginner Books series, which cut into his time even further. By May 1958, *The Cat in the Hat Comes Back* was on Random House's fall list, and the book appeared in early September 1958. As he composed the book, Seuss must have been keenly aware of "work to be done."

Dr. Seuss's well-worn drawing board.

And then I got mad.
This was no time for fun.
I said, "Cat! You get out!
There is work to be done.
I have no time for tricks.
I must go back and dig.
I can't have you in here
Eating cake like a pig!
You get out of this house!
We don't want you about!"
Then I shut off the water
And let it run out.

THE CAT IN THE HAT COMES BACK pages 12–13

A big long pink cat ring! (page 14)

In her "Democracy in America: By Dr. Seuss" (2000), Shira Wolosky suggests that "the Cat sports a stovepipe hat and bowtie based in Uncle Sam cartoons, where they in fact originated in earlier Geisel drawings and ads."[21] Three decades earlier, in "The Cat in the Hat for President," Robert Coover also portrayed the Cat as an American figure—"all red, white, and blue."[22]

Whether or not the Cat has any connection to Seuss's political cartoons is debatable, but Seuss frequently recycled earlier images in later works. So, for example, the cartoon shown here from January 1942 *may* be a visual antecedent to this scene in *The Cat in the Hat Comes Back*. In the cartoon, Seuss's top-hatted bird (representing Uncle Sam) has to contend with Nazi subs; in the book, Seuss's top-hatted Cat must deal with the pink ring. On the other hand, Seuss did several *other* wartime cartoons with a bathtub theme, and the top-hatted figure in the tub is *not* Uncle Sam: in one from May 1941, the character represents the America First organization (which Seuss criticized for leaving the U.S. vulnerable to attack). In another, from September 1941, the top-hatted person in the tub represents Japan (in hot water that signifies "war with U.S.").

The water ran out.
And then I SAW THE RING!
A ring in the tub!
And, oh boy! What a thing!
A big long pink cat ring!
It looked like pink ink!
And I said, "Will this ever
Come off? I don't think!"

THE CAT IN THE HAT COMES BACK pages 14–15

"Why, I can take cat rings" (page 16)
The ring removal (on these pages) and spot removal (on the following pages) recall Seuss's advertising work, such as this 1934 ad for Ex-tane, a spot remover manufactured by Standard Oil.

"Have no fear of that ring,"
Laughed the Cat in the Hat.
"Why, I can take cat rings
Off tubs. Just like that!"

Do you know how he did it?
WITH MOTHER'S WHITE DRESS!
Now the tub was all clean,
But her dress was a mess!

THE CAT IN THE HAT COMES BACK pages 16–17

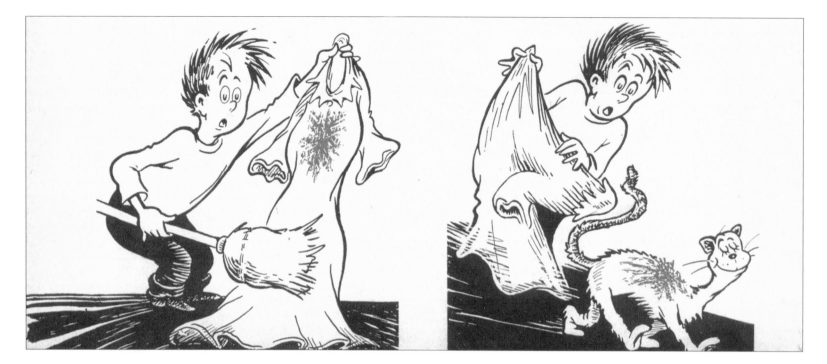

But that dress! What a spot! (page 19)

As Charles D. Cohen points out, Seuss was recycling elements of his story "The Strange Shirt Spot," published seven years earlier in the September 1951 issue of *Redbook*. In this story, a boy remembers his mother's warning to "stay out of the dirt" and tries to get rid of a spot on his "brand new white shirt." He succeeds only in moving the spot from shirt to towel, to tub, to broom, to "mother's best dress," to the cat, and then back to his shirt again. The full story is included on page 165.

Other notable instances of recycling include the To-an-Fro Marchers, who appear in *If I Ran the Circus* (1956). A version of these characters returns in "The economic situation clarified," published in *The New York Times Magazine* in June 1975. Seuss's final book, *Oh, the Places You'll Go!* (1990), reuses the *Times Magazine* drawing—with slight alteration—in the "Life's a Great Balancing Act" illustration. For another example of recycling, turn to the humor magazine *Life* (not the later *Life* founded by Henry Luce), where Seuss published "THE FACTS OF LIFE; Or, How Should I Tell My Child?" in February 1934. The accompanying illustration, "The Biological Highlights of History," included an elephant sitting on an egg. Its caption was "998,000 B.C. Elephant eggs prove impractical." Seuss revisited the elephant-on-egg idea for "Matilda, the Elephant with a Mother Complex," a 1938 *Judge* magazine story. His most famous version of this concept, of course, is *Horton Hatches the Egg* (1940).

For much more on Seuss's tendency to reuse motifs, ideas, and character names, put this book down and pick up Charles D. Cohen's *The Seuss, the Whole Seuss, and Nothing but the Seuss*. Cohen excels at tracing this fascinating aspect of Seuss's work.

Then Sally looked in.
Sally saw the dress, too!
And Sally and I
Did not know what to do.
We should work in the snow.
But that dress! What a spot!
"It may never come off!"
Sally said. "It may not!"

THE CAT IN THE HAT COMES BACK pages 18–19

"I can make the spot go." (page 20)

In this illustration, Seuss also makes the entire bathtub "go." The characters do not appear to have changed location between the previous two-page spread (pages 18–19) and this one (pages 20–21): Sally is outside the window, looking through the bottom left-hand pane; the Cat and the boy are to her right. There is no visual or textual evidence that the Cat, the boy, or Sally has moved. Yet the rug, shovel, and bathtub have suddenly disappeared in these two pages. Narrative and layout can account for the absence of the first two items. Surprise may have caused Sally to drop her shovel. And, perhaps, to accommodate the text, the rug is simply not represented—but we can assume that it is still "there," behind the text. However, the sudden appearance of a wall where the bathtub was seems to be an error in continuity.

The book contains many examples of corrected mistakes. On this page, near the far-left baseboard, Seuss has painted white over lines that run perpendicular to those on the floor (and on the baseboard). Another obvious example occurs at the bottom right-hand corner of page 6. Seuss initially had more motion lines stretching out to the left of the Cat and more wavy lines on the snow. He painted over these in the final pen-and-ink drawings, eliminating some of the lines and creating a slightly choppy effect.

But the cat laughed, "Ho! Ho!
I can make the spot go.
The way I take spots off a dress
Is just so!"

"See here!" laughed the cat.
"It is not hard at all.
The thing that takes spots
Off a dress is a wall!"
Then we saw the cat wipe
The spot off the dress.
Now the dress was all clean.
But the wall! What a mess!

THE CAT IN THE HAT COMES BACK pages 20–21

"To take spots off a wall," (page 23)

The indoor spot-removal scenes in *The Cat in the Hat Comes Back* work much as the juggling scenes do in *The Cat in the Hat*: in the first book, Seuss works in a list of required nouns (see page 44); in the second, he appears to be doing the same. In the earlier book, he gets in "ball," "fish," "cup," "book," "cake," "ship," "milk," "dish," "man," "rake," and "fan." Here, he includes "ring," "tub," "dress," "wall," "shoes," "rug," "bed," "bedroom," "broom," "milk," "pan," and "fan."

Ough! Ough!
Or Why I Believe in Simplified Spelling
By Dr. Seuss

"The Tough Coughs as he Ploughs the Dough"

It was forty-five years ago, when I first came to America as a young Roumanian student of divinity, that I first met the evils of the *"ough words."* Strolling one day in the country with my fellow students, I saw a tough, coughing as he ploughed a field which (being quite nearsighted) I mistook for pie dough.

Assuming that all *ough words* were pronounced the same, I casually remarked, "The tuff cuffs as he pluffs the duff!" "Sacrilege!" shrieked my devout companions. "He is cursing in Roumanian!" I was expelled from the school.

"Mr. Hough, Your Bough is in the Trough"

The ministry being closed to me, I then got a job as a chore boy on the farm of an eccentric Mr. Hough, who happened to spend most of his time on the bough of a tree overhanging a trough. I was watering a colt one morning when I noticed that Mr. Hough's weight had forced the bough down into the water.

"Mr. Hoo!" I shouted, "Your Boo is in the Troo!"

Thinking I was speaking lightly of his wife, Mr. Hough fired me on the spot.

"Enough! Enough! I'm Through!"

So I drifted into the prize ring. But here again the curse of the *oughs* undid me. One night at the Garden, I was receiving an unmerciful trouncing from a mauler twice my size. Near the end of the sixth round I could stand it no longer. I raised my feeble hand in surrender.

"Eno! Eno!" I gulped. "I'm thruff!"

"Insults like that I take from no man!" bellowed my opponent, and he slugged me into a coma!

Something snapped! . . . a maddening flash . . . and all became black. Fifteen years later I awoke to find myself the father of three homely daughters named Xough, Yough and Zough. I had become a thorough-going Aughomaniac.

Whose shoes did he use? (page 23)

Exploiting the ambiguous relationship between spelling and pronunciation, this page plays with the idea that words ending in "-ews," "-oes," "-use," and "-ose" can all sound similar. "News," "shoes," "use," and "whose" may look very different on the page, but they rhyme. The rhyme helps children to pronounce them, despite their various spellings.

As developed in greater detail on page 140, Seuss's work often reveals his fascination with the apparent lack of connection between English spelling and pronunciation. Where this page shows how different spellings can sound the same, Seuss's "Ough! Ough! Or Why I Believe in Simplified Spelling" shows how similar spellings can sound very different. An illustrated piece from *Judge* magazine's issue of April 13, 1929, this comic tale introduces a foreign divinity student who encounters the evils of the *"ough words."* As the student says, "Strolling one day in the country with my fellow students, I saw a tough, coughing as he ploughed a field which (being quite nearsighted) I mistook for pie dough. Assuming that all *ough words* were pronounced the same, I casually remarked, 'The tuff cuffs as he pluffs the duff!' 'Sacrilege!' shrieked my devout companions. 'He is cursing in Roumanian!' I was expelled from the school."

"DAD'S $10 SHOES!" (page 23)

An unscientific sample of shoe prices indicates that in 1957, these would have been moderately priced dress shoes. A Macy's advertisement from the November 3 *New York Times* displays Italian shoes for men. The Prato, a suede shoe, and the Piavé, a hand-stitched leather shoe, cost $9.98 a pair. They were the cheapest ones advertised by Macy's; the other shoes ranged in price from $18.94 to $21.94. A Lord & Taylor ad from the May 5, 1958, *Times* advertised a "clearance of men's shoes 11.90 to 18.90," consisting of "English and American-made shoes" that were "regularly 16.95 to 26.50." On December 30, 1958, Saks was advertising its own English-made "Paddington shoes for men" at the sale price of $9.99.

"Oh, wall spots!" he laughed.
"Let me tell you some news.
To take spots off a wall,
All I need is two shoes!"

Whose shoes did he use?
I looked and saw whose!
And I said to the cat,
"This is very bad news.
Now the spot is all over
DAD'S $10 SHOES!"

THE CAT IN THE HAT COMES BACK pages 22–23

"He will never find out," (page 24)

The Cat is much more brazen in the sequel. In the first book, he falsely claims that the "mother / Will not mind" and that his "tricks are not bad," but never does he ask the children to cover up for him. The original book's conclusion poses a moral question that asks the readers to decide whether they would lie or tell the truth. In the second book, however, the Cat encourages the children to deceive their parents. As he says on this page, "your dad will not / Know about that" because he "will never find out."

The reason for the greater degree of brashness in the Cat's personality may be that *The Cat in the Hat Comes Back* was revised less than *The Cat in the Hat* was. Certainly, in earlier versions of other books, Seuss's characters have rougher edges. For example, in the manuscript of *Green Eggs and Ham,* the black-hatted character behaves more aggressively. Instead of merely saying that he does not like green eggs and ham (as he does in the published book), he goes so far as to say, "I do not like you / Sam I am." In the final version, Seuss tones down his language and the character focuses on the food, steering clear of personal attacks on Sam-I-am himself.

"But now we have rug spots!"
I yelled. "What a day!
Rug spots! What next?
Can you take THEM away?"

"But your dad will not
Know about that,"
Said the cat.
"He will never find out,"
Laughed the Cat in the Hat.
"His $10 shoes will have
No spots at all.
I will rub them right off
On this rug in the hall."

THE CAT IN THE HAT COMES BACK pages 24–25

"No spots are too hard" (page 27)

Another example of Seuss's spot removal: In the original drawing, the upper half of the Cat's front leg (from hip to knee) blended in with his torso and back leg. To make the front leg stand out, Seuss painted white along its top and bottom edges, creating contrast between the leg and the rest of the body.

"I can clean up these rug spots
Before you count three!
No spots are too hard
For a Hat Cat like me!"

"Don't ask me," he laughed.
"Why, you know that I can!"
Then he picked up the rug
And away the cat ran.

THE CAT IN THE HAT COMES BACK pages 26–27

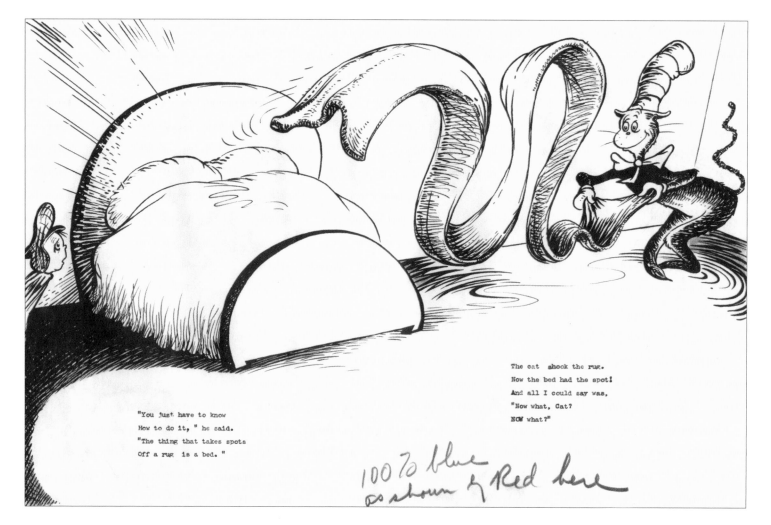

The cat shook the rug.
Now the bed had the spot!
And all I could say was,
"Now what, Cat?
NOW what?"

"You just have to know
How to do it, " he said.
"The thing that takes spots
Off a rug is a bed. "

100 % blue as shown by Red here

"Has the right kind of bed." (page 28)

A photographic print of this spread from *The Cat in the Hat Comes Back* displays an earlier version of the text:

> "You just have to know
> How to do it," he said.
> "The thing that takes spots
> Off a rug is a bed."

The revised version's more specific claim—that this is "the right kind of bed"—more neatly sets up the Cat's later admission that this is "NOT the right kind of a bed" (*CITHCB* page 30).

"NOW what?" (page 29)

An earlier version of the text for this spread also appears in the photographic print:

> The cat shook the rug.
> Now the bed had the spot!
> And all I could say was,
> "Now what, Cat?
> NOW what?"

Though less different from the final text than the passage on *CITHCB* page 28, this version lacks the onomatopoetic "CRACK!", the exclamation point at the end of the first line, and the transition "Then." It also specifies the Cat for "he."

He ran into Dad's bedroom
And then the cat said,
"It is good that your dad
Has the right kind of bed."

Then he shook the rug!
CRACK!
Now the bed had the spot!
And all I could say was,
"Now what, Cat?
NOW what?"

THE CAT IN THE HAT COMES BACK pages 28–29

Said the Cat in the Hat. (page 30)

In a 1,664-word book that uses only 290 different words, many must appear multiple times. The word "the," which appears seven times on this page, occurs the most frequently—eighty-six times in all. At fifty-four occurrences each, "cat" and "and" are tied for second place.

Words Used:

10	can	fan	him	lot	old	say	thing	we
$	can't	fast	his	lots	on	see	things	well
A	cat	fear	hit	M	one	she	think	went
about	cats	find	ho	mad	our	shoes	this	were
after	clean	for	hot	made	out	shook	those	what
again	cleaned	found	house	make	over	shots	three	when
all	cleans	fun	how	may	P	should	time	where
alone	clever	G	hurry	me	pails	shut	to	white
and	close	games	I	men	pan	small	today	who
anything	cold	get	if	mess	picked	snow	too	whose
are	come	go	in	milk	pig	so	took	why
as	comes	goes	ink	mind	pills	some	top	will
ask	could	good	into	more	pink	somebodies	town	wipe
at	count	got	is	mother	play	somebody	tricks	with
away	crack	guess	it	mother's	plays	something	true	work
B	D	guns	J	much	pop	spot	try	working
back	dad	H	jumped	must	put	spots	tub	would
bad	dad's	had	just	my	Q	stay	tubs	X
balls	day	hall	K	N	R	still	T.V.	Y
bats	deep	hand	keep	near	rakes	stood	two	yard
be	did	happy	kill	need	ran	T	U	yelled
bed	dig	hard	kind	never	red	take	up	yelp
bedroom	do	has	knew	new	right	takes	us	yes
before	does	hat	know	news	ring	talk	use	you
bet	done	have	L	next	rings	tell	V	your
big	don't	he	last	night	rub	than	very	Z
blew	down	head	laughed	no	rug	that	Voom	
boy	dress	help	let	not	run	the	W	
broom	E	helps	like	now	S	them	wall	
but	eat	her	little	O	said	then	want	
C	eating	here	long	of	Sally	there	was	
cake	ever	high	look	off	sat	these	water	
called	F	hills	looked	oh	saw	they	way	

But the cat just stood still.

He just looked at the bed.

"This is NOT the right kind of a bed,"

The cat said.

"To take spots off THIS bed

Will be hard," said the cat.

"I can't do it alone,"

Said the Cat in the Hat.

THE CAT IN THE HAT COMES BACK pages 30–31

"It is good I have some one" (page 32)

In "A Feminist, Psychoanalytic Exegesis of *The Cat in the Hat*" (1995), Naomi Goldenberg suggests that the Cat's efforts to remove the stain on the bed are an attempt to erase the role of the mother in the children's conception. The Cat, then, gives birth to Little Cats, whose "purpose is to perform linguistic razzle-dazzle and to say, 'Look, men produce language, and that is much more important than what women do.'" As Peter Steinfels writes in his article about Goldenberg's paper (which, as far as I know, was never published), "according to Professor Goldenberg . . . creating important texts compensates for not being able to give birth."[23] Although one expects that Goldenberg is speaking at least partially (if not entirely) tongue-in-cheek, the Little Cats *may* represent the Cat's offspring. On the original endpapers to *I Can Lick 30 Tigers Today! and Other Stories* (1969), the Cat identifies the younger cats in *that* book as his children (see page 160). So these cats certainly may be his, too. Or, since they come from under his hat, they may simply be the children of his imagination.

Theodor Geisel had an imaginary child, too. He had no biological children, though in 1968, when Ted married Audrey (his second wife), he acquired two teenaged stepdaughters: Lark and Lea Dimond. Helen could not have children. So, to silence friends who bragged about their own children, he liked to boast of the achievements of their "daughter" Chrysanthemum-Pearl.[24] He even dedicated *The 500 Hats of Bartholomew Cubbins* to "Chrysanthemum-Pearl (aged 89 months, going on 90)." And he and Helen included her on their Christmas cards, along with Norval, Wally, Wickersham, Miggles, Boo-Boo, Thnud, and other fictional children. Their imaginary daughter shows Ted's sense of humor but also conceals some sadness. Evidently, if Ted and Helen could have had children, they would have. As the Morgans report in their biography, Ted told his niece, Peggy (b. 1927), "who had grown up with Chrysanthemum-Pearl almost as a contemporary, that 'it was not that we didn't *want* to have children. That wasn't it.'"[25]

Ted Geisel very much enjoyed the company of his namesake—Peggy's son, Ted Owens (b. 1956). As the Morgans note, "When the boy was only a year old, Ted had dedicated *How the Grinch Stole Christmas!* to him. Later they romped in the swimming pool in La Jolla or escaped adult conversations to try on hats from Ted's closet."[26]

These are stories about my daughter and my son.... ....and my great great great great grandpa.

Greetings
from
George, Henry, Norval, Ike, Liz, Walter, Noddy,
Fairmont, Buster, Chrysanthemum-Pearl, August, Cyril,
Yvette, Miggles, Hawkshaw, Wickersham, Gordon, Norton,
Snubkin, Gretchen, Petunia, Ted, Helen, Pangborn, Pooper,
Polly, Auchinloss, Lola, Windsor, Gabrilla,
Bud, Dud, Thnud, Grimalken, Willy, Wally, Wooly,
Cindy-Lou, Boo-Boo and Go-Go GEISEL.

"It is good I have some one
To help me," he said.
"Right here in my hat
On the top of my head!
It is good that I have him
Here with me today.
He helps me a lot.
This is Little Cat A."

THE CAT IN THE HAT COMES BACK pages 32–33

Took the hat off HIS head. (page 34)

Ted Geisel was collecting hats by the 1930s, and quite possibly before then. After the publication of *And to Think That I Saw It on Mulberry Street* (1937), his hometown newspaper interviewed his sister, Margaretha (Marnie) Dahmen. She described her brother's "peculiar hobby . . . collecting hats of every descrip-

tion. Why, he must have several hundred and he is using them as the foundation of his next book," *The 500 Hats of Bartholomew Cubbins*. She added, "I have seen him put on an impromptu show for guests, using the hats as costumes. He is good at entertaining that way."[27] Seuss, however, claimed that his inspiration for *The 500 Hats* came on a train: "I was sitting in a railroad train going up somewhere in Connecticut. And there was a fellow sitting ahead of me, who I didn't like. He had a real ridiculous Wall Street broker's hat on, very stuffy, on this commuting train. And I just began playing around with the idea of what his reaction would be if I took his hat off and threw it out the window. And I said, 'He'd probably just grow another one and ignore me.'"[28]

The Cat in the Hat Comes Back's scene of hats beneath

We Always Were Suckers for Ridiculous Hats . . .

hats recalls *The 500 Hats of Bartholomew Cubbins,* in which the title character finds that each time he removes his hat, an identical hat appears beneath it—until he reaches hat 451, at which point each "new hat was fancier than the hat just before." As Seuss's sister indicated, the variety of Bartholomew's hats derives from the variety of Seuss's hats, which included a Peruvian fireman's hat, a yachting hat,

and a Mexican hat, as he described them.[29] Given Seuss's love of telling stories, it's not clear whether these hats were actually what he said they were. As his grandnephew Ted Owens recalled, Seuss loved pulling hats out of the closet: "He had a crazy story to go with each hat—where it came from, who wore it—and you were never really sure where the facts ended and where his imagination took over."[30] Seuss's imagination provided an even wider variety of hats for the animated version of *The Cat in the Hat Comes Back:* during the Cat in the Hat's signature song (". . . cat, hat. / In French, *chat, chapeau* . . ."), the Cat removes his hat to reveal different red-and-white-striped hats, each representing a different nationality or culture: French, Spanish, German, Eskimo, Scotch, Dutch, Irish, and some imaginary nationalities, too.

Hats appear in Seuss's political cartoons (such as the one at left, from April 1941) and on many Seuss characters—such as the Hoodwink from *If I Ran the Circus,* the black-hatted character from *Green Eggs and Ham,* and Mr. Brown of *Mr. Brown Can Moo! Can You?* His characters wear them, in part, because hats inspired Seuss. In his 1976 profile of Seuss, Colin Dangaard wrote, "For really stubborn blocks, he'll slip on a 'thinking cap.' He has 500 of them, including a shako made of rock-wallaby fur" and "an Ecuadorian fireman's helmet."[31] Recalling a visit to Ted's home, Michael Frith—Seuss's art director and sometime collaborator from 1967 to 1975, and the illustrator for *Because a Little Bug Went Ka-choo!* (1975, written by Seuss and Frith under the name Rosetta Stone)—also described Seuss's fondness for using the hats for inspiration. As Frith wrote in 1973, "I learned of the hats only on the last night of the first visit. We were working late and groggy, accomplishing little, and Ted announced that it was time for a thinking cap. And we worked on toward dawn, refreshed by an occasional furry fez or Madagascarian yak-herder's helm, solving all problems as they came."[32]

Seuss otherwise did not wear a hat, much to the disappointment of his fans. As Chris Dummit reported in a 1983 profile, "Neighborhood youngsters even flock to Geisel's door on his birthday. 'They get disappointed, because they expect me to wear a hat,' he said, grinning. . . . 'I have a collection of hats. But I don't have a hat that I wear. I keep them in a room at home.'"[33]

And then Little Cat A
Took the hat off HIS head.
"It is good I have some one
To help ME," he said.
"This is Little Cat B.
And I keep him about,
And when I need help
Then I let him come out."

THE CAT IN THE HAT COMES BACK pages 34–35

And then B said, (page 36)

In the Industrial Home for the Blind's 1965 edition, the words of Little Cat B—and all the characters—appear in Braille. Some of Seuss's illustrations have also been translated into a kind of Braille. This page, for example, features a rendition of the cats in black, red, and white felt.

"The three of us! Little Cats B, C and A!" (page 36)

In the photographic print, an earlier version of these words appears beneath the pasted-in type-set text:

> "Oh, yes! We will do it!"
> Laughed Little Cat B.
> "But, to do it, we have to have
> Little Cat C.
> Have no fear of that spot.
> We will clean it up now.
> We are Little Cats A, B and C!
> We know how!"

His final version offers greater variation in the language and rhymes. Instead of beginning four sentences with "we," he only begins one sentence with it. Rather than create an end rhyme between "C" and itself, he rhymes "C" and "me." Ending on "Little Cats B, C and A!" not only provides the end rhyme with "away" but also points to the Little Cats to the right of the verse. Taken separately, the changes may seem negligible; together, they add up, improving the poetry.

And then B said,

"I think we need Little Cat C.

That spot is too much

For the A cat and me.

But now, have no fear!

We will clean it away!

The three of us! Little Cats B, C and A!"

THE CAT IN THE HAT COMES BACK pages 36–37

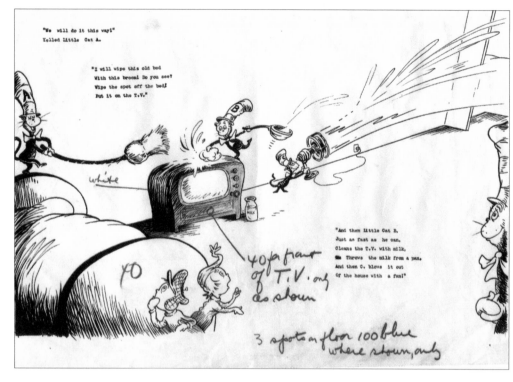

vision commercials (for Ford, in 1949). But *The Cat in the Hat Comes Back* marks the first appearance of a TV in Dr. Seuss's children's books. Its appearance in 1958 is in line with the rise in television ownership. The percentage of American homes with television sets nearly doubled between 1953 and 1960: in 1953, 46.7 percent of homes had TV sets; in 1960, 89.9 percent did.[34]

Curiously, TV doesn't show up again in a Dr. Seuss book until the 1970s. Television is in *The Cat's Quizzer, Hunches in Bunches* (1982), *I Am Not Going to Get Up Today!* (1987; illustrated by James Stevenson), and *Oh, the Places You'll Go!* (1990). TV also appears in books written under Ted Geisel's lesser-known pseudonym Theo. LeSieg: *In a People House* (1972; illustrated by Roy McKie), *Please Try to Remember the First of Octember!* (1977; illustrated by Art Cummings), and *Maybe You Should Fly a Jet! Maybe You Should Be a Vet!* (1980; illustrated by Michael J. Smollin).

"It goes on the T.V." (page 38)

Seuss had drawn illustrations of a television before (notably, in a May 1932 advertisement for Flit) and had even written tele-

And then Little Cat B (page 39)

In the typed text on the photographic print, a version of this passage is spoken by Little Cat A:

> "And then Little Cat B
> Just as fast as he can,
> Cleans the T.V. with milk,
> Throws the milk from a pan,
> And then C blows it out
> Of the house with a fan!"

As shown in the photographic print (reproduced at the top of this page), the rest of the text in the earlier version of page 38 is quite different from that in the book, too.

The primary results of Seuss's changes are clarity and concision. Instead of "Wipe the spot off the bed! / Put it on the T.V.," Seuss creates a pair of parallel sentences in "It comes off the old bed! / It goes on the T.V." "It goes on" nicely echoes "It comes off." The illustrations convey the speed of the Little Cats' activity, so "Just as fast as he can" could be safely removed. The diction of the earlier version places the emphasis on the milk instead of the spot, where the focus should be.

"Come on! Take it away!"
Yelled Little Cat A.

"I will hit that old spot
With this broom! Do you see?
It comes off the old bed!
It goes on the T.V."

And then Little Cat B
Cleaned up the T.V.

He cleaned it with milk,
Put the spot in a pan!
And then C blew it out
Of the house with a fan!

THE CAT IN THE HAT COMES BACK pages 38–39

"But look where it went!" (page 40)

Although they are not visible in the reproduction here, the final pen-and-ink drawing bears traces of a snow-covered bird and tree that were erased from the scene outside the door. For more on the snow-covered bird—the "observer" character of this book—see page 158 of the annotations.

Below Little Cats C, B, and A, Seuss had also painted white in between the "energy" lines, accentuating their resemblance to the Little Cats' tails and to the letter *S,* a visual motif introduced by the trail of the Cat's skis on page 9 and by the rug on page 29.

"Out of the house. That is true." (page 40)

The boy's words—"You blew the mess / Out of the house. That is true"—are a direct response to the Cat's words in an earlier version of the book. In the earliest surviving manuscript (pencil and ink on board) of the previous page, Seuss has written in pencil:

> It is out of the house now
> How nice said the Cat
> That spot is all gone
> Laughed the Cat in the Hat

He then erased that (although not thoroughly, so the earlier text

is still visible) and wrote the lines that appear in the photographic print (reproduced on page 136) before settling on what is in the book today.

"But now you made Snow Spots!" (page 40)

Ruth K. MacDonald writes, "It is as if Seuss and their mother have put them in charge of the whole ecosystem. . . . The pink stain looks peculiarly like a pink version of Oobleck" from *Bartholomew and the Oobleck;* "it is sticky and prone to spreading."[35] The stain also anticipates *The Lorax,* that more deftly constructed fable of environmental catastrophe.

"You can't let THEM stay!" (page 40)

In the photographic print, Seuss has a four-line version of this six-line passage, just visible beneath the pasted-in typeset text:

> I was very mad now.
> Yes, they made the spot go.
> But that spot was now lots of spots
> Out in the snow!

Were Seuss to have retained this text, it would have marked the second time the narrator described himself as "mad" (the first time is on *CITHCB* page 12, when the Cat is in the tub). The final text changes this interior monologue to an exterior dialogue, in which the boy expresses himself out loud, directing his anger toward the Cat.

Said C, B and A. (page 40)

In the photographic print, beneath the typeset text is a quite different passage:

> "Oh dear!" said the Cat.
> "To clean snow spots like that
> We will need some more help"
> Said the Cat in the Hat.

Instead of C, B, and A offering to think about the problem, the Cat simply announces, "We will need some more help." In the book, Seuss allows Little Cat C to make a similar announcement on page 42. The final version gives more power to the Little Cats, suggesting that once out of the hat, they become independent agents, acting beyond the Cat's control.

"But look where it went!"
I said. "Look where it blew!
You blew the mess
Out of the house. That is true.
But now you made Snow Spots!
You can't let THEM stay!"

"Let us think about that now,"
Said C, B and A.

THE CAT IN THE HAT COMES BACK pages 40–41

to see what they would do." At the bottom of the same page, Seuss penciled "— Bad" and below that "guns," followed by a space and "That was all that they had." Nothing more is legible.

Said Little Cats G, F, E, D, C, B, A. (page 43)

Little Cats A through Z represent Seuss's penultimate variation on the nonsense alphabet book. In 1931, Seuss wrote what he described as "an ABC book of very strange animals," including the long-necked whizzleworp and the green-striped cholmondelet.[36] Viking Press, Simon & Schuster, and Bobbs-Merrill all turned down what would have been his first children's book (and no manuscript survives). But this early work set the pattern for Seuss's later abecedarian experiments, all of which show language as both meaningful and arbitrary, practical and playful. The English proper name Cholmondeley is pronounced *chumley;* presumably, the unpublished ABC book's cholmondelet is a cousin and would have a similar pronunciation. *Dr. Seuss's ABC* (1963) also plays with the varying pronunciations of certain letters, telling us that "X is very useful / if your name is / Nixie Knox" and showing us a "camel on the ceiling." If beginning readers would never guess that "cholmondelet" might be said *chumlet,* perhaps they would also be surprised that different spellings can produce the same sounds (the initial sounds of "Nixie" and "Knox" are identical) and that the same letters can yield different sounds ("camel" has a hard "c," but "ceiling" a soft "c"). *On Beyond Zebra!*, a more radical language experiment, suggests that the alphabet is but a random pattern of symbols. Beginning after the letter "z," the book invents a new twenty-letter alphabet for words that cannot be spelled with the traditional twenty-six—or so its narrator claims. In *The Cat in the Hat Comes Back,* the Cat sends letters running pell-mell across the snowy landscape, illustrating Seuss's delight in taking the language apart.

George R. Bodmer calls these three "anti-alphabet" books that "reflect the anti-didactic mood of our time."[37] They may be "anti-alphabet," but they certainly fall in the tradition of works that use the alphabet as an occasion to explore the possibilities of language—works like Edward Lear's "Twenty-six Nonsense

Continued on page 142

"We will clean up that snow" (page 43)

In an earlier version, the Little Cats announce their mischievous intentions right away. Instead of emphasizing work (as in the published version), they promise:

> A trick that is fun.
> We call it
> Snow ball and gun.

Seuss then creates a different transition to lead the cats out of doors. He does not move directly to the scene on *CITHCB* pages 44–45 in which the cats are throwing snowballs and shooting pop guns. Instead, Little Cats D, C, B, and A leap over Sally's head, out of the door, and into the snow. In what appears to be the next illustration, Little Cats B and A continue their descent toward the snow, but now each has a pop gun in hand. Unfortunately, only two-thirds of this illustration survives, along with some of the original text. Above the cats' heads, in pencil, Seuss has written, "stood + looked to see what they would do." Likely, then, the complete couplet might have been something along the lines of "So Sally and I ran out, too. / We stood + looked

"With some help, we can do it!"
Said Little Cat C.
Then POP! On his head
We saw Little Cat D!
Then, POP! POP! POP!
Little Cats E, F and G!

"We will clean up that snow
If it takes us all day!
If it takes us all night,
We will clean it away!"
Said Little Cats G, F, E, D, C, B, A.

THE CAT IN THE HAT COMES BACK pages 42–43

Continued from page 140

Rhymes and Pictures" (1872), Maurice Sendak's *Alligators All Around* (1962), Edward Gorey's *The Utter Zoo* (1967), Chris Van Allsburg's *The Z Was Zapped* (1987), Jeanne and William Steig's *Alpha Beta Chowder* (1992), Mike Lester's *A Is for Salad* (2000), Michael Chesworth's *Alphaboat* (2002), and Jon Agee's *Z Goes Home* (2003). As Anna Quindlen has written, Dr. Seuss "took words and juggled them, twirled them, bounced them off the page. No matter what the story in his books, the message was clear and unwavering: words are fun. He hopped on Pop. He pulled an incarcerated alphabet out of a hat."[38]

For more on how Seuss's alphabet books play with the language, see also my *The Avant-Garde and American Postmodernity: Small Incisive Shocks* (2002), pages 62–64; my *Dr. Seuss: American Icon* (2004), pages 26–28; and Louis Menand's "Cat People: What Dr. Seuss Really Taught Us" (2002), pages 153–54.

They ran out of the house then (page 44)

Beneath the pasted-in typescript, Seuss's earlier typed text is still visible:

> Then out in the snow
> They ran out. We ran out.
> And the Big Cat said, "Look!
> You will see something new.
> The[y] will make lots of snow balls now
> Out of those spots.
> They will shoot them with pop guns.
> My cats are good shots."

This earlier version more suddenly places the story in the snow; the published version of the passage begins by telling us that the Little Cats "ran out of the house then," providing a visual transition from indoors to outdoors. The revised version also repeats sentence structures (three sentences in a row start with "My cats" and a verb)—such repetition is very helpful for the beginning reader.

That just could not be! (page 45)

The two-page spread here and the scenes on several subsequent pages (notably, pages 46–47, 50–51, and 52–53) adapt imagery from Palmer Cox's (1840–1924) Brownies, mischievous creatures that developed from illustrations for Arthur Gilman's alphabetical poem "The Battle of the Types" (published in *Wide*

Awake, February 1881). Gilman's verse "describes a dream about a revolt for revision in spelling led by letters of type in a printer's galley," according to Cox biographer Roger W. Cummins.[39] Echoing the lettered cats here, Cox's illustration for the poem shows lettered Brownie-like figures running around. Two years later, the Brownies made their first appearance in "The Brownies' Ride" (*St. Nicholas,* February 1883). Many other stories were published, there, in *Ladies' Home Journal,* and in thirteen successful books, starting with *The Brownies: Their Book* (1887). Speaking of his childhood favorites, Seuss told Jonathan Cott, "I loved the Brownies—they were wonderful little creatures; in fact, they probably awakened my desire to draw."[40]

Like Cox's Brownies, Seuss's Little Cats are on the move, drawing the reader's attention in several directions at once. Illustrations with action in many corners of the page recur in Seuss's work: see the arrival of friends from "all over Katroo" in *Happy Birthday to You!* (1959), or the building of the Bunglebung Bridge in *Did I Ever Tell You How Lucky You Are?* (1973). In addition to the Little Cats, the Whos most clearly bear the influence of the Brownies. See especially those scenes in which the Whos make noise—the Grinch imagining Who children playing with their toys in *How the Grinch Stole Christmas!* (1957), or the Who citizens striving to make themselves heard in *Horton Hears a Who!* (1954).

THE BROWNIES SNOWBALLING.

But this did not look
Very clever to me.
Kill snow spots with pop guns?
That just could not be!

They ran out of the house then
And we ran out, too.
And the Big Cat laughed,
"Now you will see something new!
My cats are all clever.
My cats are good shots.
My cats have good guns.
They will kill all those spots!"

THE CAT IN THE HAT COMES BACK pages 44–45

"All this does is make MORE spots!"
We yelled at the cat.
"Your cats are no good.
Put them back in your hat.

"Take your Little Cats G,
F, E, D, C, B, A.
Put them back in your hat
And you take them away!"

"Oh, no!" said the cat.
"All they need is more help.
Help is all that they need.
So keep still and don't yelp."

duced at bottom right) in which he makes an "unequivocal call for tolerance in the face of the Red Scare."[45] As I noted in *The Avant-Garde and American Postmodernity,* not only does his "paradoxical response to the children's growing fear of spreading pink ink suggest an implicit criticism of anti-Communist paranoia," but "spreading the ink actually leads to its cleaning up."[46] Perhaps, then, a third "Cold War" reading might claim that Seuss is not only calling for tolerance but also suggesting that Communism will collapse of its own internal contradictions. No need to contain it: if it spreads, its economic instability will cause it to vanish anyway.

For more on Voom, see pages 154–58.

Continued on page 146

"All this does is make MORE spots!" (page 46)

Many have interpreted the spreading pink stain as a commentary on the Cold War. In Robert Coover's "The Cat in the Hat for President," one character suggests that *The Cat in the Hat Comes Back* represents "the eradication of the, uh, Red menace by atomic power."[41] Louis Menand has written, "The association with nuclear holocaust and its sterilizing fall-out, wiping the planet clean of pinkness and pinkos, is impossible to ignore."[42] Such a reading may be persuasive if one looks to the political context, in which the House Un-American Activities Committee and the FBI were investigating alleged "subversives." As I have noted, when Voom arrives like an atomic bomb to purge the landscape of pinkness, "Seuss seems to be representing but not critiquing anti-Communist paranoia."[43]

However, as I have also suggested, we might instead see the Cat as "deliberately invert[ing] the dominant logic of the day in order to challenge it. Instead of containing the symbolic Red Menace, he deliberately, even merrily, spreads it."[44] Charles D. Cohen points out that if we wish to understand Dr. Seuss's "feelings on communism," we need only seek his 1947 cartoon (repro-

Dr. Seuss, brilliant prewar political cartoonist, came out of retirement, looked at the current American scene, and temporarily retired again.

THE ANNOTATED CAT

"All this does is make MORE spots!"
We yelled at the cat.
"Your cats are no good.
Put them back in your hat.

"Take your Little Cats G,
F, E, D, C, B, A.
Put them back in your hat
And you take them away!"

"Oh, no!" said the cat.
"All they need is more help.
Help is all that they need.
So keep still and don't yelp."

THE CAT IN THE HAT COMES BACK pages 46–47

Continued from page 144

"Take your Little Cats G," (page 47)

The text in the photographic print offers a different version of this exchange between the children and the Cat:

> "Put them back in your hat
> And you take them away!
> There is work to be done
> They are just in our way!"
> "Oh no," said the Cat.
> "They are doing just fine.
> All they need is some help now,
> Those fine cats of mine!"

Seuss deleted the earlier third and fourth lines, moving the first and second lines into their places. The new first and second lines sustain the alphabet motif. The Cat's revised retort keeps the penultimate line in anapestic dimeter and creates chiasmus.

"Help is all that they need." (page 47)

"All they need is more help. / Help is all that they need" is an example of chiasmus, a rhetorical device that, in the words of M. H. Abrams, uses a "sequence of two phrases or clauses which are parallel in syntax, but reverse the order of the correspondence words."[47] Just as the alphabetically named Little Cats show the appeal of playing games with individual letters, so the Cat's use of chiasmus confirms his interest in playing games with language.

"Little Cats H, I, J," (page 49)

Beneath the typeset text pasted on the photographic prints, Seuss's earlier text merely lists the alphabetically named Little Cats:

> "H and I
> And then J, K, L, M, N, O, P!
> And then Little Cat Q!
> And then R, S and T!
> And then Little Cat U.
> And then Little Cat V,"
> Said Little Cat G.

Replacing the repeated transition "And then" with "We need," the revised version conveys a sense of urgency. The sentence "But our work is so hard / We must have more than them" helps to emphasize this need. Seuss also improved the poetry with a greater variety of end rhymes. The earlier text rhymes only "P," "T," "V," and "G." In addition to supplying three of those end rhymes, the new version also rhymes "M" and "them," both of which offer an approximate rhyme with "N."

"U and V." (page 49)

In "Fractals and *The Cat in the Hat*" (1990), Akhlesh Lakhtakia mistakenly suggests that we consider all twenty-seven cats as fractals.[48] One can see why he might arrive at this conclusion: the simplest fractal has a shape "made of smaller copies of itself. The copies are similar to the whole: same shape but different size," as Michael Frame, Benoit Mandelbrot, and Nial Neger explain on their superb *Fractal Geometry* Web site. As Mandelbrot demonstrated in his *The Fractal Geometry of Nature* (1982), fractals can also explain natural phenomena such as ferns, snowflakes, and Queen Anne's lace—each of these is made up of smaller iterations of itself. At right is a fern from Frame, Mandelbrot, and Neger's Web site. Any fractal can be mapped by an algebraic formula. So, Lakhtakia suggests, if "cat A and its hat are the exact replicas, respectively, of the CAT and ITS HAT, and so on, there must be scaling laws for the sizes of the cats." Fractal formulae can generate increasingly smaller fractals—so small that the human eye cannot see them, just as we cannot see Little Cat Z on *CITHCB* page 56.

However, as Michael Frame points out, in *The Cat in the Hat Comes Back,* "what we have is a sequence of smaller and smaller cats," which are not the same as fractals. He explains, "In order to have a chance of being a fractal, each stage of magnification must reveal at least two copies of the previous stage. The sequence of cats is similar to nested Russian dolls, one of the most common mistakes in attempts to find fractals outside of nature." Frame continues, "In order to be a plausible fractal, cats A and B should be the same size (and both should live in the original cat's hat). Say cats A and B are ⅛ as tall as the

Continued on page 148

Then Little Cat G
Took the hat off his head.
"I have Little Cat H
Here to help us," he said.

"Little Cats H, I, J,
K, L and M.
But our work is so hard
We must have more than them.
We need Little Cat N.
We need O. We need P.
We need Little Cats Q, R, S, T,
U and V."

THE CAT IN THE HAT COMES BACK pages 48–49

Continued from page 146

original cat. Then cats C and D would live in the hat of cat A; cats E and F would live in the hat of cat B; C and D would be ⅕ as tall as A; and E and F would be ⅕ as tall as B. Each hat of C, D, E, and F would have two still smaller (by a factor of ⅕) cats, and so on." He suggests the following chart:

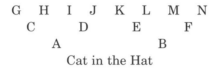

G H I J K L M N
C   D   E   F
A   B
Cat in the Hat

He points out, "Continuing in the same fashion, cats Y and Z would live in the hat of cat L. To finish the next level of the diagram, we could find cats AA and AB in the hat of cat M, and cats AC and AD in the hat of cat N." Frame proposes a better formula to describe what truly fractal cats would look like: "The appropriate scaling relation is this. At each level, each cat gives rise to 2 cats, scaled by ⅕. The dimension of the process implied by this cascade of cats is $^{\text{Log}(2)}/_{\text{Log}(1/1/5)} = {}^{\text{Log}(2)}/_{\text{Log}(5)} = .431$. If there were more cats at each level, or if they were scaled by a factor other than ⅕, a different dimension would result, but the underlying concept is the same."[49]

Although not a fractal, the cat-within-cat type of pattern recurs in nature. The nautilus shell (see cross section, left), like the cat-within-cat motif, contains many iterations of itself. If we magnify the center spiral, we will see what looks like the entire spiral; if we magnify Little Cat V (with his hat off), we should see Little Cat W (with his hat off). However, as Frame explains, if we "pick any part of the spiral other than the center and zoom in, what we see no longer looks like the whole spiral, but more and more like the edge of the spiral." Similarly, "if we look anywhere other than under the Cat's hat, say under his bowtie or in the cuff of his gloves, we won't find small cats." In other words, "With the cat and with the spiral, magnifying about one point only gives a smaller copy of the whole. Magnifying about any other point reveals no smaller copies."[50] The cat-within-cat pattern is not a fractal but does follow a naturally recurring pattern. As Chet Raymo writes in "Dr. Seuss and Dr. Einstein: Children's Books and Scientific Imagination" (1992), "Pick any Seussian invention and nature will equal it."[51]

"Come on! Kill those spots!" (page 51)
Though their aggression is playful, the warring cats here echo the quarrel in Wanda Ga'g's (1893–1946) *Millions of Cats* (1928). In Ga'g's story, a "very old man" brings back millions of cats to his wife, a "very old woman." She points out that they cannot afford to feed all of the cats and suggests that they let the cats decide which one they should keep. The man agrees and asks the cats which one is prettiest. The cats argue over this question, and Ga'g illustrates a landscape full of quarreling cats. Near each book's end, all cats (save for one) disappear suddenly. In Ga'g's book, they fight each other and then vanish, except for one little cat whom the old couple decide to keep. In Seuss's book, Voom blows all the Little Cats back under the hat of the Cat, who remains. Seuss was certainly familiar with Ga'g's book. In his lectures on children's literature at the University of Utah, he included *Millions of Cats* on "Geisel's List" of recommended children's books. Apparently, he liked the book enough to read it aloud to his class: in his notes, he has written "read aloud" next to the title of Ga'g's book.

"Kill the mess!" yelled the cats. (page 51)
In the typescript for the photographic print, the word "mess" was originally "goo." Seuss crossed out "goo" and wrote "mess" just above it. The word "goo" reinforced the connection between the spreading pink spot and oobleck (see page 154). Perhaps Seuss used "mess" instead because "goo" wasn't on the word list? Certainly, were the word "goo" used here, this would be its sole appearance in *The Cat in the Hat Comes Back*.

"Come on! Kill those spots!
Kill the mess!" yelled the cats.
And they jumped at the snow
With long rakes and red bats.
They put it in pails
And they made high pink hills!
Pink snow men! Pink snow balls!
And little pink pills!

THE CAT IN THE HAT COMES BACK pages 50–51

Oh, the things that they did! (page 52)

The Little Cat at bottom left is using what looks like a Flit gun. Dr. Seuss first became famous for the "Quick, Henry, the Flit!" campaign for Flit insecticide. For the January 14, 1928, issue of *Judge,* Seuss drew a cartoon in which a knight remarks, "Darn it all, another dragon. And just after I'd sprayed the whole castle with Flit!" The wife of an advertising executive saw the cartoon and asked her husband to hire Seuss to write ads for Flit.[52] The campaign was phenomenally successful: "Quick, Henry, the Flit!" was the "Where's the beef?" or the "Got milk?" of its day. As Robert Cahn wrote in his 1957 profile of Seuss, "'Quick, Henry, the Flit' became a standard line of repartee in radio jokes. A song was based on it. The phrase became a part of the American vernacular for use in emergencies. It was the first major advertising campaign to be based on humorous cartoons."[53]

And they did them so hard, (page 52)

As Seuss moves us from a white page (with pink accents) to a pink page (with white accents), the activities of the Little Cats suddenly seem more dangerous. On the previous two-page spread, the bird at top left merely looks surprised. Here, the bird is nearly covered in pink goo. On the previous spread, the snowman at top right is smiling. Here, the now frowning snowman's head has been severed from his body, apparently having been punched backward by an extendable boxing glove. The decapitation does appear only at the periphery of the spread—the smiling Cat and overwhelmed children are in the center. Nonetheless, it is violent, which is atypical of Seuss's work. At the very least, an image like this and language like "Kill those spots! / Kill the mess!" (from the previous page) remind us that this book is not as tightly controlled as its predecessor.

(Adv.) Copr. 1936 Stanco Inc.

Oh, the things that they did!
And they did them so hard,
It was all one big spot now
All over the yard!
But the Big Cat stood there
And he said, "This is good.
This is what they should do
And I knew that they would.

"With a little more help,
All the work will be done.
They need one more cat.
And I know just the one."

THE CAT IN THE HAT COMES BACK pages 52–53

"Now, here in my hand
I have Little Cat V.
On his head are Cats W,
X, Y and Z.

"The one that we need now
Is Little Cat Z.
You can't see him at all.
He's too little to see."

"Look close!" (page 54)

To be grammatically correct, the Cat should say, "Look closely!" One is inclined to attribute the nonstandard English to the swiftness with which Seuss wrote *The Cat in the Hat Comes Back.* However, the text in the colored photographic print indicates that "Look close! In my hand" represents a revision of "Now, here in my hand." So perhaps the change simply reflects Seuss's sense of the vitality of slang. After all, Seuss favored titles like *Oh, the Thinks You Can Think!* (1975)—using "Thinks" for "Things." And in *The Lorax,* the Once-ler proclaims, "And, for your information, you Lorax, I'm figgering / on biggering / and BIGGERING / and BIGGERING / and BIGGERING, / turning MORE Truffula Trees into Thneeds. . . ." Seuss uses "figgering" for "figuring," and "biggering" instead of "expanding" or "growing." His exuberant slang punctuates his work.

"Z is too small to see." (page 55)

In the text on the photographic prints, Seuss has:

> "The one that we need now
> Is Little Cat Z.
> You can't see him at all.
> He's too little to see."

Notice how the revised passage does a much better job of moving the action forward. The earlier version only says that Little Cat Z is both needed and small; the final version conveys his tiny size and the promise that he will "clean up that spot." The meter of the published version also does better at maintaining the momentum. The first, second, and fourth lines are all in anapestic dimeter, but the unpublished version keeps only the third and fourth lines anapestic.

"Look close! In my hand
I have Little Cat V.
On his head are Cats W,
X, Y and Z."

"Z is too small to see.
So don't try. You can not.
But Z is the cat
Who will clean up that spot!"

THE CAT IN THE HAT COMES BACK pages 54–55

"Why, Voom cleans up anything" (page 57)
In 1959, Seuss recalled receiving a letter, with a check for one dollar enclosed, "from Mrs. Jean C. Brown, whose three-year-old had just sprinkled Merthiolate on the living room rug and forestalled a scolding by telling her that 'Voom' . . . would surely clean it off." (Merthiolate is a brand of thimerosal, a cream-colored water-soluble powder used as a disinfectant.) She wrote, "*Please* send one dollar's worth of 'Voom' post haste," adding, "If you are out of 'Voom,' send a dollar's worth of 'Oobleck.'" Tongue planted firmly in cheek, Dr. Seuss wrote back that he was "frightfully embarrassed and terribly upset," but "the transportation of 'Voom' or 'Oobleck,' whether in liquid, solid or gaseous form, across state borders is to be discontinued immediately as a result of a Supreme Court decision (Justice Douglas dissenting) re the case of Grimalken vs. Drouberhanus. It seems that Drouberhanus was shoving some 'Oobleck,' which contained Voom-Impurities, across the Kentucky border, while Grimalken was smuggling 'Voom,' with Oobleck-Impurities, in the opposite direction. Nixon being out of the country at the time, the roof fell in on us. The factory closed down. Muttering, angry mobs are walking the streets, and your living room rug is gone forever."[54]

"Clean as can be!" (page 57)
Perhaps Mrs. Jean C. Brown thought Voom was a real product because its description—"Why, Voom cleans up anything / Clean as can be!"—sounds just like an advertisement. The locutions of advertising recur in Seuss's books, sometimes in the spirit of parody and other times in earnest. Sylvester McMonkey McBean in *The Sneetches* and the Once-ler in *The Lorax* speak in language that undercuts their claims. Without any concern for plausibility, the Once-ler extols the merits of Thneeds: "A Thneed's a Fine-Something-That-All-People-Need! / It's a shirt. It's a sock. It's a glove. It's a hat. / But it has *other* uses. Yes, far beyond that. / You can use it for carpets. For pillows! For sheets! / Or curtains! Or covers for bicycle seats!" While the ridiculousness of this claim mocks the salesman, Seuss presents the inflated sales pitches of other characters more sympathetically. In *Scrambled Eggs Super!*, Peter T. Hooper promises us "Scrambled eggs Super-dee-Dooper-dee-Booper," and he delivers. Voom also makes good on the Cat's promise.

Such language appears in these books because Seuss's roots were in advertising: before he wrote children's books, his campaigns for Flit bug spray and Essolube motor oil made him famous. As mentioned on page 150, his "Quick, Henry, the Flit!" became a national catchphrase. Seuss credited this phase of his career with helping him write for children: "Advertising experience was enormously helpful to me as a writer of children's books. It taught me conciseness and how to marry pictures with words."[55]

"Now here is the Z
You can't see," said the Cat.
"And I bet you can't guess
What he has in HIS hat!

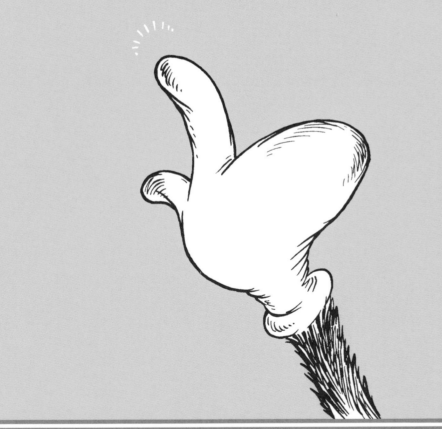

"He has something called VOOM.
Voom is so hard to get,
You never saw anything
Like it, I bet.
Why, Voom cleans up anything
Clean as can be!"
Then he yelled,
"Take your hat off now,
Little Cat Z!
Take the Voom off your head!
Make it clean up the snow!
Hurry! You Little Cat!
One! Two! Three! GO!"

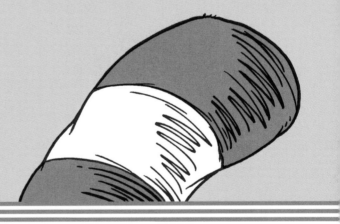

THE CAT IN THE HAT COMES BACK pages 56–57

Then the Voom . . . (page 59)

Coover, MacDonald, Menand, and I have all remarked upon the similarity between this tiny, explosive cleaner and the atomic bomb (see page 144). What fewer people realize is that Seuss invented the bomb. Well, not exactly. However, he did come up with strikingly similar ideas at about the same time. While serving in the U.S. Army's Information and Education Division

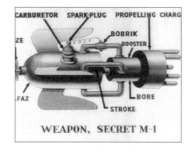

WEAPON, SECRET M-1

(a.k.a. Fort Fox) during the Second World War, Theodor Seuss Geisel co-created the animated *Private SNAFU* films, in which the title character embodies his name. In the episode "Going Home" (written by Geisel, directed by Chuck Jones), from May 1944, SNAFU returns to Podunk and begins spilling classified information. At a movie theater with his girlfriend, he sees a newsreel, "U.S. SECRET WEAPON BLASTS JAPS," showing an island and then a huge explosion that leaves nothing but a crater. SNAFU, turning to his girl, immediately begins to divulge the weapon's secrets—"I know what did it, what made the big hole. / Our new flying bazooka with radar control"—while a movie projector transmits images of his ideas from his head to another part of the movie screen. Although made over a year be-

fore the U.S. dropped its first atomic bomb on Hiroshima, the film was never released because its "portrayal of a super-bomb . . . was thought to be too close a hint at the top secret atom bomb we were developing at the time."[56]

As Judith and Neil Morgan relate in *Dr. Seuss & Mr. Geisel: A Biography*, Geisel's "next assignment at Fort Fox was to write a film spurring postwar troops to help avoid a third world war. He found inspiration in a brief *New York Times* item: there was so much energy in a glass of water, scientists said, that if it could be harnessed it could blow up half the world." During the summer of 1945, "he drafted a film treatment that

warned of the potential threat of devastating explosions." A few days later, Colonel Paul Horgan phoned from Washington asking him where he had obtained this information:

> "The *New York Times*," Ted said.
> "Burn it," he was ordered.
> "Burn the *Times*?"
> "Burn it, and report when you have carried out the order."
> Ted sent a sergeant to find a copy of the *Times*—any copy. He put it in a wastebasket, burned it in front of witnesses and telephoned the colonel to report.
> "Well done, Geisel," he was told.[57]

Horgan traveled to Europe for six weeks, during which time the U.S. dropped the first atomic bomb on Japan. As Horgan recalls, "When I returned, my secretary said Major Geisel had been making daily calls from the West Coast. So I called back and before I could say anything but 'Hi, Ted,' he said, 'I understand everything now. All is forgiven.'"[58]

Seuss explores the devastating effects of atomic weapons in the live-action musical *The 5000 Fingers of Dr. T* and in *The Butter Battle Book*. In the film, Bart Collins dreams that he is in the piano prison camp of Dr. Terwilliker (Hans Conried), forced to practice piano all day long. To escape, he and Terwilliker's plumber, Mr. Zabladowski (Peter Lind Hayes), create a bottle of "Music Fix," which, as Zabladowski warns, "might be dangerous. It might even be atomic." When Dr. T raises his baton to conduct five hundred boys at a massive piano, Bart disrupts the performance by opening the bottle, which sucks the sound out of the air. As Dr. Terwilliker's goons move toward Bart, he threatens them with the Music Fix bottle: "You come any closer, I'll blow you to smithereens!" Dr. Terwilliker asks, "Is it—is it atomic?" Bart replies, "Yes sir—very atomic!" The henchmen shout, "Atomic?!" and run away. Dr. T agrees to free Bart and the boys; the boys tear up their sheet music and take Dr. T to the dungeon while Bart conducts those remaining in a cacophonous rendition of "Chopsticks." Unbeknownst to him, toxic steam begins rising from the bottle, forming the outline of a mushroom cloud. The boys flee, and the bottle explodes into "a multi-colored Bikini-like cloud," as Seuss and Allan Scott's screenplay puts it.[59] Then Bart wakes up. No explosions occur in

Continued on page 158

Then the Voom . . .
It went VOOM!
And, oh boy! What a VOOM!

Now, don't ask me what Voom is.
I never will know.
But, boy! Let me tell you
It DOES clean up snow!

THE CAT IN THE HAT COMES BACK pages 58–59

Continued from page 156

The Butter Battle Book, which leaves the reader wondering whether anyone will dare to drop the Bitsy Big-Boy Boomeroo (Seuss's version of an atomic bomb). See the penultimate annotation to *The Cat in the Hat.*

Now, don't ask me what Voom is. (page 59)

Most interpretations see Voom as an atomic metaphor, but Robert Coover has Clark (named for a character in *One Fish Two Fish Red Fish Blue Fish,* pages 60–61) suggest other possibilities in "The Cat in the Hat for President": "*Ambiguity!* Why must it be nuclear power? All the Cat says about it is that it is too small to see, yet enormously effective. Why not Reason? Or Love? God? Perception of Infinity and Zero, or the Void? It rhymes with Womb and Tomb: Being and Nonbeing."[60] Although Clark says this in all seriousness, Coover is, of course, writing in a satirical spirit.

"So you see!" laughed the Cat, (page 61)

Seuss often includes a silent and usually unnamed bystander whose expression signals how we should respond. Here, the bird's face invites us to read the scene as he does. On *CITHCB* page 3, he is burdened by snow, amplifying the narrator's point that there is "no time" for play, fun, or games. On pages 50 and 52, he looks more anxious as the pinkness spreads and he gets covered in it. Here, on this page, after the Voom has done its work, he smiles. In the opening scene of *The Cat in the Hat,* the same bird winces as water pelts him on that "cold, cold, wet day" (*CITH* page 1).

The onlooker is usually a bird, although Seuss does use other animals and people. In *Horton Hatches the Egg* (1940), a passing fish observes a seasick, nest-sitting Horton on board a ship. *You're Only Old Once!* (1986) includes the "sympathetic" fish Norval. In *The Cat in the Hat,* the fish starts as a silent witness but soon leaves that role, becoming a main character and the Cat's most outspoken opponent.

"To come here again . . ." (page 61)

The Cat's claim that he would "be very happy / To come here again" sets up the possibility for another sequel, in which the Cat (and his accomplices) pay a return visit to Sally and her brother. Seuss never wrote such a book, although observant readers may note that the Cat sings "Happy Birthday to Little Sally Spingel Spungel Sporn" in *The Cat in the Hat Songbook*

(1967). However, it's unlikely that this is the same Sally: she does not look like the Sally of the two Cat in the Hat books, and in the manuscript for *The Cat in the Hat Songbook,* she is not called Sally but Julius Sprengelkorn. Seuss then changed Julius to Juliana, and Juliana to Sally-Anna, before settling on Sally.

In addition to the *Songbook,* the Cat did go on to star in several other works: *The Cat's Quizzer* (1976), *I Can Read with My Eyes Shut!* (1978), and the animated television special *The Grinch Grinches the Cat in the Hat* (1982). In June 1968, Seuss drew up a table of contents for a book that would have been called either *The Cat in the Hat Story Book* or *The Hat Cats' Read-Aloud Hour.* In his sketches for the cover, Seuss drew the Cat himself and wrote, "Selected and Edited by the Cat in the Hat." The Cat's planned role appears to have been rather minimal, as in *The Cat in the Hat Beginner Book Dictionary* (1964, co-written with P. D. Eastman), where the Cat is credited as author but otherwise does not appear in the book, or in *Dr. Seuss on the Loose* (1973), a cartoon adaptation of three Seuss stories in which the Cat serves as master of ceremonies, introducing each story. As planned, the story collection would have contained one original story by Dr. Seuss and forty-one by others— excerpts from Shakespeare's *Macbeth,* Lewis Carroll's *Alice's Adventures in Wonderland,* Mark Twain's *Tom Sawyer,* and Anna Sewell's *Black Beauty,* the Lilliput episode from Jonathan Swift's *Gulliver's Travels,* some of Aesop's fables, selected fairy tales (such as Hans Christian Andersen's "The Little Mermaid"), and Bible stories (such as Noah's ark and David and Goliath).

Continued on page 160

"So you see!" laughed the Cat,
"Now your snow is all white!
Now your work is all done!
Now your house is all right!
And you know where my little cats are?"
Said the cat.
"That Voom blew my little cats
Back in my hat.
And so, if you ever
Have spots, now and then,
I will be very happy
To come here again . . .

THE CAT IN THE HAT COMES BACK pages 60–61

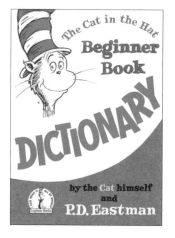

Continued from page 158

Though the Cat does not appear in Seuss's sketches for the posthumously published *Daisy-Head Mayzie* (1994), he is in both the television special and the book. While absent from current editions of *I Can Lick 30 Tigers Today! And Other Stories* (1969), the Cat is on the front endpapers of the first edition. There, he introduces his daughter (who appears in "The Glunk That Got Thunk" in that book), his son (of both "Glunk" and the title story), and King Looie Katz (of the story bearing his name). The Cat says, "These are stories about my daughter and my son . . ." The ellipsis continues to the next page, where the Cat continues, ". . . . . and my great great great great grandpa." If these characters are the Cat's relatives, then presumably the "young cat" of *I Can Read with My Eyes Shut!* is also his son.

Taking on the role of narrator in that book (as he does in most of these later works), the Cat becomes less anarchic and more conventional, but he does retain his sense of humor. He advises the young cat about reading, which (if done with eyes open) may introduce him to "fishbones . . . and wishbones. You'll learn about trombones, too. You'll learn about Jake the Pillow Snake and all about Foo-Foo the Snoo." In *The Cat's Quizzer,* he asks such absurd questions as "What would you do if you jumped in the air and you didn't come down?" and provides suitably silly answers, like "If you get stuck in the air, fly to the nearest telephone. Dial '0' and ask for a ladder."[61] Even though the Cat is less of a rebel here, he nonetheless mocks the "educational" genre to which both books belong.

In *The Grinch Grinches the Cat in the Hat,* however, the Cat is much more earnest: with the help of other townspeople, he succeeds in his plan to "ungrinch the Grinch." They sing the Grinch a song about his mother, which "softens his heart." The Cat's sense of humor emerges primarily in the way he plays with language. Early in the story, for example, when the Cat apologizes for having parked his car in the Grinch's way, he speaks in what sounds like a parody of bureaucratic language: "I do seem to be blockerizing and obstructivating your mobility." So, he concludes, "I will deblockerize and deobstructivate this roadway, allowing you to sally forth on your merry, merry way." Although his playfulness is reminiscent of *The Cat in the Hat* and *The Cat in the Hat Comes Back,* he does *exactly* what he says he'll do—making him less like his earlier self.

If less wily in later works, the Cat remains Seuss's most famous character, as well as the one who appears in more of his books than any other. In the late 1960s, Lee Bennett Hopkins told Seuss that of the "top 15 best sellers in the children's book field from 1895–1965," *The Cat in the Hat* and *The Cat in the Hat Comes Back* were already at nine and fourteen, "with total sales of 1,588,972 and 1,148,669 copies, respectively." Hopkins then asked Seuss "how this [made] him feel." Seuss replied, "Scared! Every time I start a new book, that cat squints at me and says, 'Seuss, I bet you can't top me!'"[62]

". . . with Little Cats A, B, C, D . ."(page 62)
In typed text underneath the text in the photographic prints, Seuss started the list of alphabetical Little Cats on the previous page. The speech that begins "So you see!" (*CITHCB* page 61) instead reads like this:

> "Yes. It cleaned up that spot.
> Very well," laughed the Cat.
> "And that Voom is so strong
> That it did more than that.
> It blew all my Little Cats
> Back in my hat!
> And it did all your work.
> It is done. Don't you see.
> So you should be glad.
> That you know cats like me
> And like Little Cat A
> And Cats B, C and D. . . .
> And like E, F and G . . ."

In the published version, Seuss fits the entire alphabet into one two-page spread.

" . . . with Little Cats A, B, C, D . .

E, F, G . . .

H, I, J, K . . .

L, M, N . . .

and O, P . . .

. . . and Q, R, S, T . . .

and Cat U and Cat V . . .

and Little Cats W

X

Y

and Z!"

THE CAT IN THE HAT COMES BACK pages 62–63

The Cat in the Hat Comes Back (back covers)

The backs of the jackets pictured here show the rapid growth of the Beginner Books series since it began in 1958. Judging by the titles listed on each, the first jacket is from the fall of 1958, and the second is from the fall of 1960. In a mere two years, the Beginner Books line tripled in size, increasing from six titles to eighteen.

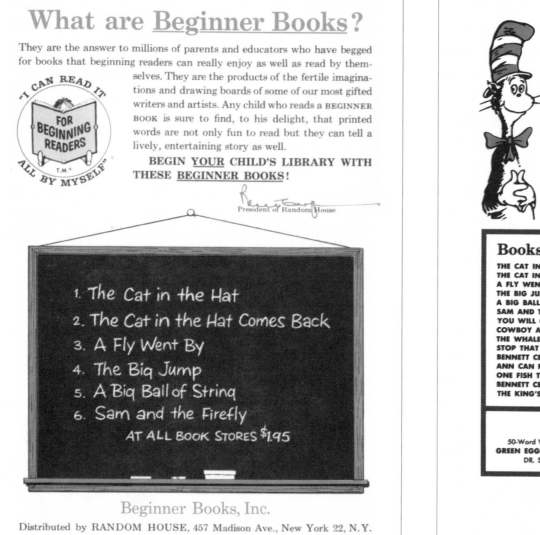

The Beginner Book Story

In 1957, Theodor Geisel, known to the world as Dr. Seuss, wrote a book called *The Cat in the Hat*.

It was fun to read aloud, easy to read alone, and impossible to put down.

From this magically right beginning came the concept of Beginner Books, exacting blends of words and pictures that encourage children to read—all by themselves. Hailed by elementary educators and remedial reading specialists, these enormously popular books are now used in schools and libraries throughout the English-speaking world.

Beginner Books®
The right reading readiness
every child needs.™

US $8.99 / $11.99 CAN
ISBN 978-0-394-80002-8

50899

9 780394 800028

Random House
www.randomhouse.com/kids
www.seussville.com

THE CAT IN THE HAT COMES BACK back cover

"The Strange Shirt Spot" is one of thirty children's stories Seuss published between 1948 and 1957 in magazines read by the parents and children of the baby boom. One appeared in *Child Life,* two in *The Junior Catholic Messenger,* four in *Children's Activities,* and twenty-three in *Redbook.* Each story was between one and three pages in length.

Seuss revised some of these stories—and recycled elements of others—for inclusion in his children's books. "The Strange Shirt Spot," first published in the September 1951 issue of *Redbook,* falls into the "recycled" category. As noted on page 116, Seuss borrowed the idea of a rogue stain for the spot-removal sequence in *The Cat in the Hat Comes Back.* An earlier version of the Grinch starred in "The Hoobub and the Grinch" (*Redbook,* May 1955) before his more famous incarnation in *How the Grinch Stole Christmas!* (1957). Another recycled story returned not in a Dr. Seuss book but in one by Helen Palmer Geisel. Seuss gave his wife the right to use "any of the situations or any of the words" from his "Gustave, the Goldfish" (*Redbook,* June 1950) in a Beginner Book.[1] Published under her maiden name, Helen Palmer, and illustrated by P. D. Eastman, *A Fish out of Water* appeared in 1961.

Dr. Seuss books that got their start as *Redbook* stories include *Yertle the Turtle and Other Stories* (Random House, 1958; *Redbook,* April 1951) and *The Sneetches and Other Stories* (1961; July 1953). Early versions of some other stories in these volumes also ran in *Redbook* first: "The Zax" (as "The Zaks," March 1954), "Gertrude McFuzz" (July 1951), and "The Big Brag" (December 1950). *Redbook* also published excerpts from several new or forthcoming Seuss stories, presumably to promote sales of the books. Abridged versions of *If I Ran the Zoo* (1950), *If I Ran the Circus* (1956), and *How the Grinch Stole Christmas!* appeared, respectively, in July 1950, June 1955, and December 1957.

However, many of Seuss's magazine stories neither served as "draft" versions of later works nor gained admission into published Seuss books. "The Hoobub and the Grinch" was reprinted on page 189 of *Your Favorite Seuss* (2004), but over a dozen of Seuss's magazine stories have not been seen since their original publication over fifty years ago.

For this little fellow, a ... spot on a shirt becomes a gigantic problem

The Strange Shirt Spot

BY DR. SEUSS

1 My mother had warned me:
"Stay out of the dirt."
But there, there I was
With a spot on my shirt!

My brand new white shirt! And that spot was so sticky,
... wouldn't shake off. It was gummy and gicky.
... terrible spot. This was real gooey goo.
... nd, brother, I knew what my mother would do
... hen Mother came home and she saw all that dirt ...!
... had to get rid of that spot on my shirt!

2 I hurried upstairs, and from over the tub
I grabbed a big towel and I started to rub.
I rubbed at that spot and I rubbed it real keen.
I rubbed it till, finally, I rubbed the shirt clean.
But then ... then I looked, and I let out a howl.
That spot from the shirt! It was now on the towel!
Now I had to get rid of the big spot of dirt
That had moved to the towel when it moved from my shirt!

3 I filled up the bathtub. I let it run hot.
I took lots of soap and I scrubbed at that spot
From quarter past three until quarter to four
Till, finally, the spot wasn't there any more.
Now the towel was all right. It was perfectly white.
My troubles were over. But ... oh-oh! Not quite!
For the spot that had moved from my shirt to the towel
Was now on the tub! I was sore as an owl!

4 What kind of a spot *was* this spot I had found?
The way the darned thing kept on jumping around!
Now the *tub* needed cleaning! I ran from the room.
I ran to the kitchen. I brought back the broom.
And I swept at that spot till I'd swept it away.
But everything seems to be crazy today!
For that spot from the tub, from the towel, from the shirt
Was now on the broom! This was mighty queer dirt!

... ad to clean up that broom before Mother would find me.
... grabbed a big cloth that was hanging behind me.
... went at that broom with a wipe and a swipe.
... hen I saw what had happened. I let out a "*Yipe!*"
... or that strange and peculiar, mysterious dirt
... rom the broom, and the tub, and the towel, and the shirt
... as now on the cloth! This was really a mess!
... or the cloth that I'd used was my mother's best dress!

6 This spot! It was driving me out of my mind!
What a spot—what a spot for a fellow to find!
My troubles were growing. The way it kept going!
Where would it go next? There was no way of knowing.
Oh, how could I stop it? Now what could I do?
Then, in walked the cat. And the next thing I knew
The cat bumped the dress. And I almost fell flat.
For the spot from the dress, it was now on the cat!

7 Then the cat started running all over the place,
With me running after. And, boy! what a chase!
I chased him downstairs. Tumbled down the whole flight.
But, finally, I nabbed him. I grabbed him real tight.
Then I got an idea! I knew just what to do.
I'd put him outside! I'd get rid of the goo!
I laughed. And I put the cat out through the door.
That spot couldn't bother me, now, any more.

8 But OOW! Then I looked and I saw that the dirt
Had rubbed off the cat. It was back on my shirt!
Right back where it started! I just couldn't win.
And then, at that moment, my mother walked in.
And, oh! the fast talking that *I* had to do!
I told her the terrible things I'd been through
With the towel, and the tub, and the broom, and the dress
And the cat, and the shirt, and she said, "Well, I guess
"You're lucky you didn't get terribly hurt.
But please, in the future, STAY OUT OF THE DIRT!"

THE STRANGE SHIRT SPOT

"rhinosaurus" (2nd paragraph)

Seuss creates a portmanteau word, combining the "rhino" component of "rhinoceros" with the common dinosaur ending "-saurus."

Wyatt Earp (7th paragraph)

Wyatt Earp (1848–1929) was a renegade lawman and saloon-keeper. He was the subject of the television series *The Life and Legend of Wyatt Earp* (1955–1961).

Governor Faubus (7th paragraph)

Orval Eugene Faubus (1910–1994) was governor of Arkansas from 1955 to 1967. In September 1957, Faubus called in the Arkansas National Guard to stop black teenagers from attending Little Rock Central High School. Later that month, to ensure the integration of the school, President Dwight D. Eisenhower (1890–1969) federalized the Arkansas National Guard (removing it from Faubus's control) and sent part of the 101st Airborne to Arkansas. The contest between Faubus and Eisenhower, as well as racist whites' persecution of the "Little Rock Nine" (as the black students were called), received considerable attention in the national and international media, landing Faubus on the cover of the September 23 issue of *Time* magazine.

Intercontinental Ballistic Missiles (7th paragraph)

The U.S.S.R. announced its first successful test of an intercontinental ballistic missile on August 26, 1957. On October 4, the U.S.S.R. launched the first artificial satellite. The United States launched its first satellite on January 31, 1958, and its first successful intercontinental ballistic missile in 1959.

Appomatox (13th paragraph)

Misspelling of "Appomattox." On April 9, 1965, at Appomattox, Virginia, Confederate general Robert E. Lee surrendered to Union general Ulysses S. Grant, thereby ending the American Civil War.

HOW ORLO GOT HIS BOOK

Every year, just a moment before Christmas, millions of Americans named Uncle George race into a book store on their only trip of the year.

"I want a book," they tell the salesman, "that my nephew Orlo can read. He's in first grade. Wants to be a rhinosaurus hunter."

"Sorry," says the salesman. "We have nothing about rhinosauri that Orlo could possibly read."

And, on Christmas morning, under millions of Christmas trees, millions of Orlos unwrap millions of books . . . all of them titled, approximately, "Bunny, Bunny, Bunny."

This causes the rhinosaurus hunters to snort, "Books stink!" And this, in turn, causes philosophers to get all het up and to write essays entitled "Why Orlo Can't Read," in which they urge that we all rush out and burn down the nearest school house.

Of course this would be just as silly as it would be to rush out and burn down the nearest Uncle George.

The reason Orlo says "Nuts to Books" is because practically every book that he is able to read is far beneath his intellectual capacity. Orlo, in the first grade, is a mighty hep guy. When he twists the knob of his television set, he meets everyone from Wyatt Earp to Governor Faubus. He attends the launchings of Intercontinental Ballistic Missiles. He observes the building of the Pyramids, flies across the South Pole and he knows what tools you have to use if you want to defang a cobra. Orlo, at 6, has seen more of life than his great-grandfather had seen when he died at the age of 90.

Yet, if you go out to get Orlo a good book he can read, even if you search the great New York Public Library, you can bring all the available books back home in a paper bag and still have room in the paper bag for three oranges and a can of tuna.

So . . . one day I got so distressed about Orlo's plight, that I put on my Don Quixote suit and went out on a crusade. I announced loudly to all those within earshot, "Within two short weeks, with one hand tied behind me, I will knock out a story that will thrill the pants right off all Orlos!"

My ensuing experience can best be described as not dissimilar to that of being lost with a witch in a tunnel of love. The only job I ever tackled that I found more difficult was when I wrote the Baedeker that Eskimos use when they travel in Siam.

In writing for kids of the middle first grade, the writer gets his first ghastly shock when he learns about a diabolical little thing known as "The List." Schoolbook publishing houses all have little lists. Lists of words that kids can be expected to read, at various stages in their progress through the elementary grades. How they compile these lists is still a mystery to me. But somehow or other . . . with divining rods or something . . . they've figured out the number of words that a teacher can ram into the average child's noodle. (Also the approximate dates on which these rammings should take place.)

Poor Orlo! At the age of 6½, his noodle has scarcely been rammed at all!

He can, of course, recognize some 1500 *spoken* words when they enter his head through the holes in his ears. But *printed* words . . . *ugh*! He can recognize only about 300 when they try to get into his head through his eyes. All the other printed words in the world all look, to Orlo, like Appomatox.

And there I was, in my shining armor, with my feet

there were no "Q" and "Z" words on my first-grade list (19th paragraph)
Though portions of this account are clearly fanciful, the claim about "Q" and "Z" words might well be true. There are no "Q" words or "Z" words in *The Cat in the Hat*. In *The Cat in the Hat Comes Back,* both "Q" and "Z" appear as names for two of the Little Cats, but these two letters do not begin any other words.

purged and sent to Siberia! (19th paragraph)
A vast area of Russia and Kazakhstan extending from the Ural Mountains to the Pacific Ocean, Siberia is famous for its remoteness, extremely cold temperatures, and prison camps. Here, in the early twentieth century, Russia and later the Soviet Union established labor camps where they sent those whom the state deemed dangerous: criminals, political opponents, dissidents, and many others. Seuss invokes Siberia as a distant, undesirable location—much as he does in the cartoon version of *The Cat in the Hat,* when the Cat announces that he's "off to Siberia" (see page 56 of annotations).

stroodle (24th paragraph)
Seuss's whimsical spelling of "strudel," evoking "noodle."

nailed down to a pathetic little vocabulary that I swear my Irish setter could master.

After the first couple of hours of staring at my Word List, I did discover a few words that might come in handy in writing a story. Words like *am* and *are* and *is*. But when you want to thrill the pants off a rhinosaurus hunter, that takes a bit of doing with words like *daddy* and *kitten* and *pot*.

After the first few weeks, I was still looking for a subject to write about. Then, suddenly one night, I dreamed the answer. Two simple little romantic words! Every last kid in the United States knew them! They were even printed on kindergarten building blocks!

I leapt from my beddie house. I rushed for my typewriter. Even before I got there, my happy fingers were already typing in the air. "The Queen Zebra" was the title of my story!

I had dashed off thirty-two red hot pages when, suddenly, I felt sort of all-over-queasy. Out of the corners of my eyes, I snuck a look at the Word List. *Queen* and *Zebra* weren't there after all!

Then, to make things even more befuddling, I noticed something new that had escaped my attention up to now. Maybe the letters "Q" and "Z" were perfectly kosher in kindergarten, but there were no "Q" and "Z" words on my first-grade list whatever. "Q" and "Z" had been purged and sent to Siberia!

Befuddled? At the end of the first four months, my Befuddlement Index had zoomed so high that my befuddlement thermometer blew up in my mouth. I was now trying to sweat out a story about a bird . . . at the same time refraining from using the word *bird*. (The list, you see, declares a permanent closed season.)

But *wing* was on the list. And *thing* was on the list. So I COULD write about a bird IF I called the bird a WING THING! And then I discovered I could use the word *fly*! Now, at last, I could really be moving! This enabled me to write a sentence.

That first sentence was also the last sentence of that story. After six weeks of trying to get my *wing thing* off the ground and into the sky, I had to give up due to numerous unbelievable reasons. *Ground* and *sky* were both taboo. Furthermore, my *wing thing* couldn't have *legs* or a *beak* or a *tail*. Not even a *foot*! Neither a *left* foot nor a *right* foot. And she couldn't lay *eggs*. Because *eggs*, according to the word list, are to be eaten, not read.

At this point, in order to get control of my emotions, I spent half a year working in my Uncle George's coal mine.

When I came up, I solved my problem by writing "The Cat in the Hat." How I did this is no trade secret. The method I used is the same method you use when you sit down to make apple stroodle without stroodles.

You forget all about time. You go to work with what you have! You take your limited, uninteresting ingredients (in my case 223 words) and day and night, month after month, you mix them up into thousands of different combinations. You bake a batch. You taste it. Then you hurl it out of the window. Until finally one night, when it is darkest just before dawn, a plausible stroodle-less stroodle begins to take shape before your eyes!

Since "The Cat" I've been trying to invent some easier method. But I am afraid the above procedure will always be par for the course. At least it will be just as long as the course is laid out on a word list.

[This essay was first published in the *New York Times Book Review,* 17 Nov. 1957, on pages 2 and 60.]

Norval (3rd paragraph)

Norval is a fiction. Seuss's niece Peggy Owens had a son—Theodor "Teddy" Owens, named for Peggy's uncle Theodor Seuss Geisel. But Teddy Owens was a one-year-old in 1957.

nautch dancers (3rd paragraph)

Professional dancers in a performance of an intricate, sinuous dance that probably originated in India.

scaling Mt. Everest (3rd paragraph)

Located on the border between Nepal and Tibet, Mount Everest reaches over 29,000 feet, making it the tallest mountain in the world. In May 1953, Sir Edmund Hillary and Tenzing Norgay became the first to reach the peak and to return safely. (Two members of a 1924 expedition tried to climb to the peak but perished on the mountain, and it is not known whether they reached the summit. When asked why he wanted to climb Everest, one of the men, George Mallory, famously replied, "Because it's there.") In May 1956, Ernst Schmied, Jürg Marmet, Dölf Reist, and Hans-Rudolf von Gunten made a successful ascent and descent. In 1957, Seuss would have been aware of these well-publicized adventures.

MY HASSLE WITH THE FIRST GRADE LANGUAGE

A while back there was a tremendous ruckus going on about the reading problems of American school kids. And I, who knew nothing about primary education, got flung into the mixer quite by accident. Somebody . . . John Hersey . . . casually suggested in an article in *Life* that I was the type of writer who should write a first grade reader.

So, with innocent conceit, I said, "Why not?" All I needed to do, I figured, was find a whale of an exciting subject. This would make the average 6-year-old want to read like crazy. None of the old dull stuff. Dick has a ball. Dick likes the ball. The ball is red, red, red, red, red.

Within an hour I found a dozen hot subjects. I merely watched my nephew Norval, who was visiting us, watch television. I discovered that Norval was fascinated by everything we adults are . . . murders, nautch dancers, beer commercials, the home life of the ant, jungle tigers . . . submarines. But the thing that thrilled the eyes practically out of his head was a chiller-diller expedition scaling Mt. Everest.

So, bright and early the very next morning, I informed a distinguished schoolbook publisher that his worries about kids reading were over forever. I would give first graders the adventures they craved, take them scaling the peaks of Everest at 60 degrees below zero.

"Truly exciting," said the publisher rather sadly. "But you can't use the word *scaling*. You can't use the word *peaks*. You can't use *Everest*. You can't use *60*. You can't use *degrees*. You can't . . ."

"Now look here!" I bristled. "You're talking old fashioned. Why, on television, that story thrilled the pants off Norval."

"Of course," sighed the publisher. "On television he understood it all. But he was looking at pictures and listening to *spoken* words. He wasn't reading *printed* words. All he knows of printed words are the pitiful few that his teacher has struggled to make him recognize. At his age he couldn't tell the printed word Everest from a pineapple-upside-down-cake."

I mulled this over. "Would you buy a book about a jungle tiger?" I asked limply.

"Certainly," said the publisher. "With two minor changes. Change the tiger into a cat. Change the jungle into a house."

Then, as gently as he could, he dropped a ton of bricks all over me. He handed me a tiny little list of words. "These are all the words that a first grade Norval *can* recognize."

I stared. I could have engraved the whole list, personally, on the head of a pin. They were thrillers . . . like *am, is, but, if, in, into, no, yes*. Words full of great adventure . . . like *milk* and *mitten* and *mop*. And a number of super-humdingers . . . like *lump* and *bun* and *string*. I saw the word *sick* and that's how I felt very.

"Now you take this list," I heard the publisher saying. "Take it home. Cut loose! Create a rollicking carefree story. Pack it with action. Make it tingle with suspense! Embellish it with gay brilliant rhymes and bubbling rhythms. And one more thing. Repeat the words. Repeat! Repeat! Taking care, of course, not to be boring."

The next thing I knew, it was six months later. I was home, staring red-eyed at the list, trying to find some usable words besides *cat* and *hat* that rhymed. The list had a *daddy*. But it didn't have a *caddy*. I found myself snarling, "faddy, maddy, saddy, waddy."

It had words like *thank*. But no *blank, crank, frank*, or *stank*. There was the word *something*. But *something* only rhymes with *numb-thing*. And even if *numb-thing* were on the list, which it wasn't, how in the blazes can you use something like *numb-thing* in a story?

"Why don't you have your cat run a Quiz show?" (17th paragraph)

Television quiz shows like *The $64,000 Question* (1955–1958), *Twenty-One* (1956–1958), and *Tic Tac Dough* (1956–1959) were popular in 1957. In 1958, investigators discovered that the producers of *Twenty-One* rigged the show by giving certain contestants—most famously, Charles Van Doren—answers in advance. (The 1994 film *Quiz Show* dramatized this story.) In the wake of the scandal, ratings for quiz shows fell, and most such programs were canceled. However, when Seuss wrote this sentence in 1957, he was merely making a reference to a popular phenomenon. The quiz show scandal would not break until August 1958, nine months after this essay was published.

And what *was* my story anyhow? At one point I spent three excruciatingly painful weeks grinding out a yarn about a King Cat and a Queen Cat. Then I called in Norval as an expert consultant to read it. When he came to the word *King,* he read it just fine. When he came to the word *Queen,* he just stood there blowing bubbles.

In a real cold sweat, I rechecked my list thoroughly. The poor queen, not being registered, died a horribly swift death. And the king died of loneliness shortly thereafter.

Norval, feeling sorry for me because I wasn't bright enough to write for him, was now dropping in occasionally after school to offer help. "Why don't you have your cat run a Quiz show?" was one of his suggestions. Nervously I fine-tooth combed the list for *quiz.* I got a shock that threw me into terrible confusion. "Q" had evidently been dropped right out of the alphabet completely!

This appalling discovery so unnerved me that for two weeks the only subjects I could think of at all were "Q" ones. Like "Quarrying for Quartz." And "The Quitter in the Quicksand." "Quilting Bees and Quails." And "A First Grade Biography of John Quincy Adams."

Then after I'd mastered *that* psychosis, I happened to notice that "Z" had been banished as a letter also! And for weeks all I could think of were Zulu zebras zipping from New Zealand to the Zuider Zee.

By this time, my first grade nephew, Norval, mysteriously stopped dropping in and I had to bungle along entirely on my own. How I ever managed to manipulate that maddening jigsaw puzzle of itsy-bitsy-witsy wordies into any kind of story at all, I don't know.

All I know is that when we finished, I was dealt the most painful blow of all. I took it around to Norval to see how he liked it.

Norval looked down his nose at the manuscript. "Don't bother me with that kid stuff," he snorted. "I've long since graduated from the first grade. *I'm* already learning calculus."

[This essay was first published in the *Chicago Tribune,* 17 Nov. 1957.]

ENDNOTES

Introduction

1. Judith Morgan and Neil Morgan, *Dr. Seuss & Mr. Geisel,* 7–8.
2. *Ibid.,* 7.
3. Edward Connery Lathem, "Words and Pictures Married: The Beginnings of Dr. Seuss," 17.
4. Judith Morgan and Neil Morgan, *Dr. Seuss & Mr. Geisel,* 45.
5. Edward Connery Lathem, "Words and Pictures Married: The Beginnings of Dr. Seuss," 20.
6. Judith Morgan and Neil Morgan, *Dr. Seuss & Mr. Geisel,* 90.
7. *Ibid.,* 81.
8. Edward Connery Lathem, "Words and Pictures Married: The Beginnings of Dr. Seuss," 21.
9. Judith Morgan and Neil Morgan, *Dr. Seuss & Mr. Geisel,* 106.
10. *Ibid.,* 127.
11. "The 25th Anniversary of Dr. Seuss," 13.
12. Dr. Seuss, "How Orlo Got His Book," 2.
13. Dr. Seuss, letter to Random House, 11 June 1956.
14. Judith Morgan and Neil Morgan, *Dr. Seuss & Mr. Geisel,* 154.
15. Jonathan Cott, *Pipers at the Gates of Dawn: The Wisdom of Children's Literature,* 25.
16. Dorothy Barclay, "See the Book? It Is Made with 6-Year-Old's Words."
17. Judith Morgan and Neil Morgan, *Dr. Seuss & Mr. Geisel,* 156.
18. "The Cat in the Hat," *Kirkus Reviews,* 216.
19. Ellen Lewis Buell, "High Jinks at Home," 40.
20. Helen Adams Masten, "The Cat in the Hat," 54.
21. Polly Goodwin, "Hurray for Dr. Seuss!"
22. Helen E. Walker, "Seuss, Dr. *The Cat in the Hat,*" 1356.
23. Emily Maxwell, "Books: Christmas for First and Second Readers," 232.
24. Heloise P. Mailloux, "Late Spring Book List," 215.
25. Margaret S. Libby, "Fun, Beauty, Fancy for First Readers," 24.
26. David Dempsey, "The Significance of Dr. Seuss," 30; Edward S. Kitch, "Modern Mother Goose: He Deals in Lilliputian Humor."
27. E. J. Kahn, Jr., "Children's Friend," 48, 50.
28. "Sneetches, Sugar, and Success: The Boom in Books for Children," 74.
29. U.S. Bureau of the Census, "Table 1-1. Live Births, Birth Rates, and Fertility Rates, by Race: United States, 1909–2000"; "Table 2. Fall School Enrollment of the Civilian Noninstitutional Population 5 to 34 Years Old, by Type of School and Age, for the United States: October 1953 to 1958."
30. "He Makes C-A-T Spell Big Money," 72.
31. David Sheff, "Seuss on Wry," 55.
32. Leonard S. Marcus, *Dear Genius: The Letters of Ursula Nordstrom,* xxvi.
33. "Humor to Start Six-Year-Olds on a Lifetime of Reading," 8.
34. Ellen Lewis Buell, "A Few New Books for All the New Readers," 36.
35. "The One and Only Dr. Seuss and His Wonderful Autographing Tour," 14.
36. *Ibid.,* 14.
37. *Ibid.,* 15.
38. *Ibid.*
39. *Ibid.,* 13.
40. E. J. Kahn, Jr., "Children's Friend," 48.
41. "He Makes C-A-T Spell Big Money," 72.
42. "Children's Best Sellers," 48.

43. Judith Morgan and Neil Morgan, *Dr. Seuss & Mr. Geisel,* 158.
44. Richard H. F. Lindemann, *The Dr. Seuss Catalog,* 28–30, 35; Jill Jones, e-mail to author, 1 Apr. 2005.
45. *An Awfully Big Adventure: The Making of Modern Children's Literature.*
46. Janice H. Dohm, "The Curious Case of Dr. Seuss: A Minority Report from America," 323.
47. *Ibid.,* 324.
48. *Ibid.,* 325.
49. *Ibid.,* 329.
50. Myra Barrs, "Laughing Your Way to Literacy," 21.
51. Ted Dewan, "The Cat in the Hat Comes Back," 12.
52. David Dempsey, "The Significance of Dr. Seuss," 30.
53. Clifton Fadiman, "Professionals and Confessionals: Dr. Seuss and Kenneth Grahame," 282.
54. Judith Morgan and Neil Morgan, *Dr. Seuss & Mr. Geisel,* 162.
55. "200 Books Given to White House."
56. Robert Coover, "The Cat in the Hat for President," 12.
57. "No Call to Be Mean."
58. Judith Morgan and Neil Morgan, *Dr. Seuss & Mr. Geisel,* 292.
59. Joanna Powell, "Tops in Hat Tricks."
60. Robert Coover, "The Cat in the Hat for President," 20.
61. Charles D. Cohen, *The Seuss, the Whole Seuss, and Nothing but the Seuss,* 338, 343, 352–53.
62. Judith Morgan and Neil Morgan, *Dr. Seuss & Mr. Geisel,* 265.
63. Eric Pace, "Dr. Seuss, Modern Mother Goose, Dies at 87," A1.
64. Miles Corwin, "Author Isn't Just a Cat in the Hat."
65. Digby Diehl, "Q & A 'Dr. Seuss,'" 39.
66. Don Freeman, "Dr. Seuss from Then to Now," 243.
67. Edward Connery Lathem, ed., *Theodor Seuss Geisel: Reminiscences & Tributes,* 20.
68. Carol Olten, "To a Living Literary Legend . . ."
69. Digby Diehl, "Q & A 'Dr. Seuss,'" 39.
70. Edward Connery Lathem, "Words and Pictures Married: The Beginnings of Dr. Seuss," 18.
71. Judith Morgan and Neil Morgan, *Dr. Seuss & Mr. Geisel,* 54.
72. Rochelle Girson, profile of Dr. Seuss, 52.
73. Lewis Nichols, "Then I Doodled a Tree," 2.
74. Dennis Georgatos, "Dr. Seuss Sets Sights on Adults."
75. "Sneetches, Sugar, and Success: The Boom in Books for Children," 74.
76. David Dempsey, "The Significance of Dr. Seuss," 30.

The Cat in the Hat

1. Judith Morgan and Neil Morgan, *Dr. Seuss & Mr. Geisel,* 159.
2. John C. Waugh, "Kingdom of Seuss," 9.
3. Michael J. Bandler, "Portrait of a Man Reading," 2.
4. Helen Younger, Marc Younger, and Dan Hirsch, *First Editions of Dr. Seuss Books: A Guide to Identification,* 27–28.
5. Karla Kuskin, "Seuss at 75," 42.
6. Judith Morgan and Neil Morgan, *Dr. Seuss & Mr. Geisel,* 245.
7. Bob Warren, "Dr. Seuss, Former *Jacko* Editor, Tells How Boredom May Lead to Success."

8. Judith Morgan and Neil Morgan, *Dr. Seuss & Mr. Geisel,* 154; Robert Cahn, "The Wonderful World of Dr. Seuss," 42.

9. Ruth K. MacDonald, *Dr. Seuss,* 107.

10. Dan Carlinsky, "The Wily Ruse of Doctor Seuss," 15.

11. Robert Cahn, "The Wonderful World of Dr. Seuss."

12. *Ibid.*

13. Glenn Edward Sadler, *Teaching Children's Literature: Issues, Pedagogy, Resources,* 249.

14. Judith Morgan and Neil Morgan, *Dr. Seuss & Mr. Geisel,* 153.

15. Edward Connery Lathem, *Theodor Seuss Geisel: Reminiscences & Tributes,* 21–22.

16. Glenn Edward Sadler, *Teaching Children's Literature: Issues, Pedagogy, Resources,* 245.

17. Ruth K. MacDonald, *Dr. Seuss,* 105–06.

18. John Hersey, "Why Do Students Bog Down on First R?" 148.

19. Donald Freeman, "The Nonsensical World of Dr. Seuss," 201.

20. Jonathan Cott, *Pipers at the Gates of Dawn: The Wisdom of Children's Literature,* 25.

21. Ellen Goodman, "What Dr. Seuss Started with That 'Cat in the Hat.'"

22. John Hersey, "Why Do Students Bog Down on First R?" 136.

23. E. J. Kahn, Jr., "Children's Friend," 50.

24. May Hill Arbuthnot, *Children's Reading in the Home,* 86.

25. U.S. Bureau of the Census, "Table 4. Characteristics of Families, by Type, for the United States, Total and Nonfarm: March 1958," 10.

26. Molly Bang, *Picture This: How Pictures Work,* 42, 44, 46.

27. *Ibid.,* 70–71.

28. "'Somebody's Got to Win' in Kids' Books," 69.

29. Mike Salzhauer, "A Carnival Cavort with Dr. Seuss," 6.

30. Ruth K. MacDonald, *Dr. Seuss,* 117.

31. E. J. Kahn, Jr., "Children's Friend," 50.

32. Judith Morgan and Neil Morgan, *Dr. Seuss & Mr. Geisel,* 9.

33. *Ibid.,* 108.

34. Charles D. Cohen, *The Seuss, the Whole Seuss, and Nothing but the Seuss,* 324–25.

35. *Ibid.,* 327–28.

36. *Ibid.,* 325.

37. *Ibid.*

38. *Ibid.,* 326–27.

39. *Ibid.,* 325.

40. *Ibid.,* 326.

41. Charles Perrault, "Master Cat, or Puss in Boots," 236.

42. Louis Menand, "Cat People: What Dr. Seuss Really Taught Us," 148.

43. Henry C. Lajewski, *Child Care Arrangements of Full-Time Working Mothers,* 3.

44. *Ibid.,* 16–17.

45. Liza Mundy, "When Mom's Away . . . the Cat Will Play."

46. *Ibid.,* 9.

47. Jonathan Cott, *Pipers at the Gates of Dawn: The Wisdom of Children's Literature,* 26.

48. Cotton Mather, *A Family Well-Ordered, or An Essay to Render Parents and Children Happy in One Another,* 45–46.

49. Louis Menand, "Cat People: What Dr. Seuss Really Taught Us," 154.

50. Jonathan Cott, *Pipers at the Gates of Dawn: The Wisdom of Children's Literature,* 26.

51. Betty Mensch and Alan Freeman, "Getting to Solla Sollew: The Existential Politics of Dr. Seuss," 32.

52. Ruth K. MacDonald, *Dr. Seuss,* 115.

53. Betty Mensch and Alan Freeman, "Getting to Solla Sollew: The Existential Politics of Dr. Seuss," 32.

54. Dorothy Barclay, "See the Book? It Is Made with 6-Year-Old's Words."

55. Kevin Shortsleeve, "The Politics of Nonsense: Civil Unrest, Otherness and National Mythology in Nonsense Literature," 276.

56. Edward Connery Lathem, "Notes in preparation for an exhibition on the life and works of Dr. Seuss," 153.

57. Rudolf Flesch, *Why Johnny Can't Read—and What You Can Do About It,* 6.

58. *Ibid.,* 5.

59. *Ibid.,* 15.

60. *Ibid.,* 21, 116.

61. Betsy Marden Silverman, "Dr. Seuss Talks to Parents About Learning to Read and What Makes Children Want to Do It," 136.

62. Ruth K. MacDonald, *Dr. Seuss,* 120.

63. Mary Elisabeth Coleman, "Reading for Recreation," 205.

64. Don L. F. Nilsen, "Dr. Seuss as Grammar Consultant," 569.

65. Ruth K. MacDonald, *Dr. Seuss,* 122.

66. Robert Coover, "The Cat in the Hat for President," 24.

67. *Ibid.,* 27.

68. Desmond Devlin, "The Strange Similarities Between the Bush Administration and Dr. Seuss," 39.

69. May Hill Arbuthnot, *Children and Books,* 42.

70. Lee Bennett Hopkins, "Dr. Seuss (Theodor S. Geisel)," 257.

71. Sybil S. Steinberg, "What Makes a Funny Children's Book?" 87.

72. Diane Clark, "He Is Waking Children to a World of Words."

73. *An Awfully Big Adventure: The Making of Modern Children's Literature.*

74. Judith Morgan and Neil Morgan, *Dr. Seuss & Mr. Geisel,* 232.

75. *Ibid.,* 73.

76. *Ibid.,* 271.

77. Glenn Edward Sadler, *Teaching Children's Literature: Issues, Pedagogy, Resources,* 247.

78. Larry Rohter, "After 60 Years, Dr. Seuss Goes Home."

79. Judith Morgan and Neil Morgan, *Dr. Seuss & Mr. Geisel,* 106.

80. *Ibid.,* 107.

81. Eric O. Costello, "Private SNAFU & Mr. Hook," 44; Michael Barrier, *Hollywood Cartoons: American Animation in Its Golden Age,* 502; Michael Norris, "Bugs Bunny Creator Puts Face on Private SNAFU: The Legacy of Animator Chuck Jones."

82. Betty Mensch and Alan Freeman, "Getting to Solla Sollew: The Existential Politics of Dr. Seuss," 31.

83. Thomas Bullfinch, *The Age of Fable: Stories of the Gods of Greece and Rome, the Deities of Egypt, and the Eastern and Hindu Mythology,* 26–27.

84. Christine Pelisek, "Snoopy's Revenge," 14; Harrison Sheppard, "T.V. Actress Facing Jail Time in 4-Year-Old Circus Protest."

85. Mike Salzhauer, "A Carnival Cavort with Dr. Seuss," 6.

86. Jonathan Cott, *Pipers at the Gates of Dawn: The Wisdom of Children's Literature,* 19; *The Tough Coughs as He Ploughs the Dough: Early Writings and Cartoons by Dr. Seuss,* 42.

87. Jack Webb, "Dr. Seuss Also Has Worn Many Hats."

88. Selma G. Lanes, *Down the Rabbit Hole: Adventures & Misadventures in the Realm of Children's Literature,* 81.

89. *Ibid.,* 79–80.

90. Judith Morgan and Neil Morgan, *Dr. Seuss & Mr. Geisel,* 214.

91. Jonathan Cott, *Pipers at the Gates of Dawn: The Wisdom of Children's Literature,* 19; Michael J. Bandler, "Portrait of a Man Reading," 2.

92. Fredric Wertham, *Seduction of the Innocent,* 10.
93. *Ibid.,* 13.
94. "Humor for Children."
95. Ellen Lewis Buell, "High Jinks at Home," 40.
96. Emily Maxwell, "Books: Christmas for First and Second Readers," 232.
97. Henry Jenkins, "'No Matter How Small': The Democratic Imagination of Dr. Seuss," 188.
98. Charles D. Cohen, *The Seuss, The Whole Seuss, and Nothing but the Seuss,* 144.
99. Michael Joseph, e-mail to author, 7 Apr. 2005.
100. David Dempsey, "The Significance of Dr. Seuss," 30.
101. Dr. Seuss and unidentified reporter at May Road School, Mt. Roskill, New Zealand, c. May 1964. Recorded for unidentified New Zealand television station.
102. Jonathan Cott, *Pipers at the Gates of Dawn: The Wisdom of Children's Literature,* 28.
103. *Ibid.,* 28.
104. Kathleen Smith, "Dr. Seuss Battles with Butter to Drive Home a Message for Children and Adults," 13.
105. Frank R. Stockton, *The Lady, or the Tiger? and Other Stories,* 1–3, 5, 8–10.
106. Jill P. May, "Frank R. Stockton," 332–38.
107. Ruth K. MacDonald, *Dr. Seuss,* 107.
108. *Ibid.,* 109.
109. Alison Lurie, "The Cabinet of Dr. Seuss," 50.
110. Betty Mensch and Alan Freeman, "Getting to Solla Sollew: The Existential Politics of Dr. Seuss," 117.
111. Philip Nel, *The Avant-Garde and American Postmodernity,* 55.
112. Kathy Hacker, "Happy 80th Birthday, Dr. Seuss."

The Cat in the Hat Comes Back
1. "Beginner Books: New Trade Learn-to-Read Juveniles," 116.
2. David Dempsey, "The Significance of Dr. Seuss," 30.
3. Edward Connery Lathem, Notes in preparation for an exhibition on the life and works of Dr. Seuss, 176.
4. Ruth K. MacDonald, *Dr. Seuss,* 130.
5. *Ibid.,* 125.
6. "City in Heart of Storm," "Yesterday's Weather in Springfield," "City Digs Out of the Snow," "Ready Today."
7. Alison Lurie, "The Cabinet of Dr. Seuss," 51.
8. Judith Morgan and Neil Morgan, *Dr. Seuss & Mr. Geisel,* 286.
9. Ruth K. MacDonald, *Dr. Seuss,* 126.
10. *Ibid.,* 127.
11. *Ibid.*
12. "The Other Cool Cat," 24.
13. Jonathan Cott, *Pipers at the Gates of Dawn: The Wisdom of Children's Literature,* 28, 30.
14. Hilaire Belloc, *Cautionary Verses,* 157, 27, 303.
15. Jill P. May, "Dr. Seuss and *The 500 Hats of Bartholomew Cubbins,*" 8.
16. Jack Webb, "Dr. Seuss Also Has Worn Many Hats."
17. See Clark; Diehl, 37; Frutig, 18.
18. Chris Dummit, "The Man Behind the Cat in the Hat."
19. Michael Frith, "Dr. Seuss at Home."
20. Rochelle Girson, profile of Dr. Seuss, 52.
21. Shira Wolosky, "Democracy in America: By Dr. Seuss," 174.
22. Robert Coover, "The Cat in the Hat for President," 43.
23. Peter Steinfels, "Beliefs."

24. Judith Morgan and Neil Morgan, *Dr. Seuss & Mr. Geisel,* 90.
25. *Ibid.,* 91.
26. *Ibid.,* 221.
27. "Gay Menagerie of Queer Animals Fills the Apartment of Dr. Seuss."
28. Cynthia Gorney, "Dr. Seuss Alive and Well, but Not on Mulberry Street."
29. Sam Burchell, "*Architectural Digest* Visits Dr. Seuss," 91.
30. Judith Morgan and Neil Morgan, *Dr. Seuss & Mr. Geisel,* 221.
31. Colin Dangaard, "Dr. Seuss Reigns Supreme as King of the Kids."
32. Michael Frith, "Dr. Seuss at Home."
33. Chris Dummit, "The Man Behind the Cat in the Hat."
34. U.S. Bureau of the Census, "Homes with Selected Electrical Appliances," 671.
35. Ruth K. MacDonald, *Dr. Seuss,* 126.
36. Judith Morgan and Neil Morgan, *Dr. Seuss & Mr. Geisel,* 72; E. J. Kahn, Jr., "Children's Friend," 64.
37. George R. Bodmer, "The Post-Modern Alphabet: Extending the Limits of the Contemporary Alphabet Book, from Seuss to Gorey," 115–16.
38. Anna Quindlen, "The One Who Had Fun."
39. Roger W. Cummins, *Humorous but Wholesome: A History of Palmer Cox and the Brownies,* 183.
40. Jonathan Cott, *Pipers at the Gates of Dawn: The Wisdom of Children's Literature,* 19.
41. Robert Coover, "The Cat in the Hat for President," 22.
42. Louis Menand, "Cat People: What Dr. Seuss Really Taught Us," 154.
43. Philip Nel, *The Avant-Garde and American Postmodernity,* 65.
44. *Ibid.*
45. Charles D. Cohen, *The Seuss, the Whole Seuss, and Nothing but the Seuss,* 337.
46. Philip Nel, *The Avant-Garde and American Postmodernity,* 66.
47. M. H. Abrams, *A Glossary of Literary Terms,* 183.
48. Akhlesh Lakhtakia, "Fractals and *The Cat in the Hat,*" 161–64.
49. Michael Frame, e-mail to author, 7 Feb. 2005.
50. *Ibid.*
51. Chet Raymo, "Dr. Seuss and Dr. Einstein: Children's Books and Scientific Imagination," 560–67.
52. Judith Morgan and Neil Morgan, *Dr. Seuss & Mr. Geisel,* 65.
53. Robert Cahn, "The Wonderful World of Dr. Seuss."
54. "Currents," 23.
55. Justin Wintle and Emma Fisher, "Two Letters: Dr. Seuss and E. B. White," 115.
56. *The Complete Uncensored Private SNAFU,* introduction.
57. Judith Morgan and Neil Morgan, *Dr. Seuss & Mr. Geisel,* 115.
58. *Ibid.,* 115–16.
59. Dr. Seuss and Allan Scott, *The 5000 Fingers of Dr. T.*
60. Robert Coover, "The Cat in the Hat for President," 23.
61. Dr. Seuss, *I Can Read with My Eyes Shut!,* 41, 60.
62. Lee Bennett Hopkins, "Dr. Seuss (Theodor S. Geisel)," 255–58.

"The Strange Shirt Spot"
1. Judith Morgan and Neil Morgan, *Dr. Seuss & Mr. Geisel,* 168.

SELECTED REFERENCES

REVIEWS: *THE CAT IN THE HAT*

"The Cat in the Hat." Kirkus Reviews, 15 Mar. 1957, p. 216.

Buell, Ellen Lewis. "High Jinks at Home." *The New York Times Book Review,* 17 Mar. 1957, p. 40.

"Some Early Spring Books for Children and Young People." *The Bookmark,* Apr. 1957, p. 163.

"The Cat in the Hat." Kirkus Reviews, 1 Apr. 1957, p. 276.

"Children's Books." *Booklist and Subscription Books Bulletin,* 1 May 1957, p. 459.

Hormel, Olive Deane. "For New Readers and the Little Tots." *The Christian Science Monitor,* 9 May 1957, p. 14.

Masten, Helen Adams. "The Cat in the Hat." *The Saturday Review,* 11 May 1957, p. 54.

Goodwin, Polly. "Hurray for Dr. Seuss!" *Chicago Sunday Tribune,* 12 May 1957.

Libby, Margaret S. "Fun, Beauty, Fancy for First Readers." *The New York Herald Tribune Book Review,* 12 May 1957, p. 24.

Walker, Helen E. "Seuss, Dr. *The Cat in the Hat.*" *Library Journal,* 15 May 1957, p. 1356.

Hines, L. G. "The Cat and the Hat." *Dartmouth Alumni Magazine,* June 1957, p. 6.

Mailloux, Heloise P. "Late Spring Book List." *The Horn Book Magazine,* June 1957, p. 215.

Burr, Elizabeth. [Review of *The Cat in the Hat.*] *Wisconsin Library Bulletin,* July 1957, p. 455.

"Seuss, Dr. *The Cat in the Hat.*" *Bulletin of the Children's Book Center,* Sept. 1957, p. 19.

Maxwell, Emily. "Books: Christmas for First and Second Readers." [Review of both *How the Grinch Stole Christmas!* and *The Cat in the Hat.*] *The New Yorker,* 23 Nov. 1957, pp. 232, 234.

"The Cat in the Hat." Childhood Education, Dec. 1957, p. 188.

Coleman, Mary Elisabeth. "Reading for Recreation." *The Reading Teacher,* Feb. 1958, pp. 205–06.

REVIEWS: *THE CAT IN THE HAT COMES BACK*

Buell, Ellen Lewis. "A Few New Books for All the New Readers." *The New York Times Book Review,* 5 Oct. 1958, p. 36.

Burr, Elizabeth. [Review of *The Cat in the Hat Comes Back.*] *Wisconsin Library Bulletin,* Nov. 1958, p. 525.

"Beginner Books Series." *Kirkus Reviews,* 1 Nov. 1958, p. 824.

"Geisel, Theodor Seuss. The Cat in the Hat Comes Back!" *Booklist and Subscription Books Bulletin,* 1 Nov. 1958, p. 136.

"Humor to Start Six-Year-Olds on a Lifetime of Reading." *The New York Herald Tribune Book Review,* 2 Nov. 1958.

Mann, Elizabeth Cannon. "Beginners thru 3d Grade—A Bonanza for All." *Chicago Tribune,* 2 Nov. 1958.

Doh, Barbara M. "Seuss, Dr. *The Cat in the Hat Comes Back.*" *Library Journal,* 15 Nov. 1958, p. 34.

Jackson, Charlotte. "Books for Children: A Christmas List." *The Atlantic Monthly,* Dec. 1958, pp. 97–98.

MANUSCRIPTS AND OTHER MATERIALS FROM THE DR. SEUSS COLLECTION

Courtesy of Mandeville Special Collections Library, UCSD Libraries, University of California at San Diego. Unless otherwise indicated, all items are by Dr. Seuss.

The Cat in the Hat, cover layout [MSS 0230, MC-078-01].

The Cat in the Hat, pen-and-ink drawings with tissue overlays and a set of 4x5 photographs of the finished drawings [MSS 0230, MC-078-02].

The Cat in the Hat, pen-and-ink drawings with tissue overlays [MSS 0230, MC-078-03].

The Cat in the Hat, pencil and colored-pencil sketches on paper with typescript captions [MSS 0230, MC-079-01].

The Cat in the Hat, pencil and colored-pencil sketches with typescript captions [MSS 0230, MC-079-02].

The Cat in the Hat, screenplay, typescript with holograph corrections [MSS 0230, Box 9, Folder 3].

The Cat in the Hat, television script [MSS 0230, Box 9, Folder 31].

The Cat in the Hat, television script, first draft—typescript with holograph corrections [MSS 0230, Box 9, Folder 33].

The Cat in the Hat, television script, first draft—photocopy [MSS 0230, Box 9, Folder 32].

The Cat in the Hat, television script, photocopy [MSS 0230, Box 9, Folder 34].

The Cat in the Hat Comes Back, pencil and ink on board [MSS 0230, MC-079-32].

The Cat in the Hat Comes Back, pencil and ink on board [MSS 0230, MC-079-33].

The Cat in the Hat Comes Back, photographic print and colored marker with caption [MSS 0230, MC-080-01].

The Cat in the Hat Comes Back, photographic print and colored marker with caption [MSS 0230, MC-080-02].

The Cat in the Hat Comes Back, poorly printed edition with corrections [MSS 0230, MC-081-01].

The Cat in the Hat Comes Back, transcribed in English Braille by Evelyn Paulson, Hampton Bays, New York, for the Industrial Home for the Blind, Brooklyn, New York, 1965 [MSS 0230, MC-081-02].

The Cat in the Hat Songbook, color roughs [MSS 0230, MC-081-06].

The Cat in the Hat Songbook, hand-colored photographic prints [MSS 0230, MC-082-01].

The Cat in the Hat Songbook, manuscript [MSS 0230, MC-081-03].

The Cat in the Hat Songbook, mounted materials [MSS 0230, MC-082-02].

The Cat in the Hat Songbook, pencil and ink on board [MSS 0230, MC-081-07].

The Cat in the Hat Songbook, rough sketches [MSS 0230, MC-081-05].

The Cat in the Hat Songbook, rough sketches and text [MSS 0230, MC-081-04].

The Cat in the Hat Songbook, three pencil sketches, mounted [MSS 0230, MC-118-01].

The Cat in the Hat Story Book, "Anthology," sketches with holograph and typescript outline [MSS 0230, Box 7, Folder 1].

Daisy-Head Mayzie, rough sketches, photographs of an early version by Geisel [MSS 0230, MC-083-19].

"Dr. Seuss, Brilliant Prewar Political Cartoonist, Came out of Retirement, Looked at the Current American Scene, and Temporarily Retired Again" [a.k.a. "COMMUNIST!"]. *The New Republic,* 28 July 1947, p. 7 [MSS 0230, Box 18, Folder 9].

"Enter a carefree Ormie in festive mood." Sketch for Ford advertisement [MSS 0230, MC-120, Folder 8].

Flit advertisement. Published in *The New Yorker,* 25 July 1936 [MSS 0230, MC-121, Folder 1].

The Grinch Grinches the Cat in the Hat, storyboard; pencil, ink, and crayon with holograph; bone pile [MSS 0230, Box 10, Folder 28].

The Grinch Grinches the Cat in the Hat, typescript, 6 pp.; bone pile [MSS 0230, Box 10, Folder 29].

Scott, Allan, and Dr. Seuss. *The 5000 Fingers of Dr. T,* screenplay, final draft, 30 Jan. 1952 [MSS 0230, Box 8, Folder 4].

University of Utah Workshops: lecture notes, July 1949 [MSS 0230, Box 19, Folder 6].

University of Utah Workshops: Mrs. Mulvaney and the Billion Dollar Bunny, July 1949 [MSS 0230, Box 19, Folder 7].

FOREIGN-LANGUAGE TRANSLATIONS

Richard H. F. Lindemann's *The Dr. Seuss Catalog* (McFarland, 2005) supplied most of the information for this list. For a more comprehensive list, see Lindemann, pages 28–30 and 35.

The Cat in the Hat

Dai mao zi di mao. Translated by Zhan Hongzhi. Taipei: Yuan-Liou, 1992. [Chinese]

Katten med hatten. Translated by Karl Nielsen. Copenhagen: Carlsen, 1979. [Danish]

De kat met de hoed. Translated by Katja and Kees Stip. Huizen: Goede Boek, 1975. [Dutch]

Le Chat au chapeau. Translated by Jean Vallier. New York: Random House, 1967. [English and French]

Le Chat chapeauté. Translated by Anne-Laure Fournier Le Ray. Paris: Pocket jeunesse, 2004. [French]

Der Kater mit Hut. Translated by Eike Schönfeld. 1999. Zürich: Piper München, 2004. [German]

Der Katz mit dem Latz. Translated by Hans A. Halbey. Hamburg: Carlsen Verlag, 1979. [German]

'Enas gatos me kapélo. Athens: Libanes, 2003. [Greek]

Hatul ta'alul. Translated by Le'ah Na'or. 1971. Jerusalem: Keter, 1990. [Hebrew]

Il Gatto col cappello. Translated by Anna Sarfatti. 1996. Firenze: Giunti Gruppo Editoriale, 1997. [Italian]

Cattus Petasatus. Translated by Guenevera [Jennifer] Tunberg and Terentio [Terence] Tunberg. Wauconda, IL: Bolchazy-Carducci Publishers, 2000. [Latin]

Kot Prot. Translated by Stanislaw Baranczak. Poznan: Media Rodzina, 1996. [Polish]

El gato ensombrerado. Translated by Carlos Rivera. 1967. New York: Random House, 1985. [Spanish and English]

El gato garabato. Translated by P. Rozarena. Madrid: Altea, 2003. [Spanish]

Katten i hatten. Translated by Lennart Hellsing. Stockholm: Carlsen, 1978. [Swedish]

Di Kats der Payats. Translated by Sholem Berger. New York: Twenty-fourth Street Books, 2003. [Yiddish]

The Cat in the Hat Comes Back

Die kat kom weer. Translated by Leon Rousseau. Cape Town: Human & Rousseau, 1972. [Afrikaans]

The Cat in the Hat Comes Back. Louisville: American Printing House for the Blind, 1960. [Braille]

The Cat in the Hat Comes Back. Transcribed by Evelyn Paulson. Brooklyn: The Industrial Home for the Blind, 1965. [Braille]

Dai mao zi di mao hui lai le! Translated by Zhan Hongzhi. Taipei: Yuan-Liou, 1992. [Chinese]

De kat met de hoed komt terug. Translated by Katja and Kees Stip. Huizen: Goede Boek, 1975. [Dutch]

Hatul ta'alul hozer! Translated by Le'ah Na'or. Jerusalem: Keter, 1979. [Hebrew]

El gato con sombrero viene de nuevo. Translated by Yanitzia Canetti. New York: Lectorum, 2004. [Spanish]

ADAPTATIONS OF *THE CAT IN THE HAT* AND *THE CAT IN THE HAT COMES BACK*

Lindemann's *The Dr. Seuss Catalog* was immensely helpful in preparing this list.

Animated

The Cat in the Hat. TV movie. Storyboard by Chuck Jones, teleplay by Dr. Seuss, music by Dean Elliott, lyrics by Dr. Seuss, directed by Hawley Pratt, produced by Chuck Jones and Ted Geisel. Voices: Allan Sherman [as the Cat], Daws Butler [as Mr. Krinklebein the Fish], Pamelyn Ferdin [as Sally], Tony Frazier [as Boy], Gloria Camacho [as Mother], Thurl Ravenscroft [as Thing One], and Lewis Morford [as Thing Two]. First broadcast on CBS-TV, March 10, 1971. 25 min.

The Cat in the Hat Comes Back. A video adaptation using the book's illustrations, suggesting movement via sound cues and the camera panning across the pages, with some stop-motion animation. Executive Producers: Ron Nicodemus and Chris Campbell; Producer/Director: Ken Hoin; Project Manager: Linda Morgenstern; Production Designer: Craig Rogers; Music Composer/Arranger: Nick Hubbell; Art Director: Dorria Marsh; Voices: Lynn Blair, Colin Carman, Earl Hammond, Barton Heyman, Marion Hailey Moss, Angelique-Claire Sirois, and Jim Thurman. Praxis Media and Random House Home Video, 1989. 12 min.

The Cat in the Hat Comes Back and Hop on Pop plus 4 More Dr. Seuss Stories. Video. Executive Producer: Sharon Lerner; Project Manager: Linda Morgenstern; Art Director: Cathy Goldsmith. Sony Wonder/Random House Home Video, 2003.

Film

Dr. Seuss' The Cat in the Hat. Movie. Directed by Bo Welch; produced by Brian Grazer; screenplay by Alec Berg, David Mandel, and Jeff Schaffer; music by David Newman. Featuring Mike Myers [as the Cat], Spencer Breslin [as Conrad], Dakota Fanning [as Sally], Kelly Preston [as Mom], Sean Hayes [as the voice of the Fish], Dan Castellaneta [as the voices of Thing One and Thing Two], and Alec Baldwin [as Quinn]. Universal Pictures, 2003. 82 min.

Games and CD-ROMs

The Cat in the Hat. CD-ROM. The Learning Company, 1997.

The Cat in the Hat. Game for PlayStation2, inspired by the 2003 movie. Vivendi Universal, 2003.

Movie Storybook

Dr. Seuss' The Cat in the Hat: Movie Storybook. Adapted by Justine and Ron Fontes. Based on the motion picture screenplay written by Alec Berg, David Mandel, and Jeff Schaffer. New York: Random House, 2003.

Recordings

Seuss, Dr. *The Cat in the Hat.* Audio recording [cassette]. Fisher-Price, 1981.
———. *The Cat in the Hat.* Audio recording [cassette]. Read by Adrian Edmondson. London: HarperCollins, 1995.
———. *The Cat in the Hat.* Audio recording [CD]. Music by Marc Levenson. Disc 1, Track 1 on *The Cat in the Hat and Other Dr. Seuss Favorites.* Executive Producer: Dan Zitt; Producer: John McElroy. New York: Random House, 2003. 8 min.
———. *The Cat in the Hat.* Book and audio recording [cassette]. *The Dr. Seuss Read-Along Library* [Beginner Books], set 1. Westminster, MD: Random House Educational Media, 1976.
———. *The Cat in the Hat Comes Back.* Book and audio recording [cassette]. *The Dr. Seuss Read-Along Library* [Beginner Books], set 2. Westminster, MD: Random House Educational Media, 1977.
———. *The Cat in the Hat Comes Back.* Audio recording [CD]. Read by Kelsey Grammer, music by Marc Levenson. Disc 2, Track 6 on *The Cat in the Hat and Other Dr. Seuss Favorites.* Executive Producer: Dan Zitt; Producer: John McElroy. New York: Random House, 2003. 9 min.

**WORKS BY DR. SEUSS THAT INCLUDE
THE CAT IN THE HAT**

For adaptations of other Seuss works that feature the Cat, see Lindemann's *The Dr. Seuss Catalog.*

The Cat in the Hat Beginner Book Dictionary (co-authored with P. D. Eastman). New York: Random House, 1964.
The Cat in the Hat Songbook. Piano score and guitar chords by Eugene Poddany. New York: Random House, 1967.
I Can Lick 30 Tigers Today! and Other Stories. New York: Random House, 1969.
Dr. Seuss on the Loose. Animated TV movie. Teleplay and lyrics by Dr. Seuss, storyboard by Bob Richardson, music by Dean Elliott, directed by Hawley Pratt, produced by Friz Freleng and Ted Geisel. Executive Producer: David H. DePatie. Voices: Allan Sherman [as the Cat], Hans Conried [as Narrator of *Green Eggs and Ham*], Paul Winchell [as Joey, Sam-I-am, and Sneetches], and Bob Holt [as Sylvester McMonkey McBean, the Zax, and Sneetches]. First broadcast on CBS-TV, October 15, 1973. 24 min.
The Cat's Quizzer. New York: Random House, 1976.
I Can Read with My Eyes Shut! New York: Random House, 1978.
The Grinch Grinches the Cat in the Hat. Animated TV movie. Directed by Bill Perez; written by Dr. Seuss; produced by Ted Geisel and Friz Freleng; executive produced by David H. DePatie; teleplay and lyrics by Ted Geisel; music by Joe Raposo and Joe Siracusa. Voices: Mason Adams [as the Cat], Bob Holt, Frank Welker, Joe Eich, Marilyn Jackson, Melissa Mackay, and Richard B. Williams. First broadcast on ABC-TV, May 20, 1982. 24 min.
Daisy-Head Mayzie. New York: Random House, 1994.
Daisy-Head Mayzie. Animated TV movie. Directed by Tony Collingwood; written by Dr. Seuss; produced by Audrey Geisel, Christopher O'Hare,

and Buzz Potamkin; music by Philip Appleby; lyrics by Dr. Seuss. Voices: Henry Gibson [as the Cat], Fran Smith [as Mayzie], Tim Curry [as Finagle], George Hearn [as the Mayor], Lewis Arquette [as the Principal], and Jonathan Winters [as Dr. Eisenbart]. First broadcast on TNT, February 5, 1995. 24 min.

**WORKS BY OTHERS THAT REFER TO
THE CAT IN THE HAT
(INCLUDING PARODIES AND CARTOONS)**

Basset, Brian. "Theodor Geisel (Dr. Seuss) 1904–1991." Cartoon. *The New York Times,* 29 Sept. 1991.
Coover, Robert. "The Cat in the Hat for President." *New American Review* 4 (Aug. 1968), pp. 7–45.
Devlin, Desmond. "The Strange Similarities Between the Bush Administration and the World of Dr. Seuss." Illustrated by Mort Drucker. *MAD,* Nov. 2004, pp. 39–43.
Gross, Sam. "He had a hat!" Cartoon. *The New Yorker,* 18 & 25 Feb. 2002, p. 134.
In Search of Dr. Seuss. TV movie. Directed by Vincent Paterson, written by Keith R. Clarke, produced by Joni Levin. Featuring Kathy Najimy [as Kathy], Matt Frewer [as the Cat], Robin Williams [as Father], Christopher Lloyd [as Mr. Hunch], David Paymer [as Ad Man], Andrea Martin [as Ad Woman], Patrick Stewart [as Sergeant Mulvaney], Eileen Brennan [as Who-Villain], Andraé Crouch [as Yertle the Turtle], Billy Crystal [as Radio Voice], and Howie Mandel [as voice of Sam-I-am]. First broadcast November 6, 1994. 96 min.
Katz, Alan. *The Cat NOT in the Hat! A Parody by Dr. Juice.* Illustrated by Chris Wrinn. Beverly Hills: Penguin, 1996. Dr. Seuss Enterprises successfully prevented distribution of this book (a comic take on the O.J. Simpson trial), but a copy can be found in the Library of Congress.
Kluger, Bruce, and David Slavin. "The Comeback Kid Meets Cat in the Hat." *Los Angeles Times,* 21 Aug. 2001.
R.E.M. "The Sidewinder Sleeps Tonite." Song. *Automatic for the People,* Warner Bros., 1992.
Seussical. Broadway musical. Book by Lynn Ahrens and Stephen Flaherty; lyrics by Lynn Ahrens; music by Stephen Flaherty; conceived by Lynn Ahrens, Stephen Flaherty, and Eric Idle; choreographed by Kathleen Marshall; directed by Frank Galati; orchestrated by Doug Besterman; original Broadway orchestra conducted by David Holcenberg. Original Broadway cast: David Shiner [as the Cat]; Kevin Chamberlain [as Horton]; Janine LaManna [as Gertrude McFuzz]; Michele Pawk [as Mayzie LaBird]; Anthony Blair Hall [as JoJo]; Sharon Wilkins [as Kangaroo]; Stuart Zagnit [as the Mayor of Whoville]; Alice Playten [as Mrs. Mayor]; Joyce Chittick, Jennifer Cody, Justin Greer, Mary Ann Lamb, Darren Lamb, and Jerome Vivona [as Cat's Helpers]; Erick Devine [as General Genghis Kahn Schmitz]; Natascia Diaz, Sara Gettelfinger, and Catrice Joseph [as Bad Girls]; David Engel, Tom Plotkin, and Eric Jordan Young [as Wickersham Brothers]; William Ryall [as the Grinch]; Darren Lee [as Vlad Vladikoff]; Devin Richards [as Judge Yertle the Turtle]; and Ann Harada [as Marshal of the Court]. Opened on November 30, 2000, at the Richard Rodgers Theatre, 226 West 46th Street, New York City.
Siers, Kevin. "Cat shedding a tear." Cartoon. *Best Editorial Cartoons of the Year,* ed. Charles Brooks (Gretna, LA: Pelican, 1992), p. 166.
Sutton, Ward. "The Cat in the Chad." Cartoon. *TV Guide,* 6 Jan. 2001.
Wilkinson, Signe. "I can hold up a thong . . ." Cartoon. *The New York Times,* 24 Jan. 1999.
The Wubbulous World of Dr. Seuss. Video and DVD series. Directed by David

Gumpel; written by Adam Felber, Richard Marcus, Bill Marsilii, Jay Martel, and Mo Rocca; produced by David Cohen, Michael K. Frith, and Brian Henson. Jim Henson Productions, 1996–2000. The Cat [played by Bruce Lanoil] appears in many episodes, including "The Song of the Zubble-Wump," "The Muckster," "The Cat in the Hat Cleans Up His Act," "The Cat in the Hat's Indoor Picnic," and "The Cat in the Hat's Big Birthday Surprise." Several episodes were also adapted for books.

OTHER DR. SEUSS WORKS CITED
(INCLUDING PSEUDONYMS DR. THEOPHRASTUS SEUSS, THEO. LeSIEG, AND RUBE GOLDBRICK)

Articles
"THE FACTS OF LIFE; Or, How Should I Tell My Child?" Part 1. *Life,* Feb. 1934, pp. 22–23, 37, 46–47.

"Matilda, the Elephant with a Mother Complex: A Dr. Seuss Fable." *Judge,* Apr. 1938, p. 17.

"The Strange Shirt Spot." *Redbook,* Sept. 1951, pp. 68–69.

"How Orlo Got His Book." *The New York Times Book Review,* 17 Nov. 1957, pp. 2, 60.

"My Hassle with the First Grade Language." *Chicago Tribune,* 17 Nov. 1957, part 4, p. 4.

[As The Dr. Seuss Surveys.] "The economic situation clarified: A prognostic re-evaluation." *The New York Times Magazine,* 15 June 1975, p. 71.

Animated Cartoons
The Complete Uncensored Private SNAFU: Cartoons from World War II. Video and DVD. Bosko Video, 1990, 1993, 1999. Cartoons produced between 1943 and 1946. Although these twenty-eight episodes were created collaboratively and individual contributors are not identified, Theodor Geisel is generally considered to be the creator or co-creator of "The Home Front" (Nov. 1943) and all eight verse cartoons: "Gripes" (July 1943), "Spies" (Aug. 1943), "The Goldbrick" (Sept. 1943), "The Infantry Blues" (Sept. 1943), "Fighting Tools" (Oct. 1943), "Rumors" (Dec. 1943), "Going Home" (May 1944), and "The Chow Hound" (June 1944). He and Munro Leaf are believed to be the co-authors of "It's Murder, She Says" (May 1945).

Books
And to Think That I Saw It on Mulberry Street. New York: Vanguard Press, 1937.

The 500 Hats of Bartholomew Cubbins. New York: Vanguard Press, 1938.

The King's Stilts. New York: Random House, 1939.

Horton Hatches the Egg. New York: Random House, 1940.

McElligot's Pool. New York: Random House, 1947.

Bartholomew and the Oobleck. New York: Random House, 1949.

If I Ran the Zoo. New York: Random House, 1950.

Scrambled Eggs Super! New York: Random House, 1953.

Horton Hears a Who! New York: Random House, 1954.

On Beyond Zebra! New York: Random House, 1955.

If I Ran the Circus. New York: Random House, 1956.

How the Grinch Stole Christmas! New York: Random House, 1957.

Green Eggs and Ham. New York: Random House, 1960.

One Fish Two Fish Red Fish Blue Fish. New York: Random House, 1960.

The Sneetches and Other Stories. New York: Random House, 1961.

Dr. Seuss's ABC. New York: Random House, 1963.

Hop on Pop. New York: Random House, 1963.

The Cat in the Hat Beginner Book Dictionary. Co-authored with P. D. Eastman. New York: Random House, 1964.

Mr. Brown Can Moo! Can You? New York: Random House, 1970.

In a People House. Illustrated by Roy McKie. New York: Random House, 1972.

The Shape of Me and Other Stuff. New York: Random House, 1973.

Oh, the Thinks You Can Think! New York: Random House, 1975.

Please Try to Remember the First of Octember! Illustrated by Art Cummings. New York: Random House, 1977.

Maybe You Should Fly a Jet! Maybe You Should Be a Vet! Illustrated by Michael J. Smollin. New York: Random House, 1980.

Hunches in Bunches. New York: Random House, 1982.

The Butter Battle Book. New York: Random House, 1984.

I Am Not Going to Get Up Today! Illustrated by James Stevenson. New York: Random House, 1987.

Marschall, Richard, ed. *The Tough Coughs as He Ploughs the Dough: Early Writings and Cartoons by Dr. Seuss.* New York: William Morrow & Company, 1987.

Oh, the Places You'll Go! New York: Random House, 1990.

Cartoons
"I am so thrilled, my dear! At last I can understand the ecstasy Lawrence experienced when he raced posthaste across the sands of Arabia in pursuit of the fleeting Arab." *The Saturday Evening Post,* 16 July 1927.

"Boids and Beasties." *Judge,* 19 Nov. 1927, p. 9.

"MEDIÆVAL TENANT—Darn it all, another dragon. And just after I'd sprayed the whole castle with Flit!" *Judge,* 14 Jan. 1928, p. 16. Marschall, Richard, ed. *The Tough Coughs as He Ploughs the Dough: Early Writings and Cartoons by Dr. Seuss* (New York: William Morrow & Company, 1987), p. 13.

"LAUGH IS LIKE THAT!" *Judge,* 19 May 1928, pp. 21, 26.

"Ough! Ough! Or Why I Believe in Simplified Spelling." *Judge,* 13 Apr. 1929, p. 18. Marschall, Richard, ed. *The Tough Coughs as He Ploughs the Dough: Early Writings and Cartoons by Dr. Seuss* (New York: William Morrow & Company, 1987), p. 57.

Goodman, Benny. "What Swing Really Does to People." Illustrations by Dr. Seuss. *Liberty,* 14 May 1938, p. 6.

"We always were suckers for ridiculous hats . . ." *PM,* 29 Apr. 1941, p. 20.

"The old family bath tub is plenty safe for me!" *PM,* 27 May 1941, p. 12.

"Man who draw his bath too hot, sit down in same velly slow." *PM,* 4 Sept. 1941, p. 5.

"Latest modern home convenience: hot and cold running subs." *PM,* 22 Jan. 1942, p. 22.

Correspondence
"Hey, you." Letter to Random House, 11 June 1956.

Screenplays
The 5000 Fingers of Dr. T. Directed by Roy Rowland; screenplay by Dr. Seuss and Allan Scott; story, conception, and lyrics by Dr. Seuss; music by Frederick Hollander and Hans J. Salter. Cast: Peter Lind Hayes [as August Zabladowski], Mary Healy [as Heloise Collins], Hans Conried [as Dr. T], Tommy Rettig [as Bart Collins]. Columbia Pictures Corp., 1953.

BIOGRAPHIES OF DR. SEUSS
Cohen, Charles D. *The Seuss, the Whole Seuss, and Nothing but the Seuss: A*

Visual Biography of Theodor Seuss Geisel. New York: Random House, 2004.

Morgan, Judith, and Neil Morgan. *Dr. Seuss & Mr. Geisel: A Biography.* New York: Random House, 1995.

Weidt, Maryann N. *Oh, the Places He Went: A Story About Dr. Seuss.* Illustrated by Kerry Maguire. Minneapolis: Carolrhoda Books, 1994. [For juvenile audience.]

BIBLIOGRAPHIES OF DR. SEUSS WORKS

Lindemann, Richard H. F. *The Dr. Seuss Catalog: An Annotated Guide to Works by Theodor Geisel in All Media, Writings About Him, and Appearances of Characters and Places in the Books, Stories and Films.* Jefferson, NC, and London: McFarland & Company, 2005.

Younger, Helen, Marc Younger, and Dan Hirsch. *First Editions of Dr. Seuss Books: A Guide to Identification.* Saco, ME: Custom Communications, 2002.

OTHER BOOKS ABOUT DR. SEUSS

Fensch, Thomas, ed. *Of Sneetches and Whos and the Good Dr. Seuss: Essays on the Writings and Life of Theodor Geisel.* Jefferson, NC, and London: McFarland & Company, 1997.

Lathem, Edward Connery. *Who's Who & What's What in the Books of Dr. Seuss.* Hanover, NH: Dartmouth College, 2000. Reproduced at www.dartmouth.edu/~drseuss/whoswho.pdf.

———, ed. *Theodor Seuss Geisel: Reminiscences & Tributes.* Introductory note by Audrey S. Geisel. Hanover, NH: Dartmouth College, 1996.

MacDonald, Ruth K. *Dr. Seuss.* New York: Twayne, 1988.

Minear, Richard H. *Dr. Seuss Goes to War: The World War II Editorial Cartoons of Theodor Seuss Geisel.* Introduction by Art Spiegelman. New York: New Press, 1999.

Nel, Philip. *Dr. Seuss: American Icon.* New York and London: Continuum Publishing, 2004.

Stofflet, Mary. *Dr. Seuss from Then to Now: A Catalogue of the Retrospective Exhibition.* Introduction by Steven L. Brezzo. New York: Random House, 1986.

LITERARY CRITICISM AND ESSAYS

Avi. "Future Classics." *The Horn Book Magazine,* Nov.–Dec. 2000, p. 647.

Bader, Barbara. "Dr. Seuss." *American Picturebooks from Noah's Ark to the Beast Within* (New York: Macmillan, 1976), pp. 302–12.

Bailey, John P., Jr. "Three Decades of Dr. Seuss." *Elementary English* 42 (Jan. 1965), pp. 7–12.

Barrs, Myra. "Laughing Your Way to Literacy." *The Times Educational Supplement,* 23 Jan. 1976, pp. 20–21.

Bodmer, George R. "The Post-Modern Alphabet: Extending the Limits of the Contemporary Alphabet Book, from Seuss to Gorey." *Children's Literature Association Quarterly* 14, no. 3 (Fall 1989), pp. 115–17.

Butler, Francelia. "Seuss as a Creator of Folklore." *Children's Literature in Education* 20, no. 3 (1989), pp. 175–81.

Clark, H. Nicholas B., Trinkett Clark, and Michael Patrick Hearn. *Myth, Magic, and Mystery: One Hundred Years of American Children's Book Illustration* (Norfolk, Boulder, and Dublin: Roberts Rinehart Publishers and the Chrysler Museum of Art, 1996), pp. 47, 49, 76, 96, 97, 101, 108, 121, 122.

Davis, David C. "What the Cat in the Hat Begat." *Elementary English* 39, no. 7 (Nov. 1962), pp. 677–79, 746.

Dewan, Ted. "The Cat in the Hat Comes Back." *The Times Educational Supplement,* 7 Nov. 1997.

Dohm, Janice H. "The Curious Case of Dr. Seuss: A Minority Report from America." *The Junior Bookshelf* 27 (Dec. 1963), pp. 323–29.

Fadiman, Clifton. "Professionals and Confessionals: Dr. Seuss and Kenneth Grahame." In *Only Connect: Readings on Children's Literature,* ed. L. F. Ashley, Sheila Egoff, and G. T. Stubbs. Toronto: Oxford University Press, 1980. Reprint of "Party of One: Children's Literature Then and Now: From Kenneth Grahame's *Wind in the Willows* to Dr. Seuss' *Cat in the Hat.*" *Holiday,* April 1959, pp. 11, 14–17.

Flesch, Rudolf R. "The Lilting World of Mr. Ted Geisel." *Los Angeles Times,* 19 July 1959.

Goldenberg, Naomi. "A Feminist, Psychoanalytic Exegesis of *The Cat in the Hat.*" Unpublished, 1995. See Steinfels, Peter.

Goodman, Ellen. "What Dr. Seuss Started with That 'Cat in the Hat.'" *Detroit Free Press,* 6 Nov. 1966.

Jenkins, Henry. "'No Matter How Small': The Democratic Imagination of Dr. Seuss." In *Hop on Pop: The Politics and Pleasures of Popular Culture*, ed. Henry Jenkins, Tara McPherson, Jane Shattuc (Durham, NC, and London: Duke University Press, 2002), pp. 187–208.

Lakhtakia, Akhlesh. "Fractals and *The Cat in the Hat.*" *Journal of Recreational Mathematics* 22, no. 3 (1990), pp. 161–64.

Lanes, Selma G. "Seuss for the Goose Is Seuss for the Gander." In *Down the Rabbit Hole: Adventures & Misadventures in the Realm of Children's Literature* (New York: Atheneum, 1971), pp. 79–89.

Lurie, Alison. "The Cabinet of Dr. Seuss." *The New York Review of Books,* 20 Dec. 1990, pp. 50–52.

Lystad, Mary. "The Cat in the Hat." In *From Mother Goose to Dr. Seuss: 200 Years of American Books for Children* (Boston: G. K. Hall, 1980), pp. 196–201.

May, Jill P. "Dr. Seuss and *The 500 Hats of Bartholomew Cubbins.*" *The Bulletin: Newsletter of the Children's Literature Assembly of the National Council of Teachers of English* 11, no. 3 (1985), pp. 8–9.

Menand, Louis. "Cat People: What Dr. Seuss Really Taught Us." *The New Yorker,* 23 & 30 Dec. 2002, pp. 148–54.

Mensch, Betty, and Alan Freeman. "Getting to Solla Sollew: The Existential Politics of Dr. Seuss." *Tikkun* 2, no. 2 (1987), pp. 30–34, 113–17.

Mundy, Liza. "When Mom's Away . . . the Cat Will Play." *The Washington Post,* 11 May 2003.

Nel, Philip. "Dada Knows Best: Growing Up 'Surreal' with Dr. Seuss." In *The Avant-Garde and American Postmodernity: Small Incisive Shocks* (Jackson, MS, and London: University Press of Mississippi, 2002), pp. 41–72.

Nilsen, Don L. F. "Dr. Seuss as Grammar Consultant." *Language Arts* 54 (May 1977), pp. 567–72.

Quindlen, Anna. "The One Who Had Fun." *The New York Times,* 28 Sept. 1991.

Raymo, Chet. "Dr. Seuss and Dr. Einstein: Children's Books and Scientific Imagination." *The Horn Book Magazine,* Sept.–Oct. 1992, pp. 560–67.

Schroth, Evelyn. "Dr. Seuss and Language Use." *The Reading Teacher* 31 (April 1978), pp. 748–50.

Shortsleeve, Kevin. "The Politics of Nonsense: Civil Unrest, Otherness and National Mythology in Nonsense Literature." Doctoral dissertation. University of Oxford, 2006.

Steinfels, Peter. "Beliefs." *The New York Times,* 19 Aug. 1995.

Wolosky, Shira. "Democracy in America: By Dr. Seuss." *Southwest Review* 85, no. 2 (Spring 2000), pp. 167–83.

INTERVIEWS AND PROFILES

An Awfully Big Adventure: The Making of Modern Children's Literature. Six-part TV documentary series, including an episode on Dr. Seuss. Produced and directed by Roger Parsons. BBC, 1998.

Bandler, Michael J. "Dr. Seuss: Still a Drawing Card." *American Way,* Dec. 1977, pp. 23–26, 28.

———. "Portrait of a Man Reading." *The Washington Post Book World,* 7 May 1972, p. 2.

Barclay, Dorothy. "See the Book? It Is Made with 6-Year-Old's Words." *The New York Times,* 15 April 1957, p. 26.

Beyette, Beverly. "Seuss: New Book on the Tip of His Tongue." *Los Angeles Times,* 29 May 1979, sec. 5, pp. 1, 5.

Burchell, Sam. "*Architectural Digest* Visits Dr. Seuss." *Architectural Digest,* Dec. 1978, pp. 88–93.

Cahn, Robert. "The Wonderful World of Dr. Seuss." *The Saturday Evening Post,* 6 July 1957, pp. 17–19, 42, 46.

Carlinsky, Dan. "The Wily Ruse of Doctor Seuss." *The Magazine of the Boston Herald American,* 4 Mar. 1979, pp. 12–15.

Clark, Diane. "He Is Waking Children to a World of Words." *San Diego Union,* 19 Dec. 1976, pp. D1, D4.

Corwin, Miles. "Author Isn't Just a Cat in the Hat." *Los Angeles Times,* 27 Nov. 1983, sec. Metro, pp. 1, 3.

Cott, Jonathan. *Pipers at the Gates of Dawn: The Wisdom of Children's Literature* (New York: Random House, 1983), pp. 1–37.

"Currents." *Publishers Weekly,* 24 Aug. 1959, p. 23.

Dangaard, Colin. "Dr. Seuss Reigns Supreme as King of the Kids." *Boston Herald American,* 21 Nov. 1976, sec. 5, pp. 1, 3.

Dempsey, David. "The Significance of Dr. Seuss." *The New York Times Book Review,* 11 May 1958, p. 30.

Diehl, Digby. "Q & A 'Dr. Seuss.'" *Los Angeles Times WEST Magazine,* 17 Sept. 1972, pp. 36–39.

"Dr. Seuss Remembered." *Publishers Weekly,* 25 Oct. 1991, pp. 32–33.

Dummit, Chris. "The Man Behind the Cat in the Hat." *Los Angeles Times,* 18 Aug. 1983, part IB, p. 7.

Freeman, Don. "Dr. Seuss from Then to Now." *San Diego Magazine,* May 1986, pp. 132–39, 242–43.

Freeman, Donald. "The Nonsensical World of Dr. Seuss." *McCall's Magazine,* Nov. 1964, pp. 115, 200–01.

———. "Who Thunk You Up, Dr. Seuss?" *San Jose Mercury News,* 15 June 1969. Reproduced in *Authors and Illustrators of Children's Books: Writings on Their Lives and Works,* ed. Miriam Hoffman and Eva Samuels (New York and London: R. R. Bowker Company, 1972), pp. 165–71.

Frith, Michael. "Dr. Seuss at Home." *Children's Book Crannie,* Jan.–Apr. 1973.

Frutig, Judith. "Dr. Seuss's Green-Eggs-and-Ham World." *The Christian Science Monitor,* 12 May 1978, pp. 18–19.

"Gay Menagerie of Queer Animals Fills the Apartment of Dr. Seuss." *Springfield Sunday Union and Republican,* 28 Nov. 1937, p. 5E.

Georgatos, Dennis. "Dr. Seuss Sets Sights on Adults." *Sunday Rutland Herald.* [No date on clipping.] Reprint of "Books and Authors: An Adult's Book in a Child Format." Associated Press, 5 July 1985. Dartmouth, Special Collections.

Girson, Rochelle. Profile of Dr. Seuss. *The Saturday Review,* 11 May 1957, p. 52.

Gorney, Cynthia. "Dr. Seuss Alive and Well, but Not on Mulberry Street." *The Indianapolis Star,* 10 June 1979, pp. 1, 10.

Hacker, Kathy. "Happy 80th Birthday, Dr. Seuss." *The Philadelphia Inquirer,* 7 Mar. 1984, pp. E1, E7–E8.

Hart, William B. "Between the Lines." *Redbook,* Dec. 1957, p. 4.

"He Makes C-A-T Spell Big Money." *Business Week,* 18 July 1964, pp. 72–73.

Hopkins, Lee Bennett. "Dr. Seuss (Theodor S. Geisel)." In *Books Are by People.* New York: Citation Press, 1969, pp. 255–58.

———. "Stoo-pendous Dr. Seuss!" *Family Weekly,* 9 Apr. 1978, p. 16.

Kahn, E. J., Jr. "Children's Friend." *The New Yorker,* 17 Dec. 1960, pp. 47–93.

Kitch, Edward S. "Modern Mother Goose: He Deals in Lilliputian Humor." *Long Island Press,* 23 Nov. 1958.

Kupferberg, Herbert. "A Seussian Celebration." *Parade,* 26 Feb. 1984, pp. 4–6.

Kuskin, Karla. "Seuss at 75." *The New York Times Book Review,* 29 Apr. 1979, Children's Books, pp. 23, 41–42.

Lathem, Edward Connery. Notes in preparation for an exhibition on the life and works of Dr. Seuss, 1975. Dartmouth College, Rauner Special Collections Library, Alumni G277n.

———. "Words and Pictures Married: The Beginnings of Dr. Seuss." *Dartmouth Alumni Magazine,* Apr. 1976, pp. 16–21.

Lingeman, Richard R. "Dr. Seuss, Theo. LeSieg. . . ." *The New York Times Book Review,* 14 Nov. 1976, pp. 24, 48.

Nichols, Lewis. "Then I Doodled a Tree." *The New York Times Book Review,* 11 Nov. 1962, pp. 2, 42.

Olten, Carol. "To a Living Literary Legend. . . ." *San Diego Union,* 17 Apr. 1984.

"The One and Only Dr. Seuss and His Wonderful Autographing Tour." *Publishers Weekly,* 8 Dec. 1958, pp. 12–15.

"The Other Cool Cat." *Early Years: A Magazine for Teachers of Preschool Through Grade 3,* Apr. 1973, pp. 22–24.

Pace, Eric. "Dr. Seuss, Modern Mother Goose, Dies at 87." *The New York Times,* 26 Sept. 1991, pp. A1, D23.

Rohter, Larry. "After 60 Years, Dr. Seuss Goes Home." *The New York Times,* 21 May 1986, p. A20.

Sadler, Glenn Edward. "A Conversation with Maurice Sendak and Dr. Seuss." [Interview on 8 Dec. 1982.] In *Teaching Children's Literature: Issues, Pedagogy, Resources,* ed. Glenn Edward Sadler (New York: Modern Language Association, 1992), pp. 241–50.

Salzhauer, Mike. "A Carnival Cavort with Dr. Seuss." *The Dartmouth Review,* 2 Feb. 1981, pp. 6–7. Reproduced in *The Dartmouth Review,* Nov. 1991, pp. 8–9.

Sheff, David. "Seuss on Wry." *Parenting,* Feb. 1987, pp. 52–57.

Silverman, Betsy Marden. "Dr. Seuss Talks to Parents About Learning to Read and What Makes Children Want to Do It." *Parents,* Nov. 1960, pp. 44–45, 135–37.

Smith, Kathleen. "Dr. Seuss Battles with Butter to Drive Home a Message for Children and Adults." *The Dartmouth's Weekend Magazine,* 18 Jan. 1985, pp. 12–13.

"Sneetches, Sugar, and Success: The Boom in Books for Children." *Newsweek,* 25 Dec. 1961, pp. 73–75.

"'Somebody's Got to Win' in Kids' Books: An Interview with Dr. Seuss on His Books for Children, Young and Old." *U.S. News & World Report,* 14 Apr. 1986, p. 69.

Steinberg, Sybil S. "What Makes a Funny Children's Book? Five Writers Talk About Their Methods." *Publishers Weekly,* 27 Feb. 1978, pp. 87–90.

"The 25th Anniversary of Dr. Seuss." *Publishers Weekly,* 17 Dec. 1962, pp. 10–13.

Warren, Bob. "Dr. Seuss, Former *Jacko* Editor, Tells How Boredom May Lead to Success." *The Dartmouth*, 10 May 1934, pp. 3, 9.

Waugh, John C. "Kingdom of Seuss." *The Christian Science Monitor,* 29 Jan. 1964, p. 9.

Webb, Jack. "Dr. Seuss Also Has Worn Many Hats." *San Diego Evening Tribune,* 11 Sept. 1974, p. A21.

Wintle, Justin, and Emma Fisher. "Two Letters: Dr. Seuss and E. B. White." *The Pied Pipers: Interviews with the Influential Creators of Children's Literature* (New York: Paddington Press, 1975), pp. 113–31.

OTHER SOURCES

3rd Bass. *Derelicts of Dialect.* Def Jam, 1991.

Abrams, M. H. *A Glossary of Literary Terms.* Sixth Edition. Fort Worth, TX: Harcourt Brace Jovanovich, 1993.

Arbuthnot, May Hill. *Children and Books.* Chicago: Scott, Foresman and Company, 1947.

———. *Children's Reading in the Home.* Glenview, IL: Scott, Foresman and Company, 1969.

Arbuthnot, May Hill, and William S. Gray. *Fun with Dick and Jane.* Illustrated by Eleanor Campbell and Keith Ward. New York: Scott, Foresman and Company, 1940.

Associated Press. "Task Force Discusses Parade Balloon Mishaps." *The Patriot Ledger* (Quincy, MA), 2 Dec. 1997.

Bang, Molly. *Picture This: How Pictures Work.* 1991. New York: SeaStar Books, 2000.

Barrier, Michael. *Hollywood Cartoons: American Animation in Its Golden Age.* New York and Oxford: Oxford University Press, 1999.

Bartlett, John. *Bartlett's Familiar Quotations.* Sixteenth Edition. Ed. Justin Kaplan. Boston, Toronto, London: Little, Brown and Company, 1992.

Beastie Boys. *Paul's Boutique.* Capital Records, 1989.

"Beginner Books: New Trade Learn-to-Read Juveniles." *Publishers Weekly,* 2 June 1958, pp. 116–17.

Belloc, Hilaire. *Cautionary Verses: Illustrated Album Edition.* With the original pictures by B. T. B. and Nicolas Bentley. New York: Alfred A. Knopf, 1945.

Bullfinch, Thomas. *The Age of Fable: Stories of the Gods of Greece and Rome, the Deities of Egypt, and the Eastern and Hindu Mythology.* Emmaus, PA: Rodale Press, 1948.

Carroll, Lewis. *Alice's Adventures in Wonderland.* Illustrated by John Tenniel. 1865. In *The Annotated Alice: The Definitive Edition.* Introduction and notes by Martin Gardner. New York: W. W. Norton, 2000.

"Children's Best Sellers." *The New York Times Book Review,* 2 Nov. 1958.

"City Digs Out of the Snow." *Springfield Daily Republican,* 15 Dec. 1915, p. 1.

"City in Heart of Storm." *Springfield Daily Republican,* 14 Dec. 1915, p. 1.

Costello, Eric O. "Private SNAFU & Mr. Hook." *ANiMATO! The Animation Fan's Magazine* 37 (Spring 1997), pp. 44–57.

Cummins, Roger W. *Humorous but Wholesome: A History of Palmer Cox and the Brownies.* Watkins Glen, NY: Century House Americana Publishers, 1973.

Dirks, Rudolph. *The Komical Katzenjammers.* First published by Frederick A. Stokes Company, 1908. New York: Dover Publications, 1974. Reprint edition includes a new introduction by August Derleth.

Flesch, Rudolf. *Why Johnny Can't Read—and What You Can Do About It.* 1955. New York: Harper & Row, 1986.

Frame, Michael, Benoit Mandelbrot, and Nial Neger. *Fractal Geometry.* http://classes.yale.edu/fractals/ [Accessed 13 Apr. 2005.]

Ga'g, Wanda. *Millions of Cats.* 1928. New York: Penguin, 1996.

The Gallup Organization. Poll 56-669, conducted 26–31 Jan. 1956. Roper Center at the University of Connecticut.

Goldberg, Rube. *Rube Goldberg vs. the Machine Age.* Ed. Clark Kinnaird. New York: Hastings House, 1968.

Hackett, Alice Payne. *50 Years of Best Sellers, 1895–1945.* New York and London: R. R. Bowker Company, 1945.

———. *70 Years of Best Sellers, 1895–1965.* New York and London: R. R. Bowker Company, 1967.

———. *60 Years of Best Sellers, 1895–1955.* New York and London: R. R. Bowker Company, 1956.

Hackett, Alice Payne, and James Henry Burke. *80 Years of Best Sellers, 1895–1975.* New York and London: R. R. Bowker Company, 1977.

Hersey, John. "Why Do Students Bog Down on First R?" *Life,* 24 May 1954, pp. 136–50.

"Humor for Children." *The New York Times,* 12 Sept. 1954.

Jacob, Brian E. *All Things Thurl.* http://members.aol.com/allthurl/thurl2 .htm

Jones, Chuck. *Chuck Reducks: Drawing from the Fun Side of Life.* New York: Warner Books, 1996.

Lajewski, Henry C. *Child Care Arrangements of Full-Time Working Mothers.* U.S. Department of Health, Education, and Welfare, Children's Bureau Publication No. 378. Washington: 1959.

Lear, Edward. *The Complete Nonsense of Edward Lear.* Collected and introduced by Holbrook Jackson. 1947. New York: Dover, 1951.

Lord & Taylor advertisement. *The New York Times,* 5 May 1958, p. 36.

Macy's advertisement. *The New York Times,* 3 Nov. 1957, p. 40.

"Macy's Presents Safer Parade." CNN.com. 26 Nov. 1998. www.cnn.com/us/ 9811/26/macys.parade.01 [Accessed 9 Oct. 2005.]

Mandelbrot, Benoit B. *The Fractal Geometry of Nature.* New York: W. H. Freeman and Company, 1982.

Marcus, Leonard, ed. *Dear Genius: The Letters of Ursula Nordstrom.* New York: HarperCollins, 1998.

Marschall, Richard. "Rudolph Dirks (1877–1968)." In *America's Great Comic Strip Artists.* 1989. New York: Stewart, Tabori & Chang, 1997, pp. 41–57.

Mather, Cotton. *A Family Well-Ordered, or An Essay to Render Parents and Children Happy in One Another.* Boston: B. Green & J. Allen, 1699.

May, Jill P. "Frank R. Stockton." In *Dictionary of Literary Biography,* Vol. 42: *American Writers for Children Before 1900.* Ed. Glenn E. Estes. Detroit: The Gale Group, 1985.

Miller, Harry S. "The Cat Came Back." Song. Chicago: Will Rossiter, 1893.

Morgan, Wayne. "Brownie Dolls and the World of Palmer Cox." Lecture. Letitia Penn Doll Club, UFDC Regional 13 Conference. Sheraton Society Hill Hotel, Philadelphia, 3–6 Oct. 1996. http://home.earthlink.net/~hellerest/ VAGABONDSONG.HTML [Accessed 17 Mar. 2005.]

Moxy Früvous. *Moxy Früvous.* Self-released cassette, 1992.

Newell, Peter. *The Hole Book.* 1908. Boston, Tokyo, and Rutland, VT: Tuttle Publishing, 1985.

———. *The Rocket Book.* 1912. Boston, Tokyo, and Rutland, VT: Tuttle Publishing, 1969.

———. *The Slant Book.* 1910. Boston, Tokyo, and Rutland, VT: Tuttle Publishing, 1967.

"No Call to Be Mean." *The Kansas City Star,* 1 Mar. 2002, p. A2.

Norris, Michael. "Bugs Bunny Creator Puts Face on Private SNAFU: The Legacy of Animator Chuck Jones." *Pentagram,* 1 Mar. 2002. www.dcmilitary.com/army/pentagram/7_08/features/14532-1.html [Accessed 2 Sept. 2003.]

The Oxford English Dictionary. Second Edition. Ed. J. A. Simpson and E. S. C. Weiner. Oxford: Clarendon Press, 1989. http://dictionary.oed.com

Pelisek, Christine. "Snoopy's Revenge." *LA Weekly,* 17 Mar. 2000, p. 14.

Perrault, Charles. "Master Cat, or Puss in Boots." 1697. In *The Annotated Classic Fairy Tales*, ed. and with an introduction and notes by Maria Tatar (New York: W. W. Norton, 2002), pp. 234–44.

Powell, Joanna. "Tops in Hat Tricks." *Entertainment Weekly,* 29 Mar. 1991, p. 8.

"Ready Today." *Springfield Daily Republican,* 16 Dec. 1915, p. 1.

Saks Fifth Avenue advertisement. *The New York Times,* 30 Dec. 1958, p. 14.

Sheppard, Harrison. "T.V. Actress Facing Jail Time in 4-Year-Old Circus Protest." *Los Angeles Daily News,* 16 July 2003, p. N1.

Stockton, Frank R. *The Lady, or the Tiger? and Other Stories.* 1886. New York: Charles Scribner's Sons, 1920.

Street, Douglas. "Howard R. Garis." In *Dictionary of Literary Biography,* Vol. 22: *American Writers for Children, 1900–1960.* Ed. John Cech (Detroit: The Gale Group, 1983), pp. 191–99.

"Table 1-1. Live Births, Birth Rates, and Fertility Rates, by Race: United States, 1909–2000." Department of Health and Human Services, Centers for Disease Control and Prevention. www.cdc.gov/nchs/data/statab/t001x01.pdf [Accessed 23 Apr. 2005.]

"Table 2. Fall School Enrollment of the Civilian Noninstitutional Population 5 to 34 Years Old, by Type of School and Age, for the United States: October 1953 to 1958." U.S. Bureau of the Census, Current Population Reports, Series P-20, No. 89. Washington: 11 Dec. 1958, p. 2.

"Table 4. Characteristics of Families, by Type, for the United States, Total and Nonfarm: March 1958." U.S. Bureau of the Census, Current Population Reports, Series P-20, No. 88. Washington: 17 Nov. 1958, p. 10.

Turvey, Debbie Hochman. "All-Time Bestselling Children's Books." *Publishers Weekly,* 17 Dec. 2001, pp. 24–27.

"200 Books Given to White House." *The New York Times,* 19 Jan. 1962, p. 29.

U.S. Bureau of the Census. "Homes with Selected Electrical Appliances." In *Statistical Abstract of the United States: 1971.* 92nd Edition. Washington: 1971, p. 677.

Wertham, Fredric. *Seduction of the Innocent.* New York: Rinehart & Co., 1954.

Wolfe, Maynard Frank. *Rube Goldberg: Inventions.* New York: Simon & Schuster, 2000.

"Yesterday's Weather in Springfield." *Springfield Daily Republican,* 15 Dec. 1915, p. 1.

CREDITS

Image details are listed by page number, from left to right, top to bottom.

p. 6, Dr. Seuss reading *The Cat in the Hat,* 1957. Photo by Phyllis Cerf. Image courtesy of Dr. Seuss Collection, Mandeville Special Collections Library, University of California, San Diego. Reproduced courtesy of Phyllis Cerf Wagner.

p. 8, *Private SNAFU,* title image.

p. 8, Dr. Seuss and his sculpture of a "Blue-Green Abelard," 1953. Image courtesy of Dr. Seuss Collection, Mandeville Special Collections Library, University of California, San Diego. Reproduced courtesy of Dr. Seuss Enterprises.

p. 8, Dr. Seuss's letter to Random House beginning "Hey, you," 11 June 1956. Image courtesy of Random House.

p. 9, cover of *The Cat in the Hat,* Houghton Mifflin edition, 1957. Image from the Oolongblue Collection of Charles D. Cohen and The Whole Seuss. Reproduced courtesy of Dr. Seuss Enterprises.

p. 9, cover of *The Cat in the Hat,* Random House first edition, 1957. Image courtesy of Random House. Reproduced courtesy of Dr. Seuss Enterprises.

p. 10, "It all starts with Dr. Seuss" button. Image courtesy of Dr. Seuss Collection, Mandeville Special Collections Library, University of California, San Diego. Reproduced courtesy of Dr. Seuss Enterprises.

p. 10, Dr. Seuss signing books, c. 1957. Image courtesy of Random House.

p. 11, cover of *The Cat in the Hat Comes Back,* Random House first edition, 1958. Image courtesy of Dr. Seuss Collection, Mandeville Special Collections Library, University of California, San Diego. Reproduced courtesy of Dr. Seuss Enterprises.

p. 11, cover of *The Cat in the Hat Comes Back,* Random House library edition, 1958. Image from the Oolongblue Collection of Charles D. Cohen and The Whole Seuss. Reproduced courtesy of Dr. Seuss Enterprises.

p. 11, Dr. Seuss talking with a toy designer about toys based on his characters, 1959. (Note the Cat in the Hat toy and book at the back of the picture.) Reproduced courtesy of John Bryson/Getty Images.

p. 12, Dr. Seuss and a person dressed as the Cat, c. 1960. Image courtesy of Dr. Seuss Collection, Mandeville Special Collections Library, University of California, San Diego. Reproduced courtesy of Dr. Seuss Enterprises.

p. 13, cover of *The Cat in the Hat* in Italian. Giunti, 1997. Reproduced courtesy of Dr. Seuss Enterprises.

p. 13, cover of *The Cat in the Hat* in Latin. Bolchazy-Carducci Publishers, 2000. Reproduced courtesy of Dr. Seuss Enterprises.

p. 13, cover of *The Cat in the Hat* in Chinese. Yuan-Liou, 1992. Image from the Oolongblue Collection of Charles D. Cohen and The Whole Seuss. Reproduced courtesy of Dr. Seuss Enterprises.

p. 13, cover of *The Cat in the Hat* in Hebrew. Keter Publishing House, 1957. Reproduced courtesy of Dr. Seuss Enterprises.

p. 13, cover of *The Cat in the Hat* in German. Piper München, 2004. Reproduced courtesy of Dr. Seuss Enterprises.

p. 13, cover of *The Cat in the Hat Comes Back* in Chinese. Yuan-Liou, 1992. Image from the Oolongblue Collection of Charles D. Cohen and The Whole Seuss. Reproduced courtesy of Dr. Seuss Enterprises.

p. 13, cover of *The Cat in the Hat Comes Back* in Hebrew. Modan, 1993. Reproduced courtesy of Dr. Seuss Enterprises.

p. 15, Ted and Audrey in J. L. Hudson Thanksgiving Day Parade, Detroit, November 1979. Image courtesy of Dr. Seuss Collection, Mandeville Special Collections Library, University of California, San Diego. Reproduced with permission from *The Detroit News.*

p. 15, "Dr. Seuss' 'The Cat in the Hat'" stamp, 1999, United States Postal Service. TM and copyright © by Dr. Seuss Enterprises, L.P. 1957, renewed 1985.

p. 15, Sam Gross, "He had a hat!" *The New Yorker,* 18 & 25 Feb. 2002, p. 134. © The New Yorker Collection 2002 Sam Gross from cartoonbank.com. All Rights Reserved.

p. 15, the Cat in the Hat sculpture, courtesy The Springfield Museums, copyright © 2002–2004 by Dr. Seuss Enterprises, L.P.

p. 16, the Cat enters in *The Cat in the Hat* television special. Copyright © 1971 Columbia Broadcasting System, Inc. All Rights Reserved. Artwork TM & © Dr. Seuss Enterprises, L.P. 1957. All Rights Reserved.

p. 16, Eric Pace, "Dr. Seuss, Modern Mother Goose, Dies at 87." *The New York Times,* 26 Sept. 1991. Copyright © 1991 by The New York Times Co. Reprinted with permission.

p. 18, penultimate page of *The Cat in the Hat.* Random House, 1957. Image courtesy of Dr. Seuss Collection, Mandeville Special Collections Library, University of California, San Diego. Reproduced courtesy of Dr. Seuss Enterprises.

p. 19, back jacket flap of *The Cat in the Hat.* Random House, 1957. Image courtesy of Dr. Seuss Collection, Mandeville Special Collections Library, University of California, San Diego. Reproduced courtesy of Dr. Seuss Enterprises.

p. 20, early front jacket of *The Cat in the Hat.* Random House, likely 1958.

p. 22, pencil and ink on board for endpapers of *The Cat in the Hat Songbook.* Random House, 1967.

p. 28, manuscript page of *The Cat in the Hat,* "I sat there with Sally." Image courtesy of Dr. Seuss Collection, Mandeville Special Collections Library, University of California, San Diego. Reproduced courtesy of Dr. Seuss Enterprises.

p. 30, illustration from "See It Go," a story in May Hill Arbuthnot and William S. Gray's *Fun with Dick and Jane,* illustrated by Eleanor Campbell and Keith Ward (Scott, Foresman and Company, 1940), pp. 6–7. Image courtesy of the Morse Department of Special Collections, Kansas State University Libraries.

p. 31, idle indoor toys in *The Cat in the Hat* television special. Copyright © 1971 Columbia Broadcasting System, Inc. All Rights Reserved. Artwork TM & © Dr. Seuss Enterprises, L.P. 1957. All Rights Reserved.

p. 31, idle indoor toys in *The Cat in the Hat* television special. Copyright © 1971 Columbia Broadcasting System, Inc. All Rights Reserved. Artwork TM & © Dr. Seuss Enterprises, L.P. 1957. All Rights Reserved.

p. 32, manuscript page of *The Cat in the Hat,* "Something went BUMP!" Image courtesy of Dr. Seuss Collection, Mandeville Special Collections Library,

University of California, San Diego. Reproduced courtesy of Dr. Seuss Enterprises.

p. 34, colored-pencil sketch for *The Cat in the Hat,* "Lots of good fun that is funny!" Image courtesy of Dr. Seuss Collection, Mandeville Special Collections Library, University of California, San Diego. Reproduced courtesy of Dr. Seuss Enterprises.

p. 36, Dr. Seuss, *The King's Stilts* (Random House, 1939), p. 15.

p. 36, illustration for "What Swing Really Does to People" by Benny Goodman. *Liberty,* 14 May 1938, p. 6. Image from the Oolongblue Collection of Charles D. Cohen and The Whole Seuss. Reproduced courtesy of Dr. Seuss Enterprises.

p. 36, Dr. Seuss, *Bartholomew and the Oobleck* (Random House, 1949), p. 18.

p. 37, sketch of Ford advertisement, "Enter a carefree Ormie in festive mood." Image courtesy of Dr. Seuss Collection, Mandeville Special Collections Library, University of California, San Diego. Reproduced courtesy of Dr. Seuss Enterprises.

p. 37, *Felix the Cat Shatters the Sheik* (poster). Educational Pictures, 1926. Image from the Oolongblue Collection of Charles D. Cohen and The Whole Seuss.

p. 42, Dr. Seuss, *The Sneetches and Other Stories* (Random House, 1961), pp. 16–17.

p. 42, fish atop stack of bubbles in *The Cat in the Hat* television special. Copyright © 1971 Columbia Broadcasting System, Inc. All Rights Reserved. Artwork TM & © Dr. Seuss Enterprises, L.P. 1957. All Rights Reserved.

p. 44, Dr. Seuss, *If I Ran the Circus* (Random House, 1956), pp. 30–31.

p. 46, advertisement, "Dr. Seuss has written a book that Johnny *can* read!" Image courtesy of Random House.

p. 48, Signe Wilkinson, "I can hold up a thong. . . ." *The New York Times,* 24 Jan. 1999. © 1999 The Washington Post Writers Group. Reprinted with Permission.

p. 48, Desmond Devlin, "The Strange Similarities Between the Bush Administration and the World of Dr. Seuss," illustrated by Mort Drucker. *MAD,* Nov. 2004, from MAD #447 © 2004 E. C. Publications, Inc. All Rights Reserved. Used with Permission.

p. 50, colored-pencil sketch for *The Cat in the Hat,* "From up there on the ball." Image courtesy of Dr. Seuss Collection, Mandeville Special Collections Library, University of California, San Diego. Reproduced courtesy of Dr. Seuss Enterprises.

p. 54, self-portrait of Dr. Seuss. *The Saturday Evening Post,* 6 July 1957, p. 17. © 1957 SEPS: Licensed by Curtis Publishing Co., Indianapolis, IN. All Rights Reserved.

p. 54, Technical Fairy, First Class, from "Private SNAFU: Gripes," July 1943.

p. 56, colored-pencil sketch for *The Cat in the Hat,* "But I like to be here." Image courtesy of Dr. Seuss Collection, Mandeville Special Collections Library, University of California, San Diego. Reproduced courtesy of Dr. Seuss Enterprises.

p. 58, images from *The Cat in the Hat* television special. Copyright © 1971 Columbia Broadcasting System, Inc. All Rights Reserved. Artwork TM & © Dr. Seuss Enterprises, L.P. 1957. All Rights Reserved.

p. 60, "bone pile" (discarded) storyboards for *The Grinch Grinches the Cat in the Hat.* Images courtesy of Dr. Seuss Collection, Mandeville Special Collections Library, University of California, San Diego. Reproduced courtesy of Dr. Seuss Enterprises.

p. 64, the fish phones the FBI in *The Cat in the Hat* television special. Copyright © 1971 Columbia Broadcasting System, Inc. All Rights Reserved. Artwork TM & © Dr. Seuss Enterprises, L.P. 1957. All Rights Reserved.

p. 64, a Thing pops out of the phone in *The Cat in the Hat* television special. Copyright © 1971 Columbia Broadcasting System, Inc. All Rights Reserved. Artwork TM & © Dr. Seuss Enterprises, L.P. 1957. All Rights Reserved.

p. 66, sketches of the Cat patting, from early sketches for *The Cat in the Hat Songbook.* Images courtesy of Dr. Seuss Collection, Mandeville Special Collections Library, University of California, San Diego. Reproduced courtesy of Dr. Seuss Enterprises.

p. 66, Dr. Seuss, *The Cat in the Hat Songbook* (Random House, 1967), pp. 52–53.

p. 68, Dr. Seuss, *The Cat in the Hat Songbook* (Random House, 1967), p. 39.

p. 70, colored-pencil sketches for *The Cat in the Hat,* "Saw them run down the hall." Image courtesy of Dr. Seuss Collection, Mandeville Special Collections Library, University of California, San Diego. Reproduced courtesy of Dr. Seuss Enterprises.

p. 72, four panels from Rudolph Dirks's *Katzenjammers* strip "An Off Day on Board the Prosit!" From Rudolph Dirks, *The Komical Katzenjammers.* First published by Frederick A. Stokes Company, 1908. Dover, 1974. Public domain.

p. 74, colored-pencil sketches for *The Cat in the Hat,* "And I said." Image courtesy of Dr. Seuss Collection, Mandeville Special Collections Library, University of California, San Diego. Reproduced courtesy of Dr. Seuss Enterprises.

p. 76, colored-pencil sketches for *The Cat in the Hat,* "Then our fish said, 'Oh, LOOK!'" Image courtesy of Dr. Seuss Collection, Mandeville Special Collections Library, University of California, San Diego. Reproduced courtesy of Dr. Seuss Enterprises.

p. 80, "Wild Tones" from Stromberg-Carlson advertising booklet (1937), p. 1. Image from the Oolongblue Collection of Charles D. Cohen and The Whole Seuss.

p. 82, colored-pencil sketches for *The Cat in the Hat,* "Then I let down my net." Image courtesy of Dr. Seuss Collection, Mandeville Special Collections Library, University of California, San Diego. Reproduced courtesy of Dr. Seuss Enterprises.

p. 82, three images of the Cat in French, German, and Mexican hats in *The Cat in the Hat* television special. Copyright © 1971 Columbia Broadcasting System, Inc. All Rights Reserved. Artwork TM & © Dr. Seuss Enterprises, L.P. 1957. All Rights Reserved.

p. 84, pen-and-ink drawings with tissue overlays and a set of 4" x 5" photographs of the finished drawings for pages 54–55 of *The Cat in the Hat.* Image courtesy of Dr. Seuss Collection, Mandeville Special Collections Library, University of California, San Diego. Reproduced courtesy of Dr. Seuss Enterprises.

p. 86, cartoon of hat-catching machine. Undated, but probably circa 1920s. From Rube Goldberg, *Rube Goldberg vs. the Machine Age.* Edited by Clark Kinnaird. Hastings House, 1968. Used by permission of Hastings House/Daytrips Publishers.

p. 86, Dr. Seuss (writing as Rube Goldbrick), "LAUGH IS LIKE THAT!" *Judge,* 19 May 1928, p. 21. Image courtesy of Dr. Seuss Collection, Mandeville Special Collections Library, University of California, San Diego. Reproduced courtesy of Dr. Seuss Enterprises.

p. 88, Brian Basset, "Theodor Geisel (Dr. Seuss) 1904–1991." *The New York Times,* 29 Sept. 1991. Reproduced courtesy of Brian Basset.

p. 92, final scene, Cat's hat passing in front of house in *The Cat in the Hat* television special. Copyright © 1971 Columbia Broadcasting System, Inc. All Rights Reserved. Artwork TM & © Dr. Seuss Enterprises, L.P. 1957. All Rights Reserved.

p. 92, original back cover of *The Cat in the Hat.* Random House, 1957.

p. 94, original front jacket of *The Cat in the Hat Comes Back,* Random House, 1958.

p. 96, left side of endpaper of *The Cat in the Hat Comes Back,* Dr. Seuss's note on deficiencies of first printing. Image courtesy of Dr. Seuss Collection, Mandeville Special Collections Library, University of California, San Diego. Reproduced courtesy of Dr. Seuss Enterprises.

p. 98, photo of six Beginner Books: *The Cat in the Hat, The Cat in the Hat Comes Back,* and the next four. Image courtesy of Dr. Seuss Collection, Mandeville Special Collections Library, University of California, San Diego. Reproduced courtesy of Random House.

p. 100, Dr. Seuss, *The Cat in the Hat* (Random House, 1957), p. 1.

p. 102, *Springfield Daily Republican,* 15 Dec. 1915, p. 1.

p. 102, from front page of *Springfield Daily News,* 14 Dec. 1915. Courtesy of the Connecticut Valley Historical Museum, Springfield, Massachusetts.

p. 106, pencil and ink on board for *The Cat in the Hat Comes Back,* "'Play tricks?' laughed the cat." Image courtesy of Dr. Seuss Collection, Mandeville Special Collections Library, University of California, San Diego. Reproduced courtesy of Dr. Seuss Enterprises.

p. 110, Dr. Seuss's drawing board and pencil cup from *The Secret Art of Dr. Seuss* (Random House, 1995), p. 6.

p. 112, Dr. Seuss, "Latest Modern Home Convenience: Hot and Cold Running Subs." *PM,* 22 Jan. 1942, p. 22. Image courtesy of Dr. Seuss Collection, Mandeville Special Collections Library, University of California, San Diego. Reproduced courtesy of Dr. Seuss Enterprises.

p. 112, Dr. Seuss, "The old Family bath tub." *PM,* 27 May 1941, p. 12. Image from the Oolongblue Collection of Charles D. Cohen and The Whole Seuss.

p. 114, Ex-tane advertisement, 1937. Image from the Oolongblue Collection of Charles D. Cohen and The Whole Seuss.

p. 116, from "The Strange Shirt Spot." *Redbook,* Sept. 1951, p. 68. Image from the Oolongblue Collection of Charles D. Cohen and The Whole Seuss. Reproduced courtesy of Dr. Seuss Enterprises.

p. 118, pencil and ink on board for *The Cat in the Hat Comes Back,* "I can make the spot go." Image courtesy of Dr. Seuss Collection, Mandeville Special Collections Library, University of California, San Diego. Reproduced courtesy of Dr. Seuss Enterprises.

p. 120, Dr. Seuss, "Ough Words." *Judge,* 13 April 1929. Image from the Oolongblue Collection of Charles D. Cohen and The Whole Seuss. Reproduced courtesy of Dr. Seuss Enterprises.

p. 124, pencil and ink on board for *The Cat in the Hat Comes Back,* "No spots are too hard." Image courtesy of Dr. Seuss Collection, Mandeville Special Collections Library, University of California, San Diego. Reproduced courtesy of Dr. Seuss Enterprises.

p. 126, photographic print, "Has the right kind of bed." Image courtesy of Dr. Seuss Collection, Mandeville Special Collections Library, University of California, San Diego. Reproduced courtesy of Dr. Seuss Enterprises.

p. 130, original front endpaper of *I Can Lick 30 Tigers Today!* Image courtesy of Dr. Seuss Collection, Mandeville Special Collections Library, University of California, San Diego. Reproduced courtesy of Dr. Seuss Enterprises.

p. 130, Dr. Seuss Christmas card (no date). Image courtesy of Rauner Alumni Library, Dartmouth College. Reproduced courtesy of Dr. Seuss Enterprises.

p. 132, original drawing for *The 500 Hats of Bartholomew Cubbins.* Vanguard, 1938. Image courtesy of Dr. Seuss Collection, Mandeville Special Collections Library, University of California, San Diego. Reproduced courtesy of Dr. Seuss Enterprises.

p. 132, some of the Cat's many hats in *The Cat in the Hat* television special. Copyright © 1971 Columbia Broadcasting System, Inc. All Rights Reserved. Artwork TM & © Dr. Seuss Enterprises, L.P. 1957. All Rights Reserved.

p. 132, Dr. Seuss, "We Always Were Suckers for Ridiculous Hats . . ." *PM,* 29 Apr. 1941, p. 20. Image courtesy of Dr. Seuss Collection, Mandeville Special Collections Library, University of California, San Diego. Reproduced courtesy of Dr. Seuss Enterprises.

p. 134, Braille edition, "And then B said." The Industrial Home for the Blind, 1965. Image courtesy of Dr. Seuss Collection, Mandeville Special Collections Library, University of California, San Diego. Reproduced courtesy of Dr. Seuss Enterprises.

p. 136, earlier, unpublished transition from indoors to outdoors for *The Cat in the Hat Comes Back.* Images courtesy of Dr. Seuss Collection, Mandeville Special Collections Library, University of California, San Diego. Reproduced courtesy of Dr. Seuss Enterprises.

p. 136, Flit advertisement featuring television, May 1932. Image from the Oolongblue Collection of Charles D. Cohen and The Whole Seuss.

p. 138, pencil and ink on board for *The Cat in the Hat Comes Back,* "But look where it went!" Image courtesy of Dr. Seuss Collection, Mandeville Special Collections Library, University of California, San Diego. Reproduced courtesy of Dr. Seuss Enterprises.

p. 140, pencil and ink on board for *The Cat in the Hat Comes Back,* Little Cats D, C, B, and A leap over Sally's head. Image courtesy of Dr. Seuss Collection, Mandeville Special Collections Library, University of California, San Diego. Reproduced courtesy of Dr. Seuss Enterprises.

p. 140, pencil and ink on board for *The Cat in the Hat Comes Back,* Little Cats A and B with pop guns. Image courtesy of Dr. Seuss Collection, Mandeville Special Collections Library, University of California, San Diego. Reproduced courtesy of Dr. Seuss Enterprises.

p. 142, "The Brownies Snowballing," first produced on blocks and puzzles by McLoughlin Brothers in 1891. Image from Roger W. Cummins, *Humorous but Wholesome: A History of Palmer Cox and the Brownies* (Watkins Glen, NY: Century House Americana Publishers, 1973), p. 222.

p. 144, photographic print, "Take your Little Cats G." Image courtesy of Dr. Seuss Collection, Mandeville Special Collections Library, University of California, San Diego. Reproduced courtesy of Dr. Seuss Enterprises.

p. 144, "Dr. Seuss, Brilliant Prewar Political Cartoonist, Came out of Retirement, Looked at the Current American Scene, and Temporarily Retired Again." Originally appeared in *The New Republic,* 28 July 1947, p. 7. Image courtesy of Dr. Seuss Collection, Mandeville Special Collections Library, University of California, San Diego. Reproduced courtesy of Dr. Seuss Enterprises.

p. 146, fern. Image from the Fractal Geometry Web site by Michael Frame, Benoit Mandelbrot, and Nial Neger. Courtesy of Michael Frame.

p. 148, shell. Image from Art Explosion 750000, distributed by Nova Development Corp., Calabasas, CA.

p. 150, Flit advertisement, published in *The New Yorker,* 25 July 1936. Image courtesy of Dr. Seuss Collection, Mandeville Special Collections Library, University of California, San Diego. Reprinted courtesy of Exxon Mobil Corporation.

p. 152, colored photographic print, "Look close!" Image courtesy of Dr. Seuss Collection, Mandeville Special Collections Library, University of California, San Diego. Reproduced courtesy of Dr. Seuss Enterprises.

p. 154, Essolube poster card, January 1933. Image from the Oolongblue Collection of Charles D. Cohen and The Whole Seuss. Reprinted courtesy of Exxon Mobil Corporation.

p. 156, secret weapon from "Private SNAFU: Going Home," May 1944.

p. 156, mushroom cloud from *The 5000 Fingers of Dr. T.* "The 5,000 Fingers of Dr. T" © 1952, renewed 1980 Columbia Pictures Industries, Inc. All Rights Reserved. Courtesy of Columbia Pictures.

p. 158, cover of *The Cat in the Hat Songbook* and sketch for cover of *The Hat Cats' Read-Aloud Hour.* Images courtesy of Dr. Seuss Collection, Mandeville Special Collections Library, University of California, San Diego. Reproduced courtesy of Dr. Seuss Enterprises.

p. 160, covers of *The Cat in the Hat Beginner Book Dictionary, I Can Read with My Eyes Shut!,* and *The Cat's Quizzer.* Random House, 1964, 1978, 1976. Images courtesy of Dr. Seuss Collection, Mandeville Special Collections Library, University of California, San Diego. Reproduced courtesy of Dr. Seuss Enterprises.

p. 162, original back jacket of *The Cat in the Hat Comes Back.* Random House, 1958.

p. 162, back jacket of *The Cat in the Hat Comes Back.* Random House, 1960.

p. 165, "The Strange Shirt Spot." *Redbook,* Sept. 1951, p. 68. Image from the Oolongblue Collection of Charles D. Cohen and The Whole Seuss. Reproduced courtesy of Dr. Seuss Enterprises.

ACKNOWLEDGMENTS

For valiant research assistance, I would like to thank: Lynda Claassen, Steve Coy, Alexandra Rosen Gagné, and Melanie Treco of the Mandeville Special Collections Library, UCSD Libraries, University of California at San Diego, and Sarah I. Hartwell and Edward Connery Lathem of the Rauner Library, Dartmouth College. Many thanks to Artie Bennett, Cathy Goldsmith, Jenny Golub, Teresa Harris, Alice Jonaitis, Kate Klimo, Alison Kolani, Linda Palladino, and Janet Schulman of Random House; Herb Cheyette and Jill Jones of Dr. Seuss Enterprises and International Creative Management; Roger Adams of the Morse Department of Special Collections, Hale Library, Kansas State University; Maggie Humbertson of the Connecticut Valley Historical Museum, Springfield, Mass.; Amy Baskette of the National Portrait Gallery; the Interlibrary Services Department at Kansas State University's Hale Library; and Patrick Murtha and Cliff Starkey, my research assistants here at Kansas State University.

For their advice and assistance, my sincere thanks to Lee Behlman, Linda Brigham, Jill Clingan, Charles D. Cohen, Jill Deans, Michael Frame, Gloria Hardman, Brian E. Jacobs, Michael Joseph, Kenneth Kidd, Linda Nel, Kevin Shortsleeve, Katie Strode, Joseph T. Thomas, Jr., and Helen Younger.

For their help in finding copyright holders and/or granting permission to quote from or reproduce copyrighted material, special thanks to Tanty Avant, Brian Basset, Zarette Beard, Jeff Burak, Margarita Harder, Russell A. James, Peter Leers, Eileen Margerum, Tracy McDonald, Trevor W. McKeown, Shirley Springman, and Terri Torretto.

For funding the research, thanks to the Friends of the UCSD Libraries and to Kansas State University, which provided a Small Research Grant.

For dreaming up a better title, special thanks to Anne Phillips.

A big caps-lock THANKS to Lane Smith for introducing me to Editor One and Editor Two.

And even more *THANKS* to Karin Westman for her patience, love, and support.

ABOUT THE AUTHOR

Like Theodor Geisel, Philip Nel was born in March, grew up in Massachusetts, enjoyed doodling, and was not an ambitious student. Phil became aware of these happy coincidences when he read Judith and Neil Morgan's *Dr. Seuss & Mr. Geisel: A Biography* in 1995 as a graduate student at Vanderbilt University. The biography also made him realize that one could study Dr. Seuss . . . and write books about him. Red books, blue books, big books, new books.

Green Eggs and Ham taught Phil to read. His parents, recent immigrants from South Africa, had never heard of Dr. Seuss. Then, at the local library, his mother discovered some books that were much funnier than anything she had read as a child—the works of Dr. Seuss.

Phil loved them. "I remember being three years old, turning the pages of *Green Eggs and Ham* and sounding out each word," he recalls. "I didn't know that the book had only fifty different words, but I did know that the repeated words made me feel smart—I'd pronounced 'house' before, and there was 'house' again. Suddenly I was reading! And it was fun!" he says. "I had so much fun that as soon as I finished reading the book, I read it again. And again. And again."

The first of his family to be born in the United States, Phil burst onto the scene in 1969, the year that *Sesame Street* made its debut. His sister Linda, born in 1971, loved P. D. Eastman's *Are You My Mother?* Her first words were "You are not my mother. You are a Snort." His were "Sunny day, sweeping the clouds away." Okay, those weren't really their first words, but public television and Beginner Books *did* teach them to read.

Although formal education was of little interest until late in his high school years, Phil has enjoyed many varied pursuits—music, art, history, comics, and literature. (Boxes of each can still be found moldering in his mother's Connecticut basement, awaiting an archivist.) His curiosity has served him well in creating *The Annotated Cat* and has made him a fan of annotated editions since, as a college student, he first read Martin Gardner's *Annotated Alice*.

In 1992, Phil received a BA in English and Psychology from the University of Rochester, as well as a handsome debt that he finally finished paying off in 2005. Next, Phil headed to Nashville, pursuing graduate degrees in English at Vanderbilt (MA '93, PhD '97) while also pursuing the charming and brilliant Ms. Karin Westman. After a whirlwind five-year courtship, they married in 1997. Both are now associate professors in Kansas State University's English Department, where he directs the graduate-level Program in Children's Literature. He regularly teaches courses in children's literature, adolescent literature, twentieth-century American picture books, and Harry Potter. In the spring of 2007, he will teach an upper-level course devoted to Dr. Seuss.

Phil is the author of three previous books: *Dr. Seuss: American Icon* (Continuum, 2004), *The Avant-Garde and American Postmodernity: Small Incisive Shocks* (University Press of Mississippi, 2002), and *J. K. Rowling's Harry Potter Novels: A Reader's Guide* (Continuum, 2001). He is working on two other books: *Crockett Johnson and Ruth Krauss: A Biography* and (with co-editor Julia Mickenberg) *Tales for Little Rebels: A Collection of Radical Children's Literature.*